Letters to a Friend

Letters
To a Friend

The Correspondence Between
T. H. White and L. J. Potts

Edited and Introduced with Notes
by François Gallix

G. P. Putnam's Sons   New York

Excerpt from the poem *Kangaroo* from *The Complete Poems of D. H. Lawrence* by D.
H. Lawrence, selected and edited with an introduction and notes by Vivian D.
Sola Pinto and F. Warren Roberts, copyright © 1964, 1971 by Angelo Ravagli
and C. M. Weekley, executors of the estate of Frieda Lawrence Ravagli. Used
by permission of Viking Penguin Inc., William Heinemann Ltd., Laurence
Pollinger Ltd., and the estate of Frieda Lawrence Ravagli.

Library of Congress Cataloging in Publication Data

White, T. H. (Terence Hanbury), 1906–1964.
  Letters to a friend.
  1. White, T. H. (Terence Hanbury), 1906–1964—
Correspondence. 2. Authors, English—20th century—
Correspondence. 3. Potts, L. J. (Leonard James),
1897–   . I. Potts, L. J. (Leonard James), 1897–
II. Gallix, François. III. Title.
PR6045.H2Z489   828'.91209 [B]   81-15749
ISBN 0-399-12693-7   AACR2

Printed in the United States of America

Contents

Acknowledgments

When I asked Sylvia Townsend Warner whom I should see in order to get a better understanding of White's life and works, the first name she mentioned was that of Mary Potts.

I went to see Mary several times in Cambridge, where she teaches the harpsichord, and she showed me White's correspondence, but it was in Paris that she suggested I edit White's letters to herself and her husband. I would like to thank her for the patience she showed in answering my seemingly never-ending questions. During one of our conversations about White, she told me:

"I think my husband was a sort of father figure. . . . He was Merlyn to Tim, just as Tim wished to be Merlyn."

I must also record my gratitude to Michael Trubshawe, who very kindly talked to me about White and showed me his letters. In one of these, on January 1, 1949, White had included a photograph of his portrait by Van Doorn (see the letter to Mary and L. J. Potts, October 4, 1948) and written on the back:

Some said: "He is saying: Just make one proposition or another, and I will contradict it!"
Others said: "He is saying: I wonder if the artist knows I am as drunk as I feel?"

The rest said: "The combination of surprise, timidity and supreme contempt is irresistible."

I am indebted to Rachael Feild, who told me about White's life in Alderney; to the late David Garnett, who retraced his long friendship with him; and to Carol Stallings, who gave me a very detailed account of White's last lecture tour in the United States.

I am grateful to Sir John Verney for the opportunity to read the letters and diary written by White during his Italian visits of 1962 and 1963; to the late Harry Griffiths, who was my guide in Alderney; and to Patsy, Charles, and Timmy Lane, who shared with me some of the best moments they spent with their cousin.

I would also like to thank Patricia Bullen, who passed on her personal impression of White and let me read his letters, particularly one written somewhat tongue in cheek on October 15, 1959: "I happen to know that I am a genius—there is no boastfulness about this at all, it is like knowing that you squint."

I gratefully acknowledge the assistance given me by the Humanities Research Center, the University of Texas at Austin and by Ellen S. Dunlap, the research librarian, for giving me permission to quote from the White collection (particularly Mary Potts' letter of November 31, 1944). I am also indebted to Queens College, Cambridge for their permission to publish two articles from *The Dial*. Finally, I would like to thank M. Pierre Vincent, who helped me with the typing.

Introduction

Sylvia Townsend Warner once told me that T. H. White was a sort of mirror, quickly summing up the expectations of the person he was talking to and providing him with the character he chose to see. When she started to write his biography she was faced with dozens of different Whites, a plethora of incompatibles, which this remarkable man endeavored to forge into one complicated, vivacious life.

White was a consummate performer, playing myriad parts and assuming many different masks, perhaps as defenses against disclosure of the vulnerable real self behind the roles. He acquired more and more personae as he grew older, rarely dropping any, so that his range of motifs constantly increased. As would be the case with his great fictional creation, Merlyn the Magician, he drew from both the once and the future realms of his experience; even at the end of his life he retained the buoyant expectancy of a schoolboy, and as a schoolboy one could see in him a blustery eccentricity more appropriate to his middle years.

Stories about White abound: in Alderney he used to welcome his guests in a scarlet dressing-gown, ushering them to his bright, red-painted kitchen; he was fond of serving visitors meals in a different room each day, so as to leave behind the washing up; he resorted to

11

tinned milk in his tea because his dog didn't like the milkman. He once suddenly stopped paying his bills and opening his letters and dumped them in the back of his car. He had a phase of paying accounts to the nearest zero: if he got a bill for £34.15, he would send a check for £30, and if the bill was £36.04, he would send a check for £40. White once sent a check signed "Santa Claus" to a firm of photographic chemists in Jersey to prove their inefficiency and to show that they would not even notice: the receipted account was sent back to him! White's favorite party list was made up of people he *knew* would hate each other, so that he, the perpetual student and scientist of natures, could watch their reactions in a sort of infernal experiment. The most widely known White anecdote is probably his answer to a young American who had knocked at his door in Alderney, announcing to him that he was a Jehovah's Witness. White grabbed the collecting box and replied: "And *I* am Jehovah! Hand over the takings!"

Always an enthusiast, White was full of ideas and projects; he had a genuine desire to learn about everything and was always ready to experience some new thing, so as to be able to write fully about it afterwards. Perhaps the most significant statement on White to come from his works is this passage from *The Once and Future King*: "'The best thing for being sad,' replied Merlyn, beginning to puff and blow, 'is to learn something. That is the only thing that never fails.'" White firmly believed that one had to experience everything one wrote about, whether it was riding a horse, shooting a bow and arrow, or wearing a suit of armor. This enthusiasm never failed. During his American lecture tour, for example, he became so interested in the history of the Mormons that he planned to write a book about them; only death stopped him from doing so.

His range of avocations was incredibly wide, including painting, shooting, hawking, salmon fishing, deep-sea diving, gardening, knitting, making films, and trying to hypnotize himself. He was as drawn to such pastimes as cutting silhouettes out of cigarette packets and learning to play the pennywhistle as to such great undertakings as piloting a plane or sailing a boat.

White's learning was never purely theoretical; he believed in putting his knowledge into action and always tried to go as deeply

12

into a subject as he could. After reading a treatise on hawking he decided to tame a goshawk according to the seventeenth-century method of "watching" the raptor. The hawker had to stay awake with his captive for as long as three days and nights in order to break its will. When the bird flew off, White was despondent but not defeated. Disappointment, after all, was merely part of the learning experience.

After listening to a BBC program on the deaf and blind, White was struck by the misery of such a state, but unlike most of us, he also felt impelled to act: he wrote to the Association in Aid of the Deaf and Blind, extending an open invitation to its members to visit him in his Channel Islands home. First learning, with his extraordinary facility for acquiring knowledge, finger-talking, lip-reading, and Braille, he then gave much of his time to those new friends who crowded his house at Alderney for their holidays.

In his later years, troubled by deteriorating health and the burden of middle age, White drank excessively, both to raise his spirits when he was unhappy and to restore his flagging attention when life got boring, but he was also capable of "putting himself on the water-waggon" as soon as a new interest cropped up. In his cups, he could turn tedious, and his stock phrases were heard rather too often: he used to grumble about the "Farewell State" that had taken all his money from him, and to complain about "Urinal Bevan."

White was also a lover of animals. He gave up going to libraries and seeing people in order to look after Brownie, his beloved red setter, and the unbearable sorrow he felt when she died is chronicled in this correspondence. He tamed hawks and at one time kept toads and grass snakes (at liberty in his sitting room—a frightful ordeal for the maid who cleaned his rooms!).

But of all the pictures of White, the one that will most probably remain is that of the patriarch, the prophet, White the sage, the magus, with his magnificent beard bristling in all directions. Once, in Ireland during a pilgrimage, White had been made to feel like St. Patrick, and on another occasion, in the States, he had been mistaken for Hemingway, but without a doubt, he was first and foremost Merlyn the Enchanter.

He was a handsome man all his life, never more so than in his later years, with his white hair and beard and his brilliant blue eyes. Well over six feet tall, he had a swinging stride, and even when his leg was giving him trouble, he managed to turn this to his advantage by limping majestically. As for his voice, it comes to us through the recordings he made, the voice of the patriarch, deep, warm, refined and reassuring.

White was a great letter-writer; he wrote to David Garnett, Sir Sydney Cockerell, Siegfried Sassoon, Sir John Verney, and the actor Michael Trubshawe, among many others, but from 1930 until his death in 1964 he certainly sent more letters to L. J. and Mary Potts than to anyone else. The Pottses, David Garnett, and Michael Trubshawe are some of the very few people who can claim to have had an unbroken friendship with the author of *The Sword in the Stone*.

L. J. Potts was White's tutor at Queens' College, where White read for the English tripos under his supervision for a year, but their lasting friendship did not start until White's second year at Cambridge:

> My tutor was L. J. Potts, whom I disliked to the point of rage for about a year. It took me all that time to discover that he was going to be the great literary influence in my life, as well as being the most noble gentleman I have ever met.

L. J. Potts was only nine years older than his student, although the student/mentor motif was always an ingredient of their association, and the two men liked and admired one another. White valued his friend's judgments, and L. J. Potts was one of the first to discover, praise, and encourage White's talent as a creative writer.

Even if White could write to Mary Potts on December 4, 1936, "I have no friends—I have never considered other people, so why should they consider me?" it obviously did not apply to the Pottses. White could find no better friends to talk to about his love affairs, his psychoanalysis, his hesitations as to whether he should get married and whether he ought to join in the war effort.

Mary and L. J. Potts were usually White's first readers, or listeners, for he would read whole chapters aloud to them and ask them what they thought. He also sent them his typescripts so that they could use their blue pencils. Whole chapters in *The Witch in the Wood* (volume two of what would become *The Once and Future King*) were entirely modified on Potts's advice, and when his friend declared against his novel "You Can't Keep a Good Man Down," he decided not to publish it. White knew he wasn't at ease with the female characters of his novels and he always welcomed Mary Potts's comments and guidelines. As for L. J. Potts, he was certainly White's best literary critic when he wrote: "The one character you can dramatise perfectly is yourself."

White's rich sense of humor underlies many of these letters, as it does most of his best novels. One will remember the man who decided that he would live asexually for forty days or play the recorder "with no clothes on, like a debauched merman" and rebuild London as a pyramid over the river Severn. When he knew that Mary Potts had had her third baby, he felt "like shouting Snap, or whatever one does in Happy Families." He asked, "Why not just arrange to have the next one smaller?" and when he was told he was going to be a godfather, he wrote, "It is almost nicer being a godfather than a father, like having white mice but making your nanny feed them for you!"

Most of White's letters to Potts are in the present book, with a few overly arcane exceptions. Many names are mentioned; they have been left as they were in most cases. Very few had to be altered in order to avoid libel. White's often eccentric spelling and punctuation have usually been retained; only the most confusing irregularities have been altered to conform with standard style.

White and Potts had half-seriously agreed that whoever outlived the other would publish their correspondence, and White would probably have kept his word after L. J. Potts's death if most of his friend's letters had not been destroyed in David Garnett's leaking shed, where they had been stored. Yet White was still hoping to publish the remaining letters: "It will be a crying scandal if his [Potts's] letters are not collected and published at some future date."

Of all of T. H. White's large and varied correspondence, the letters to L. J. and Mary Potts are, as Sylvia Townsend Warner put it in a letter to me (May 13, 1976), "among the best of White's letters, and the most typical, bragging, confiding, asking for advice he won't take. In a way they are better than the letters to Garnett, because they are without the desire to impress."

The secret of this complex personality is perhaps expressed on his tomb in Athens, not far from Hadrian's Arch:

Author
Who
From a troubled heart
Delighted others
Loving and praising
This Life.

CHAPTER 1

Cheltenham, Cambridge, Reigate

Terence Hanbury White was born on May 29, 1906, in Bombay, where his father, Garrick White, was a district superintendent of police. He was an only child.

In 1911 Garrick White took a year's leave, and the family visited England. When the parents returned to India (separately—Garrick when his leave ended and Constance eighteen months later) Terence was left with his mother's parents. By this time there was not much love left between Constance and Garrick White, and the quarrels between them reached such a state that in 1915 Constance left her husband and, with her son, moved into her parents' house in St. Leonards in England.

The years White spent with his grandparents, Mr. and Mrs. Aston, were very peaceful until 1920, when he was sent to Cheltenham College. Discipline was strict in this school, which had a military section. Caning was part of the rules, and the ceremony that took place before and during the punishment was an ordeal that seems to have left deep marks on the adolescent's mind. White said later that it had turned him into a flagellant.

On January 25, 1923, there was an article in *The Evening Standard* entitled: "Judge Puzzled by Husband, Sought Restitution but did not want wife back"; it went on to explain in detail Garrick White's drinking habits and cruelty to his wife. Full names were given and the seventeen-year-old boy, still at college, had his parents' private life exposed for anyone to read.

White left Cheltenham in 1924 and had to give private lessons for a year before going to Cambridge; he entered Queens' College the next year to read for the English tripos. His supervisor was L. J. Potts.

For the English tripos, White wrote an essay on Malory—his first contribution to the Matter of Britain, and an excellent choice, as it led to his tetralogy on the Arthurian legend.

In 1927, the doctor diagnosed tuberculosis and some of his teachers in Cambridge decided to start a subscription to send the young White to Italy. L. J. Potts gave a very large sum. (Thirty-three years later, when L. J. Potts died, White paid back the sum to his friend's widow.)

This first journey to Italy had a great influence on White. While he was in Capri, he started to write two books, which were to be published under the name of James Aston: *They Winter Abroad* and *First Lesson*. Both are about British people visiting Italy. White had intended the latter to be a novel about a homosexual couple in Italy; it was first to be called "Of Whom the World." In its final version, Mr. Belfry, a forty-seven-year-old teacher from Cambridge, and Beatrice were substituted for John and Tonino. It was during this first stay in Italy that White really tried to understand and sympathize with homosexual love. As Sylvia Townsend Warner put it: "In Italy, unsupported by English disapproval or approval, he had to decide for himself—or maybe have the question decided for him."[1]

Back in Cambridge, White published *Loved Helen*, a book of poetry dedicated to his mother,[2] and got a First Class with Distinction in English. In 1930, he went as an Assistant Master to

St. David's, a preparatory school in Reigate. He took a form in classics and mathematics, another in French and geography, and was also in charge of the physical drill, "managing most efficiently to combine discipline with amusement," according to his headmaster's testimonial. With a friend, R. McNair Scott, White wrote a murder story with a very complicated plot, *Dead Mr. Nixon*, in which the villain is a lecturer at the London University!

White would stay at St. David's for two years, feeling all the while, as he wrote to Potts, that "it's rather preposterous to teach Latin in a prep. school after getting a First in English." Still, as Sylvia Townsend Warner observes in her biography of White, "If the employment was preposterous, its perquisites were valuable; limited responsibility, regular holidays, time to call his own, freedom to pursue his private intentions." Those intentions were to make money off his writing as well as to pursue more scholarly publication, and to investigate the possibilities of becoming a "Toff," at the same time as he disparaged the class snobbery of those around him. To Potts and his new wife, as perhaps to no one else, White was able to express the duality of his own nature in a totally open, undisguised way. This divided nature manifests itself not only in matters of class and artistic pursuit but also in his highly conflicting feelings toward marriage. That he could pour out his thoughts to the Pottses is an indication of the special importance of his favorite mentor in his life. If White was to become Merlyn, it may very well have been Potts who first implanted in his sensibility the myth of the playful, unbridled, and irreplaceable relationship between teacher and student.

[October 12, 1930]
The Dingle, Reigate, Surrey

Dear L.J.P.

Forgive my tardiness in writing about your POEMS. I despised them heartily at first and put them by me in despair, not knowing

19

what I could say to you. Just now I thought I really must face them again and make a dreadful effort at diplomacy. So I started reading them again, and I've only got as far as 3 b (not a very good one, by the way) and I'm writing *at once*, because its past ten o'clock and I have a full day's work before me tomorrow. I just haven't time to read them right through tonight, so I'm going to write about the first five or six and perhaps continue this letter when I've had time to finish them off with a considered judgement.[3]

Well, first of all, it has just dawned upon me that I disliked them for a very good and superficial reason, i.e., the diction. And secondly and finally and lastly and in conclusion I've just had the excitement of seeing the poems *through* the diction. In spite of it, I mean. They say something superlatively worth saying and once you have got through the language they even justify that. I should by all means urge you to publish them—so long as you are going to go on writing, and preferably in a modern tongue. Unless you will do this it will be useless to publish them, for your personality will require a *weight* of evidence before it can break through the present medium enough to impinge upon the consciousness of the reader. The reason why it has impinged on mine is that I already know you personally to some extent. You see, they are *reflection* poems (that is why I like them so much) and it takes a lot of familiarity to find out the way a man reflects. If one hadn't discovered the mental angle of Blake what bosh all that stuff about caterpillars in a cage would be. So with your mental angle. It will need a lot of publication before you can establish it to any but those who know you. It is not facile like mine.

But to return to this diction. Have you ever heard of the English language? And will you give me your no doubt all-sufficient reasons for saying: "life is *but* a task" instead of *"only"*; "nought" instead of "nothing" and so forth *ad nauseam*. Why should your bitch be called "Thou"? Or have you reverted to Quakerism?

You are writing in the idiom of the 1820s. It is so pronounced that I can date it to within a decade, except where it is tainted with Rupert Brooke. And then I could say "by 1823 out of 1914" just as if it were a horse. The things positively reek of retrogression.

20

I am so emphatic for a rather dreadful reason: they almost convert me to the retrograde. But not quite, but not quite.

On second thoughts I shall send this off but keep the poems for a further onslaught and instalment.

So tremble. I daresay I shall burn them.

    yours,
    Timothy

Down in pocket, down in spirits, having failed to complete the letter of criticism about Potts's poems, White writes instead to Mary Potts in apology. "Tilly" is the great Shakespearean scholar, E.M.W. Tillyard, Potts's university supervisor and close friend, whom White had met often while both were visiting the Pottses. The detective story White refers to is *Dead Mr. Nixon*.

[November 17, 1930]
The Dingle, Reigate, Surrey

Dear Mary,

I feel just too miserable about these poems of your respected husband's. I liked and like them to the point of envy, but a conspiracy of circumstances have prevented my getting a letter about them *finished*. I have it by me, half done, and now I'm almost too ashamed to go on with it. First, I was broke. You will think it ridiculous, but I couldn't afford to register them and hoped to be able to send them back by Tillyard, who was going to come to see me. That fell through. Then I paid a visit to a friend near here and suggested that he should collaborate in a detective story in which I had got bored. He agreed, and waded in to such good purpose that I became enthusiastic too, and we have been in hopes of getting it finished by Xmas. That may have been selfish of me, but it rather took my mind off literary criticism and I shirked. Now the whole

21

school is down with chicken pox, which means extra work, not less of it, and I myself have 'flu. You see how ill at ease I am by the way I multiply excuses. However, though dastardly, it may shew that I am not lost to all decent feeling.

I am particularly miserable to think that L.J.P. may have thought my silence meant a low opinion of the work. Of course it didn't—not anything of the sort—only a wicked, slothful, selfish nature. Having said this I feel much better.

Thank you for your invitation. Could I perhaps come to see you next holidays? After Xmas? Is L.J.P. in a great hurry to have his poems back? Shall I send them off now, with half a letter, or wait till Tilly does really come, or bring them after Xmas? It is truly good of you to invite me after such a wickedness.

How do you like being a don's wife? I do hope you will be able to keep off muffins and undergraduates for tea. And sitting on the floor.

Yours
Timothy

White and his friends all had pet names: David Garnett was Bunny, Leonard James Potts was Pottës, E.M.W. Tillyard was Tilly, and Terence Hanbury White was always called Tim—an association of his name with that of the multiple-store chemist, "Timothy White."

[January 3(?), 1931]
47 Carisbrooke Rd., St. Leonards on Sea

Dear Mary,

I'm very sorry to hear about the illness, and hope it's only 'flu or liver. Or it might be the biodynamical changes consequent upon getting married. As a matter of fact he must have had a tremendous constitution not to have broken sooner. I expect women are too

22

callous to feel these nervous alterations so much as man. I daresay you won't be bowled over yourself for another two years or so, and then it will be by Cambridge, not by L.J.P. A propos of those initials, have you come to any practical solution of the problem of what to call him? I mean other than "Boo-boo" or whatever wives do privately call their husbands. If so I should be glad to hear of it, so that I can call him so myself. "Potts" seems rather Edwardian, and L.J.P. is not practicable in the spoken conversation. He has never divulged whether the L. stands for Lorenzo or Lancelot, and I might feel shy in calling him either.

But I must get on to the purpose of this letter. Will you tell me frankly whether he will be well enough for me to come on the 28th and leave early on the 30th? If not one could easily put it off. Or if these dates don't suit my other possibles would be the 24th 25th. Whichever you like, if either is convenient.

It was very kind of you to ask me, but I shouldn't dream of coming if he wasn't well.

Yours
Timothy

While Potts seemed quite willing to put up with many of White's eccentricities, he apparently objected to the younger man's designs for moving up in the world.

[February 2, 1931]
The Dingle, Reigate, Surrey

Dear L.J.P.

Thanks for your letter.

I am sorry that you can't be bothered with my convictions about gentility. It is an absorbing topic. The real gentleman is so easily defined. You can do it in a sentence. He must have been educated

23

at Eton and Christchurch or Magdalen Oxford or Trinity Cambridge, and he must have £10,000 a year. No other requirements. Fairly good Ersatz-gentleman can be manufactured on other principles (though rigid ones: such as £5,000 a year & peerage obtained in the civil services) but they are all eventually substitutes. No nonsense.

As for snobbery, it is one of the best parlour games known to me—for persons not among the gentry. The gentry don't need the games, for they have the genuine article. So when they want to play games they have to take to poetry and that sort of thing. Hence my desertion of poetry (my possession) for gentility (my sport) in vice versa. And of course all Englishmen take games seriously.

I have started on Hopkins (I mean the book on him) and should be really obliged if you could afford me a little help. He is a tougher proposition than I thought. I am pencilling queries in the margin of my copy, and I propose to send it to you for consideration, if you will permit. Will you?

Answer this when you write.

I am too busy for more.

Best love to Mary

Timothy

White's two years at St. David's were prolific in terms of his writing. The "blood-story" described in the following letter is *Dead Mr. Nixon*, while the second story, in which he arranges to have Potts fictionally murdered by an actual university colleague, is *Darkness at Pemberley*. Sir Bernard Spilsbury was a well-known expert in forensic medicine.

Dear L.J.P.

I'm sorry I've been so long in answering your letter: purely through idleness, I assure you. Thank you for paying my fine. I must endeavour not to forget to pay you back. As a step in this direction may I ask leave to pay you when I see you, instead of going out for a postal order?

I dont know whether I've written to you since my blood-story was accepted by Messrs. Cassels? If not, it has. They were the first publishers we sent it to, so I may be able to afford to be a quasi-gentleman eventually after all. I am just going to start another one—the one I told you about, in which you are murdered by Laffan. Gerard Hopkins will take me another year at least, and this book will be in the nature of a holiday from him. My school holidays begin next Tuesday, the day after tomorrow, and I'm going to Malvern to take a course in Advanced Equitation. This is all directed at gentility. I must try to get in parliament sooner or later, as that is quite one of the recognised short cuts. If as a conservation, naturally. The blood-story is not to be called "Gunmen in England" but "Dead Mr Nixon." I feel it will be a tremendous failure. We fall between two stools.

Now, when you do next write to me (if before 15th April, then to

8 Wellington House
Great Malvern),   will you please tell me all about your dead undergraduate mystery? Was he murdered? Did Sir Bernard Spilsbury do it? How has the university managed to lead this English Reformation? For it is a reformation—the re-Americanisation of England—when taken in conjunction with the late massacre at Kings. I rather expect that you and Tilly will be the next to go. Cambridge seems to be getting more and more of a live wire.

By the way, about that cutting I sent you. I had doubts whether it might make you unhappy, but I decided it was too futile. I should never have sent you any attack which seemed to make a hit, or

25

which could have been sufficiently near the truth to be wounding. But the one I sent you was so silly and obviously beside the point, so very much written by a creature definitely not human and mentally a slur upon the intelligent apes, that I thought it couldn't disturb you at all. It is the kind of attack which is always being made or intruded upon myself, and which inflicts wounds which I preserve with a melancholy pride. Melancholy for the mental age of the human race. Of *course* it isn't *remotely* justified for a *moment*.

White's self-consciously Swiftian satirical attitudes toward child-rearing find perfect expression in the following letter to Potts. The Dolmetsch concert referred to was a program given at Cambridge by Rudolph Dolmetsch, Mary Potts's harpsichord teacher, and his wife, Millicent; the Clarke Lectures are a series of addresses by well-known literary characters from outside the university, which are still held annually at Cambridge.

Saturday [May 9, 1931]
The Dingle, Reigate, Surrey

Dear L. J. P.

Were you amused in Paris, and have you grown jealous with Mary? I mean more jealous? Did you know that you are, or aren't you, and if not why did I think so, and does it annoy you to be told? I think you ought to have a baby. It's unkind to Mary, but it'll be for both your good (is that grammar?) in the long run. Also I am rather in favour of babies. Perhaps you could lend me one to bring up when you have some to spare. It will be taught the three I's (Inversion, Introversion, and Intellect), the three R's (Riding, Rogering and Rumination), and the three G's (Grace, Government and Gentility). If it isn't an Extrovert after that I shall boil it for my hounds. And yet I suppose I should be selfishly sorry if it was.

On mature consideration I should like it to be nicely balanced between the two.

I suppose it's hell to have a child really. It would eat one eventually, if left to itself in natural surroundings.

My book on Hopkins has come to a complete full stop. It never got beyond the first joyous chapter of demolishing previous critics. I must be content to be a wash-out until I've made enough money to afford leisure. Then I shall write well, for I find that I'm naturally strenuous and should be driven into writing by having nothing else to do. This school-mastering business is a bad idea really—however pleasant. So was your idea that I ought to be driven to write by writing for a living. The need of money has never driven me to anything but despair. It is leisure only that will ever pull me through. And that I don't seem likely to get. My only hope is to write detective stories till I have an income. Even then I spend it as it comes in—I mean the money made out of detective stories—and so shan't ever have an income.

I wonder whether this perpetual egoism bores you, but excuse myself by reflecting that it probably embodies a general truth. Indeed, it may be the best way to express a G.T.

I am writing a perfectly hellish detective story [*Darkness at Pemberley*]. I started it at Malvern and must have written nearly 20,000 words in a week (whilst riding 5 hours a day) quite cheerfully. Since then I haven't written a word. I kept saying "I must! I will!" Pathetic industry!

How is your scrap book of meditations going on? I tried to begin one but found that when working at school I was too busy to have any. When enjoying myself in the holidays I'm too happy to want any.

I hope the Dolmetsch concert was a success and that Mary is still enjoying the harpsichord. What does she think of Cambridge now?

Who is doing the Clarke Lectures, and how about the Festival Theatre? Are you taking Mary to a May week ball, and why not?

As I had nothing to say in the first place I think this letter might as well stop now.

love
Timothy

P.S. (About that child)—or I should eat it.

* * *

From the very beginning, Potts had attempted to convince White that he could do better in the world than teach, since his talent as a creative writer would bring him great esteem and a more comfortable livelihood. The D. H. Lawrence poem that White praises is as follows:

But the yellow antipodal Kangaroo, when she sits up,
Who can unseat her, like a liquid drop that is heavy, and just
     touches earth,
The downward drip
The down-urge.
So much denser than cold-blooded frogs.[4]

[Monday May 11, 1931]
The Dingle, Reigate

Dear L.J.P.

    Last night I happened to turn up one of my hidden caches of your letters, and read them all through. It has made me feel desperately sorry that you got married, and I hope you will tell Mary so. How long will it take you to both realize how ruined you are? There you sit, squat rather, or positively subside (like the Kangaroo of D.H. Lawrence's—do you know that poem?—it is *such* a good one; in the 2nd volume) in a sort of welter of domesticity, pots, pans, bidets, babies, meals and bedmaking. The trouble about it all is that you don't have to lie in the bed because you've made it. You've got to make the damned thing before you can lie in it, and that's what you're going to spend the rest of your life doing. Faugh! You talk to me about my not becoming a don because it would be bad for me, but after all I haven't yet offered to slip into somebody's bosom and be lost in them. You and Mary have slipped into each

28

other's bosoms reciprocally, and both disappeared, like a conjuring trick.

I just thought I'd let you know.

love from
Timothy

In May 1931 White turned twenty-five. He was halfway through his stint at St. David's and was awaiting publication of his first mystery, *Dead Mr. Nixon*. He and Mary Potts were engaged in a left-handed handwriting competition (the last two sentences of the following letter were a specimen of White's left-hand writing). The books he recommends to Mary are David Garnett's *The Grasshoppers Come* and A. J. Cronin's *Hatter's Castle*. J. C. Squire was literary editor of *The New Statesman* and *The London Mercury*.

[May 25, 1931]
The Dingle, Reigate

Dear Mary,

I was absolutely *transported* to have a birthday present and I shall never forget you. Nobody ever sends me any nowadays, although I am just as keen as ever on having them. So this was a tremendous surprise and made me feel quite happy all day. It is the first present I've had for two years—except from my mother. The last one was a one and sixpenny cigarette lighter, given me by a boy. His and your names will be engraved upon my heart. Do you read the Pooh books? I felt like Eyore with his popped balloon and the empty honey pot. Not that His Monkey Wife was comparable to either of these, but I mean as regards rarity.

I changed the book, by the way, for I have a copy (and believe it was myself who recommended you to read it in the first place).

Naturally I changed it for the worse—giving it in part exchange for a foul book called "IF."

If you want some books to read, I am told there is a new David Garnett coming out—called something about grasshoppers—and a book called Hatter's Castle which is said to be brilliant. As this is said by the J. C. Squire coterie I can't vouch for it. My own book comes out on 30th July and I will send you a copy, for Potts as well. I shall be too mean to give you one each, and in any case it's not worth it, as the thing will be merely a curiosity.

Thank you for your offer of one twin. I accept it, provided it takes my name. What a shame to have to have babies, but I suppose it's all for the best. I expect they will all be cross-eyed, or piebald or something of the sort. They do always so seem to be. I am dismayed by the paucity of presentable children. Mind, I shan't accept the demi-twin unless it's blond.

How is the harpsichord and the husband? Was he offended when I told him he was jealous of you, and were you pleased? If he is not too angry to answer you might ask him whether I am examining this year, and, if so, whether he knows on what books?

I won't try another page. I did admire your left hand writing.

Love,
Timothy

In due time, *Dead Mr. Nixon* appeared and Potts responded favorably to it, delighting the neophyte novelist. "Scott" refers to White's collaborator, R. McNair Scott. White wrote the first four chapters, part of chapter five, chapters 12, 13, part of chapter 14, and the last five chapters.

47 Carisbrooke Rd., St. Leonards-on-Sea

Dear L.J.P.

Time seems to have passed over our heads rather dreadfully since you last wrote, and I notice that you have changed the character of your signature. It was splendid of you to say just the right things about *Dead Mr. N* (Tilly failed to do so) and I must tell you that all the parts applauded by you are my own, and the hunt and the battle are not. So you guessed very cleverly. I wrote approximately the beginning, the middle and the end, Scott doing intermediate bits on either side of the middle. I am in process of quarrelling with Scott (it seems my fate) and am *delighted* to hear that his piffling little rivers flowed up hill. Did you notice, too, the absurdity of the hunt? An exhausted jade plodding—indeed *lurching* was the word used—across fields but able to take stiff fences at the end of them; all this apart from childish improbability of hired hack leading good class hunters and so on? I have since written a detective story on my own (in 3 weeks) to pay for my hunting next winter. It will be much better. Naturally tongue is still in cheek, but one can't do it otherwise and anyway it's as honest as keeping a fried fish shop—a trade it much resembles. This new book I'm touting at the moment with Hodder & Stoughton and after that I propose to capture the mezzo-brow market with a book on the Rad Ike or Constant Nymph level, thus making £10,000 in America through the Bk. of Month Club.

At the same time I am salving my conscience by writing the first 1st class poetry I've ever written—though infrequently.

But I expect all this is boring news. You have made me a great stranger in the past few months, and I have suspected you of being angry about something. If this is the case you obviously won't believe me when I say that I haven't the remotest idea what you're annoyed about, and so the matter is best left unopened.

I'm sorry to hear about Mary.

Timothy

Dear L.J.P.

I cannot suggest about your lady friend's book, but Hodders themselves might consider it if she can introduce some sentiment. The detective story market has dropped out and all publishers are clamouring for serious (!) works. All she can do is to keep touting it round, beginning with Jonathan Cape and working downwards. I hope she will have the guts to go on waiting and touting, as almost any book is bound to go in the end, somewhere, if one doesn't get discouraged. She could get the work done for her by sending it to an agent, if bored, but agents demand 10% of profits. Priestley's agent for *Good Companions* made his fortune over it.

The poem in *The Listener* was a good one, I think, but unimportant.[5] It would have been α if its content had been vital, but as it is remains a good B +. Since writing to you I have looked through the poems which I was pleased about and am dashed to find that only one bears out my statement. This one is called "The Skull" and is α + in its modest way.

This skull is the deserted egg of an extinct species,
Bleached, blown, and long past being stale or rotten:
A mineral remnant, one of the collector's pieces,
In which the Dodo of the mind was once begotten.

I feel my own skull, through its warm and motive coating
Of quick comfortable hair and the neck's firm soft flesh:
Nestling in rosy enclosure, cushioned & cradled, floating
In the fruit's womb, a nutty Kernel, a fledgeling fresh.

How smoothly it articulates upon its nervous column,
Nourished with scarlet sap in the rich autumn;
How fruitfully it snuffs up balmy aromas through its five living
      issues,
Warm and ripening in a cradle of juicy tissues.

* * *

Strange but natural that this cosy Kernel,
Its flesh fermented, must later bleach above:
A fruit no longer but self-sufficient, an eternal
Hard-shrivelled, clean-nibbled, pleasant peachless stone.[6]

I am not clear as to what is the best order for the lines in verse 3 (whether abab would not be best) nor whether the two common adjectives "firm" & "soft" are justifiable so close together in verse 2. But they are more or less what I mean.

My serious historical novel [Farewell Victoria] is giving me much entertainment, tho' I have not yet written a word of it. I find that the two decades following the year 1840 marked the apogee of the 2nd golden age in English Civility. And it was the most golden of the lot. The great Georgian times were all right for the *spirit*, I suppose, but lacked the necessary material comforts. It seems to have been all a matter of *wit* and *tea*, perched on a dunghill. Sewers and so forth quite deadly—cholera—plague—smallpox. But in the '50s and '60s we were *cives romani*. The 18th century was the age of improving landlords (see Trevelyan) and things were looking up in the country parts, when everything was put back by the Industrial Revolution. So the real fruits of civility were put off. Till (about) 1840, on 2nd thoughts, I should say that there had been *no* golden ages at all. I find from Punch that the aristocracy really were the cads that Thackeray makes them out (and of course the Charles II class were cads all over). They never paid their bills. Punch is full of jokes about duns. And till then there were no middle classes to make a buffer between debtor and creditor. The state of affairs was grave in your Restoration period; but it was infinitely worse, tho' less swashbuckling, in the reign of George 3. For one thing the lower classes had increased numerically in that reign alone from 7½ to 14 millions.

I think I should be wiser to hastily drop this subject before I get pedantic about it. Besides, it is still only partially digested in my head. What I set out to say is that I've fallen in love with the years 1840–60 and am starting a book on them. I have rediscovered the brandy of history. I wish I'd read it at Cambridge. It is the only humane study, as foxhunting is the only rational sport.

I am glad that Mary's operation was successful, and here is a list of some books which might amuse her.

α. The only great book *since* I saw you: *The Grasshoppers Come* by David Garnett   α +

β.   *Hatter's Castle* by   ?   Dud but compelling   β −
       The Longest Journey by E. M. Forster   α −
       In the Beginning by Norman Douglas   β +
       The Midnight Folk by John Masefield   α +
       Afternoon Men by   ? (scandalous & ephemeral)   β +
       The Prisoner in the Opal by A. E. W. Mason   (detective)[7]   β +

N. B. Most of the books in the second heading have been out a good long time. Note the Masefield book. You will probably loathe it because I say it is good. If you miss the point, and I'm not sure that it is entirely your type, of course you will. But in my opinion it is his *only* claim to the consideration of posterity, and a *chef d'oeuvre* of the *imagination*. A *poet*. I shall talk to you for hours about its points when I next see you. I admire it so much that I daren't try to begin telling you why. This letter would never end. I must say just one thing. I read it all through to my form last term (illicitly)—their average age being about 10½—and *each* boy in the form enjoyed it as much as I did. Considering how much less mentally alert we are in comparison with boys of that age I need say no more. Do not answer this letter for a long time, but, when you do, tell me that your donnish god forsaken soul was not too far gone to enjoy that book.
       love from
       Timothy

Glad you are to be praelector. You must be making a considerable fortune. I wish I were. Unfortunately the people who know how to spend never have it. No, I have not decided against marriage. I think it's excellent when you can afford it. I never objected to anything but love in a cottage. Cottages were made for free love alone. When are you going to introduce me to the Gabriels? Yes, I shall be delighted to play bowls. Though actually I despise all games that have rules. You would be much happier, really, if you were allowed to simply roll the things about on Granchester Meadows. Children are the only people who know how to play games, and theirs are all like that for example.

White's lifelong battle with alcoholism, as well as his ambivalent relationship with his mother, appear as topics for discussion in the following letter. He alludes to an unrequited love, one of many such affairs he was to have over the years. The book he hated writing would be published under the name James Aston as *First Lesson*, and was dedicated to L. J. and Mary Potts.

Saturday [October 10, 1931]
The Dingle, Reigate

Dear L.J.P.

I have just been reading a letter which you wrote to me in rather a tearing good humour before you were married, and it has prompted me to write to you, or to your past self, or to the humour in which it was written. I think I must be in a good humour myself, although I'm half way into an attack of 'flu and struggling in one of my numerous unrequited love affairs.

I seem doomed to sterility and can't help feeling it a waste. My body, poor creature, though as weak as a kitten at far too many points, is superficially well made, I am sure of it, and seems so pathetically *deserving* that I feel a cad to baulk it all the time. However, this is a delicate and amusing subject which must be put off till I can inflict it upon you in its true proportions by word of mouth. I think I may say that I have reached the valuable critical pitch at which all sexual tragedies appear richly comic. Long may I retain it. The good humour must be due to other than physical causes. I am writing a book about a don called Mr. Belfry who goes to Italy a virgin, takes a mistress, falls passionately in love with her, is jilted because she falls in love with somebody else, and returns to Cambridge, taking up his duties where he left them off. I shall be pleased to have written this book, I suppose, though I hate writing it. Then I'm feeling cheerful because I had the strength of mind to practice shots in the squash court by myself, for an hour, this afternoon. I did this α. because I am suffering from 'flu, β. because I want to be good at squash. I ask myself whether you will find these satisfactory reasons. Then I had a bath, and lots of whisky, and I think perhaps on the whole that's enough explanation of good humour and a sufficient apology for writing.

I got a letter this morning from some pundit at the B.B.C. actually *soliciting* a poem for *The Listener*,[8] because they liked the last one. Hence more good humour. I shall be positively bubbling over by the time I've finished the whisky and this letter.

The detective story which I wrote last vac. has soured on me. Hodders refused it, and so did Collins. So I have sent it to a literary agent and washed my hands of it.

Isn't this crisis awful? My mother has just bought a house [at Mount Pleasant, Burwash, Sussex], and I've implored her to move into it quickly, so that at least she can have some ponderable possession when the currency collapses. Next holidays I am going to have to hunt with a very unfashionable pack, on account of financial strain, but I hope to get my don's adventures finished then and make a little pocket money. Fame comes slowly, but I intend to have it sooner or later. For one thing my body (q.v. supra) can't have its sop until I can afford it. And all the time one's rosebuds are slipping away. Never mind, I insist upon being a roué sooner or later, even if I have to wait till I dodder. I'm afraid I shall be a scandal as a poet laureate.

How is Mary? Has she had any of those children yet—of which she promised me one for immoral purposes? I am glad they have cut off her feet successfully, or whatever they did.

I send you a poem, with my love. ["Dr. Prisonface." See Appendix B]

    Timothy

In case this handwriting has tried your eyes I may mention that it was you who put me up to it. You said that writing small and carefully was an excellent sedation when tired. You must be careful of your chance remarks to pupils.

In 1932 White, as Sylvia Townsend Warner suggests, was "considerably nearer in age to his pupils than to their headmaster . . . Combative and chivalrous, White was drawn to defenseless causes as others are drawn to lost ones. An incident had inflamed both his pity and his satire. Two little boys had been found in the same bed, and were expelled. White was charged to accompany them to London. During the journey, he asked what they had been doing. They admitted that they had been talking. Asked what they had been talking about, they replied, 'Buses and trains.'"[9] Clearly, his championing of his students played a large role in the eventual fate which he reported to Potts on January 22, 1932.

Ian Parsons and Tony Tendall were contemporaries of White's at Cambridge. In 1926, White had gone with Parsons on a walking tour in Lapland.

                                   [January 22, 1932]
                            Laker's Hotel, Redhill, Surrey

Dear L.J.P.
    To all intents and purposes I have been fired from this school

37

owing to my socratic intransigeance. There was nothing wrong, or anything of that sort, and Dr. Prisonface had to invent a rambling plaintive excuse about the lack of people to teach the boys cricket now that he is suffering from rheumatoid arthritis. He also expressed his great regret, and he will be bound to provide me with the testimonial in which he doesn't believe. Well, are you going to let poor Nelly starve?

I go at the end of next term. What ought I to do? I feel that it's rather preposterous to teach Latin in a prep. school after getting a First in English. I am writing to Ian Parsons, to see if he can get me a job in a publisher's; to Tony Tendall, to see if he can wangle me on to the B.B.C.; to the late headmaster of Cheltenham, who has just gone to Shrewsbury and might give me a job there; to Gabbitas; and to Laffan, in case his influence can manage one of the better public schools.

But can *you* get me anything in Cambridge? As you know, I had rather have that than anything. If you want to shew this letter to Tilly, do. But not to Laffan or anybody else. I shall be telling him and all my other correspondents that I leave through boredom. I think I should have done in one more term, so don't commiserate. I may add that I believe I have a novel coming out in April [*They Winter Abroad*] which would have resulted in my being expelled with ignominy. So perhaps this is all for the best.

Recollect, however, that I shall have no reserves to draw upon. I must get a new job quick. I know it would need a titanic effort to get me into Cambridge, but now you can at any rate dismiss the doubt as to whether Cambridge would be good for me. It's no longer a question of good or not, but of needing a job. The only question is whether you are fond enough of me to make the effort.

Is that an *appalle au coeur*? And how do you spell it?

Love from
Timothy

Love to Mary.

Despite his dismissal from St. David's, White was not destined to starve. Through a stroke of luck, his First in English, and aid from an influential person, he secured a position as head of the English department at Stowe, a ten-year-old public school that was already being spoken of as "the new Eton." Although the identity of White's benefactor is not known for sure, he is thought to have been E.M.W. Tillyard.

[February 28, 1932]
The Dingle, Reigate

Dear L.J.P.

I am very sorry I put you in the boresome position of having to write that last letter, but you will admit that one can't be scrupulous about one's bread and butter. Fortunately I have succeeded by my own efforts, to a certain extent, and am to be the head of the English department at Stowe from next September.

I leave here in April. I shall pay a month's round of visits or so, and then go to Paris to see a rich demising aunt: thence to Warsaw, or any other convenient place for wild oats and local colour. China is too far, or I would. It would be difficult to get back in time.

But now to the purpose of this letter. As head of the English faculty at Stowe I am ready to treat with the English faculty at Cambridge (like William IV with God—see Max Beerbohm). If you will give all my boys credits in School Certificate I will teach them anything you specially want. And then, of course, they will get Firsts with Distinction at Cambridge, throwing credit upon both of us. Seriously, with me at Stowe and you at Queens (not to mention I. A. Richards and Tilly) I believe we can reform the world. In thirty years we will have Gerard Hopkins canonised in Westminster Abbey, Tilly on the throne (on account of his tact and practical ability), yourself as Canterbury (because of your moral priggish-ness), myself as C. in C. of the army (my moustache), and Richards, obviously, at the Home Office.

But this is what I am trying to say: Presumably one gets notice from the University as to what the set books are every year. It will be easy enough to cram them. But is the unhappy entrant for School Certificate expected to have any background of general literary acquaintance besides? If so, how much, and how would you advise me to administer it? How most easily?

Lastly, I am too moral to content myself with merely getting credits in School Cert. My accursed proselitising conscience bids me do something for literature: even, perhaps, to "put it across," to popularise, to James-Douglas. Well, I am enclosing a couple of abortive lists which purport to recommend books for holiday tasks (if one still calls them that). They are calculated to *give boys a background of literary appreciation* quite distinct from examination knowledge. In a small way they try to suggest that one *could enjoy reading!* I want you, if you can be so very kind, to tell me what I have left out. As you see, it is mostly modern stuff. This is a weakness, I am sure, but I can't think of "classics" (Doctor Prisonface's word) which boys would really be unable to put down. This is what I want from you. Remember the limited experience of boys. They range from twelve or thirteen to embryo undergraduates.

My policy is to be jesuitical. If necessary I am ready, as you see, to recommend things like Rupert Brooke (like to like, puerile to puerile) because I myself founded my literary appreciation on an early passion for Ruby M. Ayres.

I believe that real enjoyment of reading must develop itself naturally from the bloodiest tripe upwards. So if you can think of a Dickens which ought to be on the list I am even ready to recommend that. (To the lowest forms.)

If you will look at the VERSE columns you will catch the idea. The bottom begins on Flecker and Masefield (visual or narrative). As it reaches puberty Brooke is thrown in. (He would have been lower on the grade, except that you have to be pubic in order to swoon in him, and that raises the age level fortuitously.) De la Mare is added, as a stepping stone to higher things. Then Thomas (perhaps also a very little Sassoon, Owen, and certainly Housman). And *then* we begin to read *poetry.*

40

Now are you going to help me? You had better. I am bringing out between three and four books this year, novels, not all under my own name,[10] and I shall neither send you a single copy nor write a single initial in a copy bought by you, nor even reveal my pseudonym, unless you add to these lists and return them. If you won't do it for me or the books, you ought to do it for literature. I know exactly what you are going to say:

Dear Timothy,

At last I am beginning to answer letters again. Mary and I were so delighted to hear your good news. I must say you deserved a little luck. But I am sorry I cannot help you over those lists. I should have been delighted. . . . English dons not the people for literary appreciation. . . . get so out of touch . . . no time to read new books . . . absolute hermit . . . busy . . . busy . . . busy . . . etc. . . . etc. . . . etc. . . . andsoforth . . . andsoforth . . . andsoforth.

love from
L. J. P.

If you write me anything of the sort I shall send you a bomb by parcel post, like in America.

There is one aspect of the question which I ought to mention, and that is that the headmaster of Stowe [J. F. Roxburgh] is *practically conscious*. More so than any other headmaster known to me at any rate. He does not mind how sexual the books recommended to elderley specialists may be—Joyce if necessary. But he very reasonably points out that the younger boys are sexual powder magazines. He never forbids a boy to read a book if he has come by it in the normal course of events, but he prefers that I should not *recommend* books of a suggestive nature to the middle and lower school. I don't grudge this restriction when you consider the somewhat special nature of the institution in which they live, and when you consider that their necessarily small experience of the *fact* makes the recommendation of its *literature* stupid. They have nothing to judge the literature by. Also they might make the mistake of learning theory before practice—the bane of the modern world.

Personally I shall be chary of recommending books which hinge on these subjects even to the highest forms—for the reasons I gave above: the uselessness of fancy before fact.

And lastly I have a doubt about my list (Prose) for the lower forms. On my (I am convinced correct) theory of starting with tripe—something which the child really wants to read—ought I not to be recommending Edgar Wallace (actually, as I expect I've told you, he was *quite* one of the greatest tripe writers because of his sincerity. Nobody in Edgar Wallace is a pose. Nobody exists except to further the plot, or speaks except for that reason.)? I wonder if you would have an opportunity of asking Richards this?

And if he says, as I am convinced he will, that I ought to be recommending Nat Gould, how am I to reconcile this with the prejudices of the parents?

Love from
Timothy

White, preparing for his new life at Stowe, wrote at length advising Potts on his impending fatherhood, although, of course, it was a subject in which White was thoroughly inexperienced.

[March 22, 1932]
The Dingle, Reigate

Dear L.J.P.

She is quite robust enough to have nothing to fear from babies: I mean nothing serious, because after all the quite hellish pain is not an important matter fundamentally. Anybody can stand pain. It may even be good for them, and one knows that it will be over. No

42

human beings ever suffer more pain than they can bear. It balances itself. At the high levels of pain one knows that one won't be called to face what is beyond one's powers, because there is a sort of saturation point. The only boresome thing is being so sick before the baby for so long, and having to put up with the baby when one's got it. I am not talking hot air. I have discussed maternity with quite a number of frank and sincere women: in fact it has always interested me. Now there is one thing which I must beg you to see to, and to impress upon Mary, and that is that nobody tries to be Spartan or considerate towards the doctor. The last mother I talked to had guts like Mary, and had been told that it would be hell, and had reconciled herself to bearing it. Not knowing quite what degree of hell it would be, and not wanting to be laughed at for being fussy and getting the doctor too soon, she practically had the baby before the doctor was fetched. You must get the doctor as soon as Mary feels ill, even if it means a false alarm and getting him again. If you are going to be fussed yourself I will come to stay round about the critical date, and walk you up and down Sedley Taylor Road to keep you out of the way. I believe this is what friends do for each other in novels. Personally I should think it would be about the most brutal thing I could possibly do to you.

Wish Mary good luck and give her my love. Tell her also that this will mean a temporary breakdown in our relations, as I cannot have anything to do with a household which has a baby in it. The whole thing is too much of a strain.

By the way, I am in the midst of an animated correspondence with Rubinstein's, the criminal lawyers, in regard to the murder story (shortly coming out with Gollancz) which had a murder in your rooms [Darkness at Pemberley]. Apparently I have libelled almost everybody in Queens', and I am having to write to the worst sufferers (the book is already in page proofs) asking whether they mind. Perhaps I ought to ask you whether you mind an exact plan, furniture included, being published of your late rooms on A staircase? The plan even marks your tin bath. The murdered man is the don occupying these rooms, and he is described as an intransigeant & affluent drug-addict. If the cap fits wear it.

43

There is no reason why this letter should ever stop, nor why it should ever have begun, so perhaps I had better end it peacefully here.

Love from
Timothy

[April 3, 1932]
The Dingle, Reigate, Surrey

Dear POTTËS,

Thank you and Mary for your invitation. May I accept it, but fix a date later on? I am going home tomorrow (MOUNT PLEASANT, BURWASH, SUSSEX) to write two novels, and this, combined with the grisly environment with which my mother usually surrounds me, is likely to reduce me to a nervous wreck sooner or later, and probably more than once. I am rather wanting to save up my visits to friends so that I can take them when matters become critical. There is going to be additional trouble because I have embarked upon an experiment in living which, although possibly interesting and certainly valuable in several queer ways, is arduous. I am trying to live asexually for forty days. I am afraid you will think it rather typical of me. I was always by nature a pole-squatter and marathon dancer. The forty is of course for Hebraic reasons.

I prefer POTTËS to the Greek POES, because there is something Chaucerian about you.

Love from
Timothy

Under the name James Aston, White had published another novel, *They Winter Abroad*. His fears of Stowe students' parents finding the book "immoral" can be understood from this brief quotation from David Garnett's review: "The novel is a description of a hotel for

44

English people in Italy and the effect which the southern springtime has upon them, awakening desires which have been dormant during the winter. Sex. Yes, indeed."[11]

[May 12, 1932]
Mount Pleasant, Burwash, Sussex

My Dear POTTËS,

Herewith a book by a friend of mine, whom you may know. I have got him to autograph it for you. If you happen to recognise him, he says that he won't mind your hinting strongly at the authorship. In fact he would be very glad if you did. He wants it pushed in Cambridge. The only reason for the pseudonym is that he wants to hold down a job in a public school, where parents are the oddest people and may find the book immoral. So the pseudonym leaves him and his headmaster (who knows) able to deny culpability if necessary. I hope you will like it. Will you lend it to Tilly, and ask him to push it too? I am so poor that I can't afford to send him a copy; though I should dearly like to. Mrs. Gordon has also been asked to assist with publicity.

Forgive this short note, in the midst of other necessary correspondence.

    Love from
    Timothy

And to Mary.

During the summer of 1932, T. H. White had composed a "Pirate Story," called "Rather Rum," which, in spite of several attempts, was never published.

Mount Pleasant, Burwash, Sussex

Dear Pottës,

We don't take in *The Times* and I have no means of telling how Mary's affair is going on. Will you let me know whether it is a boy or a girl, when it is?

But I am ashamed to say that Mary is far too healthy to provoke any of my sympathy, and this letter is not really about her at all.

Your interest (which seemed not to be entirely pretended) in my Pirate Story has put new life into me, and I propose to get it published. But I can't forget that Chatto's sent it back to me as a dud. I am sure it isn't a dud, but the business has shaken my confidence. I want to know whether you will allow me to send you the typescript (as a well-disposed person) for correction? I am willing to entirely re-write five eighths of it. If you would read it through, cutting out as much as you like, and making as many corrections as you like of any sort, it would help me simply tremendously. If you send it back unaltered I shall publish it so, and it may mean the ruination of my reputation as a seller. So you must remember that we have got to make concessions to a barbaric public. If, on the other hand, you send it back with all but two chapters cut out the odds are approximately five to two that I shall cut out all but two chapters. So you must not be too severe. Now then, will you take it on? These are the only kinds of babies that I can manage at present. I think as a proud father you ought to be sympathetic.

THEY WINTER ABROAD has gone into three impressions already.

Best love, and especially to Mary,
from
Timothy

White is at his most whimsical and his most gracious in his letter of congratulation on the birth of the Pottses' daughter, Margaret. The capitalized "She" at the end of the first paragraph replaces the word "it," which was intentionally crossed out. (The letter was written on Chatto and Windus stationery, with the heading crossed out.)

[July 7, 1932]
33 Grosvenor Rd., S.W. 1

My dear Mary,

I didn't answer your magnificent letter at once, because I intended to send Miss Margaret Potts the largest bunch of lilies. It seems silly to tell you this, because I am not sending them: and not wholly as a result of poverty. But at the moment (though I have quite enough) and so it is stinginess purely. (There seems to be some confusion in that sentence.) Anyway, what I meant to say is that I *ought* to have sent you many pounds worth of lilies for having such a magnificent baby as I am sure she is, and for having her so sensibly, and for being the only friend's wife of mine that I have ever approved of. All the others have had babies, and when I refer to their babies I call them "it." But your baby shall always be "she": the highest award possible in the class. In fact, as you and Pottës are the only two godly people I know, I shall have to break down my prejudice against being used as a Po, and come to visit your baby, and even handle her, and give you the benefit of my extensive experience as a wet nurse. Do they call them so because of what the baby does? But come, I am really not at all flippant. Will you believe me that I worried for a week before it happened, and made pretexts all over Sussex to borrow copies of *The Times*? I had just written to Pottës to ask, when I got this letter. It is magnificent news that you are well, and I hope not too much wrecked. Don't dare to have another unless you want it ("it" because we don't know yet). Frankly I am glad She was a girl, though I usually prefer boys. You and Pottës will be better with girls. I don't know why.

I so seldom see virtue rewarded that I dislike it when I do. I cannot sincerely congratulate people whom I envy. So I shall stop writing.

Love from
Timothy

In August of 1932, White published a novel under his own name, *Darkness at Pemberley*. Although he calls it "that ridiculous little book," he cannot disguise his pleasure in its appearance. As James Aston, he would be represented in the fall by *First Lesson*, which he refers to as "the Belfry book." Describing it in a paragraph heavy with parentheses as "my experience grafted on your pre-marital nature," he goes on to assure Potts of the complimentary nature of his borrowing from his mentor's own experience. Sylvia Townsend Warner has written of this paragraph as follows: "That Potts's pupil should entangle himself in such a fluster of parentheses suggests embarrassment; but embarrassment from a sense of having made too free with Potts's premarital nature was not in keeping with White's character—or with Potts's either . . . [White] was afraid of being thought a prig. . . . It was the disclosure of his old-fashioned esteem for Potts as a man with a sense of duty that embarrassed him."[12] The novel he speaks of as "Old Mundy's Garner" would be published as *Farewell Victoria*, and his "book about three great failures" would be called "Three Lives" (which was left unpublished); the lives he had chosen were those of Joanna Southcott, Admiral Byng, and Sir Jeffrey Hudson, Henrietta Maria's dwarf.

[August 25, 1932]
47 Carisbroke Rd., St. Leonards-on-Sea

My dear Pottës,
    You really might have spared me serious comment on that ridiculous little book. It was only sent to you out of affection, or as

the domestic cat lays the tragic corpses of the household mice before her master's door. I wrote that book in little over 3 weeks, putting down anything that came along on the spur of the moment. Everybody at home thinks it splendid. I know it to be bloody, because it won't even be bad enough to succeed in its object, viz: £. s. d. There was one thing that amused me, however, when I read it in print after not seeing it for a long time, and that was to watch my instructive literary reserve compelling itself to gush. I felt that I was watching the Dean of Canterbury in pink tights, trying to keep step with the other members of the chorus. For, though you won't admit it, I have a sixth sense against helotry and am naturally timid about leaving myself open to accusations of rhetoric and sentimentality. It cost me a good deal to write some of the things in that book: the characters! Prigs and imbeciles.

Just before I leave these dullish subjects, I must tell you that the Belfry book (wh. describes my experiences grafted on your premarital nature, and which I hope you will recognise as complimentary—I have had to *laugh* gently at the hero now and then, to provoke sympathy for him and to save myself from being a prig, but the basic picture [of the man who recognises responsibilities] is the greatest compliment I shall ever pay to anyone) will be out fairly soon in England. But I am going to ask you not to read it (I shan't send you a copy) until the *American* edition comes out. That will not be for some months. But Chatto's have funked, and forced me to cut out, all the most essential bits. I am in hopes of getting America to include them, and should like you to read the full book (which is good) rather than the mutilatee (which is trivial). Meanwhile (yesterday) I have just finished my great full length heroic picture of the XIXth century. It will come out in January or Feb. (I hope) and will be called OLD MUNDY'S GARNER. I am not sure that it isn't as bad as everything else I have written, and if so, after the pirates (title "RATHER RUM") I shall write no more. I will send you the pirates as soon as I can get at them. They are packed away at Reigate.

As for your baby, I scorn her. I am buying a horse this week.

But yes, I do suffer from Weltschmerz: but not a temporary one. It is not clear to me that anybody can say in advance whether they are justified in having babies, quite apart from the present depression. You and Mary were happy. I should have thought you could have carried on at that without thrusting life on an innocent party. It is quite probable that she will be happy too but was it worth it? I mean will it be worth it, for the baby? Nobody, I believe, has ever completely solved that problem. Now that I am alive I can see no excuse for ceasing to be so. But I cannot either see any excuse for having begun to be in the first place. The situation about life seems to me to be on all fours with the situation about God. As regards the latter we are at a balance which makes him equally possible and impossible i.e. there is no evidence, and we are therefore scientifically *refused* agnosticism. We have no right to make any hypothesis and so even agnosticism is cut out. Until there is a hint one must be an atheist. It seems to me that the value of life is just the same. Is it or is it not "worth it"? Nobody knows. Have you then the right to postulate a baby? Fine words to address to a new parent, but I console myself by thinking that you will have got round them long ago. Don't consider me pessimistic. I bathe all day, have a negro complexion, and a promising beard. *Nota*. Had I a right to bring that beard into the world?

Pottës, you are not enough of a flâneur (whatever that may mean) and dilettante. I think you ought to take steps to rectify it. Soon I am going to write a book of letters to my grandson, in which I shall lay down the law about madeira, cigars, getting drunk, and other vital matters. But like that Stanhope boy, you will never be a credit to me. I am also going to write a book about great failures: Joanna who failed to parturate the Messiah, Byng, Chelmsford, and that Elizabethan nobleman who failed and voyaged seven years to court forgetfulness without effect. I should like to include you, but I am afraid you are your own success.

Don't be so rude to me about your dirty little baby. I am not a homosexual, as I shall explain to you when I see you.

Enough of this letter, which is boring me as much as it is boring you.

love from
Timothy

47 Carisbroke Rd., St. Leonards-on-Sea

Dear Pottës,

Wd. you let me have a p.c. by return of post saying whether you wd. object to my dedicating my book about the don in Italy [*First Lesson*] to you and Mary? It has been emasculated by Chatto and I shd. only use your initials. But I shall understand *perfectly* if you wd. rather not. If I don't hear directly I shall take silence to mean refusal. [*First Lesson* was dedicated "To L. J. P. and Mary."]

    love from
    Timothy

Having managed to get himself in debt to his mother, White writes simultaneously both to Mary Potts and to her husband to ask for a loan with which to pay her back. Always short on cash, he immensely disliked asking for money, and so he tells Potts "I hate writing this letter (but not so much as I hate my mother)."

[September 16, 1932]
Laker's Hotel, Redhill

Dear Mary,

This is a *delicate* letter, adressed to you in the strictest confidence in the hope that I can rely on your *vision* and *sincerity!* (Excuse all this underlining: it is a form of graveyard jocularity.) Well, I am slightly up the pole financially and as I once paid back some money which I had borrowed off Pottës, I have written to ask him for more. But the letter is enclosed with this because I don't want him to get it unless he is in a sound position himself. I have asked him for twenty pound (and I may say that if it had been for myself I should have done without it: but it is for my mother, who is plaguing me to pay

51

her 3 guineas a week for the fourteen weeks which I spent at home, and as I loathe the woman I shall have to pay her) and as it really doesn't matter (i.e., I am in no danger of the judgement, since it is a debt inside the family) I honestly don't want him to be asked at all if it is going to be the least bit difficult for him. Now then, Mary, this is where you come in. I expect Pottës keeps you in complete ignorance of his finances, but if you have by any chance managed to *worm* something out of him, you will be able to judge how he stands. If you think it may be an annoyance to him, tear up the enclosed envelope. Will you do that? Get hold of the fact that it is not a matter of importance except to my private feelings. I owe nothing to any tradesman and have in fact a balance of ten pounds. I can easily tell my mother to wait. But personally, because I dislike her very much and should like to have done with her altogether, it has seemed best to borrow so long as nobody is put out unduly. I wonder if you grasp the situation and are reliable, or whether you think this to be a great deal of insincere fuss about a small matter. It is not a small matter. Money is the most important thing in the world, and it slips through my fingers.

Don't, on the other hand, read any pathos into this appeal. I am nowhere near the workhouse, and have just bought a horse (a beauty). I am quite happy financially and it is only for emotional reasons that I want the money. The woman is a vampire. I really do mean it when I ask you to use your discretion with the enclosed. It will bother me not to have paid my mother, it will bother Pottës to pay me. Sum up the comparative bothers and act according.

Now enough of this miserable topic. Send me a long letter about Margaret, whatever you do. I am very good with babies and am coming to see her when she is about a year old, as I propose to teach her her first word, which shall be "bugger."

Best love from
Timothy

My dear Pottës,

Are you in a sufficiently safe position to lend me £20 possibly till 20th December, but I hope sooner? I am not in any great need of the money as I only owe it to my charming mother (who charges me 3 guineas a week for the pleasure of staying with her). I am solvent, but not sufficiently solvent to pay her this sum and live till they pay me at Stowe. At the moment it is only a question of doing one or the other, and there will be no difficulty in refusing to pay her at once, as it is a family matter. But I dislike her so very much that it would be a pleasure to escape any obligations which I shd. be under as her debtor. I explain this in order to make it clear that the matter is a trivial one. Your refusal wd. not surprise me (indeed, if anything, the loan wd.) nor inconvenience my finances (only my family emotions) and certainly wd. not diminish, (as nothing cd.) my admiration for yourself. I shd. be very sorry to think that you were putting yourself out at all—but I thought it was worth asking, in case you are really rolling secretly in money all the time.

I hate writing this letter (but not so much as I hate my mother) and so I shall stop writing it.

Best love from
Timothy

CHAPTER 2

Stowe

White stayed four years at Stowe and he was so impressed by the place that it formed the background of *Mistress Masham's Repose*—Malplaquet being a mixture of Stowe and Blenheim: "It was surrounded by Vistas, Obelisks, Pyramids, Columns, Temples, Rotundas, and Palladian Bridges . . ."

Stowe's headmaster, J. F. Roxburgh, was considered to be responsible for the school's success but, as had been the case with L. J. Potts, White first disliked him, and only did him justice years later:

Roxburgh—whom I envied at that time and consequently disliked but later, after leaving, made real friends with—was a genius. He allowed people enormous latitude to do what they enjoyed doing.

The young teacher drove around in his old Bentley and was extremely busy during his free time—riding, hunting, shooting, fishing and learning to fly; every activity was very carefully recorded in a different diary and some of this material was used in *England Have My Bones*.

As White had feared, the publication of *First Lesson* in 1932 indeed created a minor scandal in the school. A parent of one of the boys recognized White under the pseudonym of James Aston, read the book about the Cambridge don in love, and was shocked and alarmed. Roxburgh stood by his young teacher, but White had to write a letter promising that he would write no more such books.

While he was at Stowe, White started being psychoanalyzed and wrote down many of his dreams in his private journals. He had a great opinion of his psychoanalyst and believed that a Harley Street specialist could put an end to the loneliness that was the price he had to pay for his sexual fantasies. The episode of the barmaid he unsuccessfully wooed for seven months may be considered as part of the treatment.

His teaching left him time to write, and in *Farewell Victoria* he showed for the first time his feeling for the past and his dislike of the modern state, where the individual is over-ruled—one of his favorite themes: "The end of the Victorian era had banished man from the world. The greatest acceleration in history had expelled the individual, reducing him to the unrecognized status of the country labourer."

Stowe was the last school at which White formally taught, but his continuing need to educate would be manifest in his warm and supportive relationships with the young. Ever an ardent student, he was always able to inspire others with the desire to acquire knowledge.

[October 20(?), 1932]
Ye Olde Crowne Hotel, Brackley, Northants.

My dear Pottës,

Herewith [*First Lesson*]. I hope you will be able to detect in it some vaguely amusing resemblance to a forecast of yourself, twenty years hence, if you hadn't married Mary. But perhaps not much. It has become entangled with my own emotions. You need only take the noble side of Belfry's character as your own. The events are purely autobiographical with a difference. In any case it comes with my best love to both of you.

I feel no letter from me will be complete without a mention of your £20. The sudden 3 weeks holiday over paralysis at Stowe has set me back a little financially, and my new (detective) American publisher has evidently been drinking too much in Europe, for he has sailed away again with a depleted banking account and the mere promise to pay me when he gets back to America. So I think you will be poor for 3 more weeks.

Thank you *very much indeed* for your 1st rate letter re the boy Gell. I am at present insisting that he take the 2nd group and go to Peterhouse, though his mother, who is a snob, is still standing out for Trinity. I'll soon settle her, however.

What a boon this holiday is! I was going mad, and not only mad but tubercular. Did I tell you that Stowe was a whited sepulchre? It is. It happens to have some first rate underpaid masters, who do a great deal for the boys, but otherwise is completely hellish— understaffed and pure shew-ring. J. F. Roxburgh is a circus master, nothing else. A stinking little snob of a protestant at heart.

How is that baby of yours? You don't tell me anything. How much does she weigh, and when do you think she will get whooping cough? Give her a linseed mash every saturday, with a condition powder, and two hours regular exercise daily. You will find that she will do better if you damp her bran slightly, just enough to make it stick to the hand. Above all ball her cautiously.

And how are (1) Mary (2) Harpsichord (3) Bowls (4) Recorder? How are the vegetables in the front garden? How, in fact, are all the 100% successes which nobody but you wd. have managed to achieve?

Best love from
Timothy

P.S. I have just remembered that the first person I ever managed to seduce was a girl called Winifred, in a hotel at Crowhurst. This I think is rather important. She was only six. I was only 6.30. She was a sweet creature and had shimmering white buttocks. But we were caught, just when she had consented to let me smack them. How typical!

Just how prophetic were the young teacher/novelist's fears of problems with *First Lesson* is evidenced by this irate letter to Potts.

[January 20, 1933]
Stowe, Bucks

Dear Pottës,

First of all I must clear up the points about which I might have written to you before. I can't say how grateful I am for the criticisms of "Rather Rum": except by letting you know that I have adopted every single one—even to the extent of making a feeble attempt to condense some of the conversations to which you objected. The only thing I want to do now is to return the revised M.S. to you, for further pruning. I haven't the heart to ask you to do this, but if you are sufficiently interested you might write and ask me for it, when I should send it off at once. The point is that it is now hovering on the verge of being a very good book and I am ready to sacrifice myself and you, as Milton did himself and his daughters. It is still halting at the start and needs revision.

But now to the sad sequel. I am as usual in a devil of a mess. *First Lesson* was read by a stinking evangelical parent of one of the boys here (the pseudonym had leaked out owing to the imbecility of Chatto's, who kept sending my correspondence to James Aston, Stowe, Bucks: with the result that, there being a boy here called James Ashton, everything got wrongly delivered and the arrival finally of a photograph exploded the plot entirely. The boy came to me with the picture, asked if it was me, and turned over a considerable arrears of correspondence which he had kept in a puzzled way) and this perfectly bloody parent complained to the headmaster. The headmaster (from whom I had not concealed the pseudonym) bought the book, and was shocked too. Now there is a tremendous fuss, as the parent wants my blood (what a foul mind he must have) and nearly withdrew his boy. The headmaster seems to be kindly, though intellectually dim, and keeps telling me that he knows "The book does not reflect its author." He wants me to give him a written recantation, condemning *First Lesson* as an "undergraduate scrape," and promising that James Aston will write no more such books. I am going to give him this letter, with mental reservations. It is, after all, intended for a cad (the parent) (And also for the governors, who, the H.M. assures me, will soon be in the fuss as well) and may as well be caddish.

The point now is, or rather the points are:

1. Is "Rather Rum" obscene?

2. Shall I publish it, if so, only in America and drop a lot of money?

3. Or shall I change the pseudonym again, and make everybody be damned careful of the next one? This will also drop money, by throwing away all previous publicity gained by the name Aston.

But there is another alternative. I showed Rather Rum to the headmaster and put the three above points to him. He replied that the book was only obscene in a few isolated phrases, and that without them it could perfectly well be published in England under the Aston name. He objected to Saugling being mentioned as a castrato, to the suggestion that he might have been preserved from the world had he been actually castrated, to Sir John being perched upon Lady Calcutta "definitely astraddle." At this point his intellect gave out and he must have stopped reading the book. He did not get as far as the willy-nilly ideas of flagellation, or Madge seeing life at last. Also, though he had reached Mr. Faith, he didn't guess what the secret sin might be.

Now what am I to do? Am I to cut out anything of this sort which might offend the sort of stinkers that one gets as parents, or will this harm the book? Is it a good enough book for it to matter whether it is harmed or not?

Here is a list of queries, like the one that Byng gave to his council of war:

1. Must I choose between being an author or a schoolmaster? If so, which am I to be, and how am I to support myself as an author?

58

2. If the choice is not yet imperative, shall I mutilate "Rather Rum" and publish it in England under Aston, or shall I not mutilate it, publish it in America, and keep the English edition up my sleeve against a rainy day, or shall I start a new pseudonym altogether?

My own feelings are (a) I want to go on being a schoolmaster because I have just bought a lot of furniture, (b) if "Rather Rum" really might be a good book unmutilated I had rather defer profits than mutilate it, (c) if the mutilation might actually do it good (and I suppose it might?) then I am perfectly willing to do that.

Meanwhile I am giving the H.M. his cringing letter (cringing letters for cringing people) and I should like to have an unbiassed opinion of the book, in the light of this problem. Do you think that if I sent it to you, you could (a) read it again yourself ad hoc (is that the right latinism? It was meant to mean "in the light of this problem" as above—but I thought it would be a change) (b) solicit the interest of I. A. Richards? In the first place Tilly says that he remembers me, and, in the second, the book was discussed with him originally. He was one of its begetters. He is unbiassed. I trust his judgement as to whether it is worth my while trying to be a writer of integrity or not. And on this point I am vain. I enjoy my expensive hunting too much to care much about the question, except as one of honour.

Now it is not absolutely necessary for you to read it again yourself. I don't see how I can inflict a second reading of typescript on a slow reader who is also very busy. (The only point in my favour is that so far I am bona fide.) But Richards is a quick reader and I have not bothered him before. Can you do it? Can you let me have a p.c. on this subject (whether to send you the M.S. or not) by return of post? The other queries must, I fear, be answered at leisure.

Don't, if you can help it, tell me to write all this screed out again for Richards and send him the M.S. myself. For one thing I am still a responsible tutor, and the time to write even this is sadly hewn out of the hours of the night. It would be a far kinder thing simply to transfer this letter to him and let him give you a verbal answer over the telephone. *Then*, if he will look at it, I will write to him in full.

N.B. I suppose all this must be rather confidential, as it reflects

some discredit on somebody. If it is on the school, which I stand
pledged to defend, then the common-rooms of Cambridge ought
not to be talking about the obscenantism of Stowe. I suppose,
anyway, that other schools would have been even worse. But what
a life! Tell Tilly that it makes me feel half a communist already. I
wonder if King Amanullah will follow us into that as well?

    love from
    Timothy

"When Timothy White arrived at Stowe he fell in love with country
things" reports one of his former students, and this delight in village
life, in going to the local pub, in hunting and fishing, was to stay
with him all his life.

[April 23, 1933
Bull Hotel, Fairford, Glos.

Dear Pottés,
    I have been meaning not to answer your letter for quite a long
time, but now it's time I did. After my play [*Miracle at Verdun*] which
was a howling success and made a profit of £50 for our poor boy
club, I came straight here, leaving no address, and have been
fishing in peace ever since. Publishers in all parts of the country are
howling for my blood; creditors are combing sea ports; old friends
are feeling their faith severely tested: but meanwhile I have been
chosen to represent a village pub at darts against the neighbouring
public houses. If only I had an income! For I'm coming to terms
with life at last and solving all the riddles of the Sphinx. Beer solves
them; but particularly rustic, sincere, affectionate beer. No other
kind will do, and you can't pose at it. I wish you were here too and
enjoyed the same sort of thing. Tilly wasn't at all bad. Unfor
tunately, unless you have really been a disguised aleman all along,

should recognise your novitiate and be inclined to shew off. This, of course, would be fatal, as the most important mysteries prescribe sincerity and simplicity as a sine qua non.

So that if only I had an income I could take up my real vocation, which is to be in the open air all day and get more and more sodden every night. I should never write another word, and I very much doubt whether I should ever die. Bliss.

However, to give you my dreary little smatch of news. I have taken Richards' criticism to heart and intend to re-write Rather Rum next holidays. I shall probably keep a great deal of the end. You might perhaps tell Richards this as it may flatter him to know that his advice was not asked out of pure wantonness, and if flattered his personal antipathy (rightly detected by you) may wane. The other book about the groom [*Farewell Victoria*] (which is terribly dreary except in patches) has been offered for by Collins—I told you about the quarrel with Chatto?—on certain conditions which have not reached me yet owing to my concealment of address.

There is only one other matter which needs to be dealt with and that is the one of our meeting. This fishing is making me pay through the nose, so that I can't invite you to stay with me till Collins have paid for the groom. If you are at a loose end I shall be the same till May 8th but you wd. have to pay for yourself. If however you can afford the time to snatch a weekend during term I shall have some money by then and I insist that you bring both Mary and the baby to the environs of Stowe. I can put you up either in an hotel or in a farmhouse with the most amazing feather beds. The only thing is that I refuse to take Mary with us to pubs, as this makes the habituers uncomfortable. The *proper* thing to do is for us to go off from 8 till 10 and BRING HER BACK A BOTTLE OF STOUT. We carry it back in a sort of fish bag brought for the purpose.

On second thoughts, if she takes the baby with her, and suckles it ("it" in order to evade the repetition of the feminine personal pronoun, and then keep this sentence on the high level of clarity which has been set by the limpid style of other parts of this letter— and there is no reason why I should finish the clause even there: except the reasons of common humanity, from the lack of which I have never suffered [by the grace of God]—) then it (but not, in this case, the baby) wd. probably be all right.

On third thoughts, no. This wd. only do in a town public.

Now I will leave you to work that out.

> Best love from
> Timothy

It is, I suppose, needless to thank you for reading that book again. I *expect* you to be one of the best people in the world and therefore don't trouble to thank you for it.

By the summer of 1933, White was convinced that his days at Stowe were numbered. Expressing his congenital fears of deprivation to Potts, he received an answer which, in turn, prompted the following reply.

[September 16(?), 1933]
The Nelson Head, Horsey, Norfolk

Dear Pottës,

You are quite right in saying that I can never be a failure. Neither of us, now, will ever fail so far as to be successful. There is a kind of posthumous success which isn't wicked (e. g., Hopkins) and this I expect you will achieve—not with your English Comedy, but with your pseudo-diary when published.[1] (Will you make me your literary executor in case you get run over?) But the real success is to accomplish the first death effectively and early. I am getting on well with it. For me it will mean (1) no more writing. (2) no more luxuries like cars and hunting and the upper classes. My motives for writing were never good and life has cured my snobbery. Well, it may not be an advance. One can't tell what it's like to be dead in this way any more than in the other.

Yes, please. I should much value details of scholarships when you can. I have been corresponding with Tilly and I'm not coming to Cambridge just now. Why this is, I can't quite say. It is probably something to do with the fundamental lethargy which I share with Dr. Johnson. When I make plans it costs me such an effort that I can't summon the energy to unmake them. I had fixed to go back to Stowe on the 20th for my last season's cub-hunting. It will be a frightful wrench to leave here before I would actually have had to (on the 27th) and I can't afford to re-plant and up-root in Cambridge into the bargain. Imagine the agony that it must have given Johnson to go to the Hebrides. However, I suppose Boswell bought all the tickets. I wish I had a Boswell.

This place is good. I get bed and board for 2 guineas a week. I think it might suit you next summer. The best of it happened last night, when Bernard Shaw came to the public house disguised as a tramp. He was selling paper flowers for a living and was irresistible. Fully conscious that his income was in the neighborhood of £10,000 a year, I couldn't help giving him 12/6.

My *best* love to Mary. I must come and play bowls so that the next baby is as good as the last. Do you realise that I may die without ever having seen even Margaret?

Timothy

Despite his proclamations of misery at Stowe, White was actually achieving the colorfully controversial status that he always craved. As Sylvia Townsend Warner says in her biography of White, "Stowe at that date was fashionably Red, and White had several pupils who professed and called themselves communists. Their opinions and actions—a petrol-soaked Union Jack was burned during an Empire Day celebration attended by a War Office bigwig—appealed to the *frondeur* streak in his character; he was excited and curious, and slightly dutiful. He probably felt that he ought to be a communist."[2]

The Crown Inn, Tingewick, Bucks.

Dear Pottës,

Do you remember we talked about producing at the Festival? Well, now it is not just talk: it has got to happen. I have suddenly found out that it is my mission in life to produce *Henry V* as communist propaganda, first at the Festival and afterwards in Moscow. Neither is anything going to stop me. Will you write to the man who runs the Festival and tell him that you have an amateur producer who will do it for nothing? (I mean, is it any good your doing so? I think it is. If not *somebody* has got to be found who will put it through for me. I will of course write to the manager myself—if only I knew his name—but he has got to be positively *bombarded* with letters from all quarters coincidentally.)

If you like you may *hint* to him how it is going to be done, but don't give away too much because the idea is worth its weight in gold. He will probably try to pinch it. It is going to be done like this:

Modern dress for real people like Pistol and Quickly.

Exaggerated or stylised modern dress for people with any reality at all. e.g. Top hats, tummys and false noses for bishops, peers etc. Some like Beaverbrook, some like Baldwin, some like the bishop in the Russian version of *St. Joan*.

Full armour for Henry, with Union Jack baldric and a union jack on a pin in his helmet like a flag day only much bigger. He will carry a micro- phone throughout, and speak all his speeches at it. Any- body else who has a particularly bogus speech will be allowed to have the microphone pro tem, and indeed we will probably develop several sharp tussles for its possession. Crosses and Union Jacks suddenly looming out in glorious lights and stars upon the cyclorama. Poppies. Staff officers. Big gun battles. *Prologues* by newspaper magnets with heels on desk speaking into telephone for latest edition. Big business. Publicity. Empire. Reporters, interview, flashlight photographs after Agincourt. No more paper. For Xt's sake help.

love
Timothy

* * *

Potts, perhaps taking more seriously than he needed to White's doomed picture of himself at Stowe, attempted to secure a position for his young friend as English Lektor at Uppsala, Sweden, a post he had himself formerly held. Ultimately, nothing came of the Uppsala attempt, and White remained at Stowe, all the while complaining and chomping at the bit.

Monday [August 1934?]
Stowe School, Buckingham

Dear Pottës,

It is frightfully good of you to take the trouble. I should *love* the job. They are sending me mad here: I was never born to mind my P's & Q's. Also I'm too young to vegetate yet (though I've got a frightful belly coming) and I am beginning to find that there is something horribly excessive about boys in the mass: like haddocks. As for its only lasting 6 years at most, I don't mind at all. I have finished, but am tickling up and polishing over, a book that will make my fortune. There are only two worries—(1) Are there Nazis in Uppsala? (2) If I put in for it, do you really think that I shall have annoyed my headmaster seriously, in the event of my failing to get it? Personally I am prepared to chance no (2), if you think the chances of getting it are at all sporting. I want to get away from the British Public Schools.

What am I to do? Shall I wait whilst you angle?

I'm sorry that I haven't been to see you this holidays, nor thanked for the Xmas Sermon, which I read religiously (and could see you through it distinctly). I think it was a brilliant compromise. The reason why I haven't written was of course the book, which nearly sent me raving. Now it has reached the happy stage of needing only spices, garnishments and comfits, sprinkled on the top.

By the way, you are vague about salary. When you say that it would be ample for a bachelor, what kind of bachelor do you mean? Don't forget that I shall keep a hunter and a Bentley in God's own country. In Uppsala I should be quite prepared to live on simple liquor. No. I'll drop everything if you like; but I do want to do it for

65

a worthy cause. Is it difficult to learn Swedish? Hooray! (as King Amanullah didn't remark) I feel quite hysterical and half a jar already.

If you get me the job I'll give you a Siamese cat. There! (Unlikely though it may seem, I have one.) Tell Mary: Nymph in thy orisons, be all Timothy's dreams of Uppsala remembered.

Best love from
Timothy

I shan't say anything to anybody.

[May 6, 1935]
Stowe School, Bucks. Jubilee [of King George V]

Dear Mary,

This is not a bread and butter letter, but a need to communicate. The journey was dreadful, because I kept trying to read small print and also attend to the state of agriculture out of the windows, like Cobbett, and when I arrived the whole of my sweet village was in a state of jubilee, and the publican drunk, and now so am I. I am sure you will look less disapproving than Pottès when you read this. Your horrid book has not done me *any* good: the Walford Davies atmosphere of being simply terribly careful not to hurt each other a bit, and the atrocious man who was as much a virgin as his wife and slept for three nights outside the sheets, have thrown me into a turmoil of doubt and fear. It will ruin everything for me if I have to be more considerate than I naturally am: which is very little. (However, I daresay the answer to this is that one can't be. So there is nothing to worry about except predestination.) The other *hideous* discoveries are of the nature of necessary ???? precautions. In the first place I can't possibly have all my dairymaids measured by doctors (how it wd spoil the spontaneity of the occasion: one could make quite a funny scene for a novel out of this—and the rage of the dairymaid) and so I shd have to stick to the male preservative, which seems to be 50% fallible. This wd not only jeopardise my situation but also entail such a lot of cleaning up, just like coming down in the morning to wash the glasses and sweep up all the match sticks in a soiled jubilee pub, that really I think I shall have to marry a wife and tell her we are only going to have straight copulation with the objective of children. I mean, I think there is a very good cause for the anti-contraceptive attitude e.g. it is psychologically unnatural. So it looks like either a wife and hundreds of children, or lots of dairymaids and a great drain on my income in paying maintenance. What is a poor Irishman to do? I wish to god I was an Esquimau.

Best love to Weg [Margaret]. Here is a poem for her:

> "I am Weg.
> I have one leg
> (twice).
> This is very nice."*

No need to send messages to Pottës or Beth [Elizabeth, known as Betsy, the Pottses' second daughter] (my name for her) but not for the same reason.

Tim Θ

*Excuse me if this is a bit Barrie or Milne, but it was spontaneous: perhaps the jubilee.

In March of 1935, injuries sustained in a car crash left White temporarily blind in one eye, but he used his convalescence to compile from the various sporting diaries he had been keeping a collection of essays, which would be published as *England Have My Bones*. In the words of Sylvia Townsend Warner, "Liking Stowe no better, still not sacked by Mr. Roxburgh, still alive after the car crash . . . he decided to look for another post, and learned from the Appointments Board that there was a chance of a Professorship at Presidency College, Calcutta; and it shows how sad and sensible he had become that he made the first approaches himself."[3]

[October 11, 1935]
Stowe School, Buckingham.

Dear Pottës,

I have had a letter from the Appointments Board, saying that they think I would be a strong candidate for the Professorship of English at Presidency College, Calcutta. The screw seems to be in the neighbourhood of £830 a year, on 3½ year contract. The circular makes none of the important facts clear (i.e., whether one has decent vacations, since write I must, and whether one gets the hot weather in Calcutta etc.) and I am writing to the Appointments Board to find out about these. Do you happen to know anything about the job *or* can you find out anything by ringing up a crony, if you have one, on the Appointments Board?

As a man of the world (you will strenuously deny it) but more as somebody who knows me, would you advise me to try for it?

The advantages are that it would rescue me from here and give me a chance of seeing a bit of the world while I am still young.

The disadvantages are that I am not sure whether I want to see the world. I get on very well in England.

Try to make Mary take a *fairly* light view of the case by pointing out to her that I am doing exactly three full time jobs at the moment (a) being psychoanalysed (b) being an author (c) being a schoolmaster. As a relaxation I am learning to be a farmer. Anyway, I am mentioning Weg [Margaret, then aged three] by name in my next book: so let the little toad be content with that.

I hear they have nobbled you for the tutor job and thus wrecked your books for the moment. I am sorry.

> Love from
> TIM

Under the influence and perhaps at the suggestion of his analyst, White decided to woo a local barmaid, on whom he quickly and hopelessly developed a crush. The course of the courtship and White's feelings about it and about analysis are described vividly in the following group of letters.

[January 1936]

Dear Pottës or Mary—I don't mind which of you—will that annoy either of you, and if so which? —I have just been reading the letters of D. H. Lawrence, and sprung up off a bed to write to you! I meant to, for a long time, because I have again forgotten whether Mary is going to do her stuff this month or next, and I wanted to extend support. But Lawrence made me.

How is Mary? My next book, which is just about rotten enough to catch on with the Book Society, so we all have high hopes, comes to you some time in February. In time to be read *after* the baby [William Potts], I hope. My address is a secret from everybody in the world, but I tell you so that I can get the first news. It is 65 Grafton Street, W. 1. Dont tell anybody else.

In case Mary is in a condition to appreciate a little news, I will tell you mine. It is most extraordinary. I am partially in love with a quite perfect barmaid, and spend six hours a day sitting in her pub, as temperately as is consistent with remaining in her good graces, staring at her. She doesn't feel anything in particular about me. I talk to her a lot. She has the mental age and morality of rather a nice girl guide. Dark hair, big dark eyes, boyish figures, protruding or rather *upstanding* bottom, giggles. I find that I make a *perfect* lover: I am so humble. When she is cross I just go on holding my peace for days, admitting her superiority and ordering drinks in a steady imploring voice. It will be irresistible in the long run, poor girl, and we shall be very happy. Anything but marriage is out of the question for her. We shall take a public house outside Cambridge, and you shall come to dinner every night, bringing masses of dons. N.B. You pay.

I am not really in love with her yet, or more emotionally than sexually, and I go on being psycho-analysed every day, dashing back to the pub the moment I have been done. Most exciting. A sort of Stop Press newsboy between Harley St. and the Fitzroy Arms.

Is this very selfish? No, I really do like her in a queer little way. I don't love her. She doesn't love me. Damn.

How are all your children?

love from
Tim

Tuesday [January 1936]

Dear Pottës and Mary and all your children, I write rather drunkenly I'm afraid, but courting a barmaid means that one has heavy committments in that line. The great thing is that you should realise that these letters do *not* require an answer, unless you feel like it yourself. In yourself. I use you as a safety valve merely, in the (thank God) way that all the other common people have done since adolescents (?) first required confidants. All you have to do is to exclaim Dear Me! at intervals.

Well, it is all very exciting. You must envisage quite a slim little brown creature, compact of lower middle class inhibitions. A very *sanitary* sort of girl, probably always washing her private parts like a

70

cat. Have you noticed how everybody from the suburbs always does this? She is *most* unsuitable for me. If I were to be natural with her for ten seconds I should shock her out of her wits. She won't drink or smoke or admit that there is such a thing as sex in the world, probably because she is basically sexy. She flirts with all the customers, but immediately they become at all intimate except in an obviously leg-pulling way gets withdrawn and unhappy. No brains at all (such a mercy) but loyal and hardworking and moodless and above all *very* nice to go to bed with.

Yesterday I screwed my courage and said: "Do you ever go to cinemas with your customers, or is that wicked?" She shook her head. It was wicked. This was several hours from closing time, and I fell into the dumps for half an hour. Then I realized that Suckling was right about this sort of thing. The pale wan lover was just a piss-arse. So I took it on the chin and came up again smiling, and was there this morning again, prepared to invite her to cinemas every day till she does give in. None of these dull and mute young sinners for me. The girl will break before I do. She only makes me more rife in my wrongs, more lawless and more lewd. Let her look out for herself, that's all that I can say.

Tilly invited me to read a paper to his literary soc. in Jesus. I am too lazy to write to him (or too busy) and so you have got to give him a message. The message is: "January 20th is no good, but I should *like* to read a paper on *Lady Chatterley's Lover* so long as he will make it on a saturday night and put me up, and so long as I can say what I like." It ought to be a phallic society really. Are you going to read your satire to my society next term? What about coming while Mary is in the nursing home, as soon as the son has properly arrived: I am not at all afraid of being homosexual about him now.

I go back to Stowe on tuesday, to the rugger players. Our Forward, whose arse is heaven, hollow-wed be thy shame.

Timothy

P.S. I think I am going to be a great writer after all.

P.P.S. Means keeping it till monday, so I'll send it off without consulting B.

Dear Pottës,

Bennet is the name [of White's psychoanalyst], initials E. A. and address 97 Harley St. He is a very great man—must be, for cured cases such as mine are I believe most rare, if not unique. The reason why your man didn't keep on going to him is that he never insists or lectures or assumes (except on the rarest possible occasions like those minute pushes, under the table, of Cecil's, in Strachey's *Elizabeth & Essex*) the initiative. He believes that these are fatal courses of action in his line of business. In fact almost every psychopathic case is largely complicated by refusal to accept responsibility. Your man probably went to him expecting B. to undertake the burden of his existence and direct it. This B. won't do. He appears at first sight, therefore, most vague and ineffectual. He will not even persuade a patient to go on being treated—no explanations—no pronouncements—no effort on his part to struggle with destiny. If you stay you stay, if you go you go. It depends, must depend, on you. It so happens that I have a streak of endurance (not a virtue, just a fact) and so I stayed: I am so happy that I hop about like a wagtail in the streets. Your man probably hadn't this odd obstinacy of character, and so he went. It is almost useless to urge him to try again, because then *we* shall be assuming the responsibility which ought to rest on him. However, I don't think it would do any harm to read him bits of this letter (you must not shew it him) so that he can know, at least, that Bennet is *not* a charlatan. I had to find even that out for myself, and to endure through the suspicion. I will shew your letter to Bennet. Personally I think p.a. the greatest thing in the world (how not, since it has made me happy?) and if I had any guts I should write and publish my sexual autobiography, for the benefit of other poor devils.[4] If only I had been the kind of person who went, ten years ago!

Meanwhile all goes swimmingly. I am in high favour with my Phoebe, dream *all* the right dreams, and feel in case to jostle a constable. Little does she know how close she sails to seduction, and how she will like it!

There won't be another book of poems unless you keep those I send you—they are the sole copies. I think the second one (or I thought when I sent it off) was *very* good. Pity it is so much in Lawrence's style. But to hell with *trying* to be or not to be this or that. I shall be what I am, spontaneously, like a fountain.

Glad you liked *Sponge*. Try *Mr. Romford's Hounds* next, and at all costs avoid *Handley Cross* or *Jorrocks Jaunts* until you are well at home with the others.[5]

I am busy drawing obscene pictures just now, so I can't afford the time to write you another poem.

    love from
    Tim

I will wait till I have shewn this to Bennet tomorrow, before sending it off. I don't want to spoil your fellow's psyche. This is a dereliction of duty (responsibility) on my part; but I don't mind making it since (a) this kind of thing is B's job, not mine, (b) it is somebody else's responsibility, not mine.

My only outside evidence for Bennet's ability is that the man who gave me his address was a sadistic homosexual, and now is married and has a baby. Also H. (STRICK confidence) was a total wreck at Stowe, masturbated at least once a day, couldn't shit, thought he was done for: now look at him. He has gained stones merely in weight.

P.S. Bennet says that in this type of case *relations* are very often antagonistic to the notion of analysis. Does this apply? [A poem, "Love Song for Lin," was enclosed in this letter. See Appendix B.]

[January 22, 1936]
Stowe School, Buckingham.

Dear Pottës,
    Thank you ever so much for *Mr. Sponge*. Where on earth did you

get it? It *looks* as if it might be a first edition (though it has a different cover from mine, which I thought was a facsimile of the first) and if so, must be worth pounds. My own, merely a facsimile, is worth 30/-. And what a nice inscription: I am afraid that is all I shall ever get—nice inscriptions from really intelligent people. I have got an awful feeling that I am never going to make real money from books, not till I'm dead. It is such a pity. I had far rather write like Dickens and have money to spend on my life, rather than write like Lawrence and be a great dead man. I am beginning to digress.

Thank you for the book, and for saying such a nice thing on the fly leaf. I am glad you liked Soapey. He is real. So is Romford in *Mr. Romford's Hounds* (I'll lend it you if you like) but Jorrocks is *not*.

Publication of my book *[England Have My Bones]* is put off till March 5th because there is an illusory hope of persuading the Book Society to recommend it. They have already chosen their January and February books, so we think it worth waiting. The publishers do. I don't. Things like that simply don't happen to me.

But I don't mind. They can wait as long as they like, for me. I'm not interested. I left the barmaid a virgin, for all my efforts, and likely to be. Here I am back at school and feeling physically sick at it. There was a masters meeting first thing, and we "stood in silence for a few seconds in memory of His Majesty the King." Imagine it. Not publicly. Just a lot of seedy schoolmasters standing up among themselves, hearts full of buggery and jealousy and prejudices and fear, standing in silence, feeling fools, because the ring master cracked his whip.

I can't write here nor get on with my life nor love my barmaid. I told you I was selling the car, didn't I? Something deep inside myself is making me call in my resources, either to start with a pittance to live on as an author or else to get married with. I don't know which.

Did you give that message to Tilly? I am asked to read a paper to the Christ Church essay society and should do the same one for both if he agrees. I am interested. I suppose you cant lend me a Lady C.? I have nothing new to say about Lawrence, but what I have got to say is absolutely right. Just platitudes practically. But I

74

have a feeling that even platitudes will be eye-openers to this bloody modern reading public.

Well, I suppose I had better go and lie in bed.

love from
Tim

I feel like a row of bars.

Dear Pottës,

I think as a tutor you ought to know a respectable analyst. Men, I believe, have their change of life at the undergraduate age. Bennet is going to be in Cambridge next Sunday, and will call on you for ten minutes if you like. Would you like? If so, send me a p.c. before Friday morning saying where and when.

Did you give that message to Tilly, or shall I write myself? I am reading the same paper in Oxford, and will on second thoughts keep it moderately clean. It is called The Anti-Socialist.

I went up to see my barmaid on Friday, and she was pleased to see me. I don't know quite where I am at the moment (the mere fact of being back here, surrounded by such a vast boyish subconscious, is bound to have a retrograde effect) but I carry grimly on—a kind of hermaphrodite, without desires either way. I never knew that I could fight such a long battle as this, with such optimism and tenacity and patience. My troops move on a terrific front, and I hold them in hand. I don't stick my chin out like Mussolini, but look ahead with my eyes set: an unblinking eye. Not that there aren't set-backs, reverses, but I am resilient: a staunch, slow Marshal. I admire myself very much.

How is that baby of yours going?

love from
Tim

75

My dearest Mary,

Well done! How clever and typical of you to have a son on purpose. [William Potts was born on February 21, 1936.] I was in a frightful bother here, because Pottës led me to believe that he was going to be born last Sunday. Not knowing much about these things I stayed by the telephone all Sunday and then began to dream about it every night. I daredn't ring up to ask, for fear that the telephone would be a disturbing influence, and because I felt sure that something had gone wrong. I didn't want to enquire about a baby from a newly made widower, but I was ready to dash over and kidnap Pottës (I was not going to let him out of my sight) as soon as the dreadful news came of its own accord. It was a harrowing time.

So you can imagine what a joy it was to hear that you had done *exactly* what you wanted, as usual, and how delightful it feels to be a godfather. I have forgotten what you are going to call him. Has he got a strawberry mark? (Seriously, now that I am contemplating matrimony, I think you ought to set about getting those marks off your daughters. They are removable—I have enquired—and *not* fair on their future beaux.) I wonder whether he will be a nice godson. Tell me the date he was born on, for my mug, which I shant send but bring to the christening. (N.B. I wonder whether you will be able to have that done at a time when I am not absolutely unprocurable? Bennet thinks he can finish me off next holidays, and, if so, I shall probably take a fortnight salmon fishing in Scotland to celebrate. Still, you must tell me the approximative date and I shall have to arrange my life in accordance. It is almost nicer being a godfather than a father, like having white mice but making your nanny feed them for you. Pottës, of course, will be fearfully jealous of the boy later on, and probably beastly to him. So will the boy be to Pottës. Did you notice Tilly and Stephen? (I believe they have got over it now.) You will have to lend me your son a good bit, as soon as he is ten years old, because I am afraid to have children with my barmaid. She is too much of a shrimp, and besides, I should hate her to love anybody except me. I shall teach him to fish first of all, and then, as soon as he gets into his 'teens, he shall shoot with a four-ten (a small shot-gun). Are you jealous that somebody other than yourself should be already plotting about him?

My own news is all goodish, tho' not so good as yours. The *Daily Mail* and the Book *Guild* (not society) have both chosen the next book *[England Have My Bones]* as their book of the month. It will mean a few more thousands sold and a bit of a start. With luck I may bring you a copy next week-end. Collins had pulled off a treble never before accomplished in the publishing trade—his authors have taken the Book Society, the *Evening Standard*, and the *Daily Mail* books of the month for March. It is said that each of these books will help the others. It means that I can leave at the end of the Summer term pretty optimistically now.

The barmaid loves me, and I love her. The only snag is that I don't know whether we ought to be married. There is no intellectual contact, and almost no interests in common. Do you think the first of these matters? I have a sort of feeling that it doesn't, and that between men and women there never is an *intellectual* bond, and that there oughtn't to be. The interests are much more serious. You will say why don't I just go to bed with her? Well, I had much rather, *if that were what she wanted*. I have discovered that men do not take women, but give themselves, and so the whole thing must depend on her. What I am doing at the moment is just letting things happen. Anyway, I can't run the Universe. But this is all very dull compared with Master Potts. Are you planning to have him a duke, a bishop, a field Marshal, an admiral or merely to marry into the royal family? Tell me what he looks like, or will.

On second thoughts, don't. A person with *three* babies can't possibly write letters. I shall come and see for myself at the week-end. *Clever* Mary.

Love to Pottës
    Mary Pottës

The Misses Pottës
Master Pottës
I feel like shouting Snap, or whatever one does in Happy
Families.
xxxxx
from
Tim

[February 29, 1936]
Stowe School, Buckingham.

Dear Mary,
Thanks for your very nice letter. Certainly I shouldn't have any
more babies if they are going on in arithmetical progression like
this. It is too bad.
No more now from your
arrabbiated
Timothy

P.S. Why not just arrange to have the next one smaller?
P.P.S. Tilly told me that Pottës wd see me last night, so I didn't
ring up. Then Pottës didn't.

In May of 1936, unhappy with the results of his recent attempts to
change, with his love life, his analyst, and his profession, White
resigned from Stowe. Leaving behind a more assured, orderly
portion of his life, he was setting out in unknown directions,
heading toward a future that would provide him with much that he
wanted—but not contentment.

78

Stowe School, Buckingham.

Dear Pottës,

We are very sorry to hear that our godson's bowels are not working properly, and would like to point out that this is a matter of profound importance which might have extensive consequences in his later life. Every avenue is to be explored and no stone left unturned. The best thing is probably to do little or nothing about it.

I am sorry to hear that you are having a bloody life at present. So am I. I am feeling abandoned by Bennet and scarcely at all improved.

As far as your queries are concerned; no, I am behaving badly for my last term at Stowe—which is a bad thing. But not very badly. On second thoughts I am probably behaving rather well. Anyway I spend half my life correcting essays which any sensible man would cut. I plucked up courage and resigned in the last week of the holidays. It needed courage, because Bennet has only got me about one quarter of the way. *England Have My Bones* has made a profit of about £500. I don't know what my future is going to be, if I have a future. The barmaid is a complete write-off.

I caught a 30-lb salmon in Scotland (which is a big one) and sent it to David Garnett. I wonder how he contrives to be happy.

I am sorry if this letter is stupidly morbid, but it may do me good. Ça ira. Does that mean what I think it does?

love from
Timothy

What it really means is that I am working too hard (trying to write a little piece of my next novel every day, keeping up my fan mail etc. etc.) and probably have a tummy upset or something like that. Anyway, I don't profess to take the high jump just yet. Hopkins, poem 40, line 4.[6]

P.S. I am a brave man in some ways.

CHAPTER 3

Stowe Ridings

After David Garnett's full-page review of *England Have My Bones* in *The New Statesman and Nation*, and after the book had been chosen by the *Daily Mail* and the Book Guild as their selection of the month, White felt he could devote all his time to writing. After resigning from Stowe, he moved to a cottage in Stowe Ridings where he stayed until 1938, living the rural life of which he had long dreamed. His house was "a gamekeeper's cottage in the middle of a wood, seven miles from each of the three tiny towns Buckingham, Brackley, Towcester," and it was to become Merlyn's cottage in *The Once and Future King*.

It was at Stowe Ridings that White tamed his first goshawk. It was there, too, that he started a new manuscript which he would take up again fifteen years later and publish as *The Goshawk*.

White's correspondence with David Garnett dates from that period, and by February of 1937 they had become firm enough friends for Garnett to invite White to come fishing on the Wye. The following December, White went goose-hunting in Norfolk at Wells, spent part of the next year there, then moved on to the New Inn, Holbeach St. Mark's, where Garnett was to join him for

Christmas and the New Year. During this time, White toyed with six chapters of a finally unfinished novel, "Grief for the Grey Geese," concerned in great part with the goose-hunting which had become, along with falconing, his newest avocation. He felt so strongly the ambiguity of the sportsman who kills for pleasure animals about whom he cares that he projected these feelings onto Merlyn in *The Once and Future King*, choosing the wild geese as his symbol for freedom and peace.

It was, in fact, in the quietness of his gamekeeper's cottage that White composed the first of his Arthurian novels, *The Sword in the Stone*. At last, he had written the book that would bring him the money he so desperately needed, for the volume was sufficiently successful on both sides of the Atlantic to be chosen as a selection of the American Book-of-the-Month Club.

In November 1936 White, in the course of having his appendix removed, had met a nurse called Stella, with whom he had another short, unsuccessful affair, but, by April 1938, he had shifted his affections to a thirteen-year-old, Annette, who had often come to visit him. In his journal, White confessed that he was almost in love with her, although he never admitted his feelings to the girl. He was to meet her again, but not until 1946.

[October 8, 1936]
The Cottage, Stowe Ridings, Buckingham.

Dear Mary,

What an angel you were to write twice when that accursed Pottës was too lazy. This is my second letter to you. The other I tore up. I shan't write to Pottës till he learns to be good again, stops calling me stoico-laconic, gives up talking in that smug way about "all the best people in Cambridge" disliking Peter H. (the snob), and reclaims Peter H. himself. Meanwhile he is no god-brother of mine.

My mausoleum is the wonder of the district: a victorian, semi-detached gamekeeper's cottage, it stands in the middle of a wood

81

six miles from the nearest town. But I have done it all up myself, painted every stick and stone, and inside it takes your breath away. Pile carpets and solid luxury.

I have been writing a book about falconry[1] and trying to train a goshawk. You begin by sitting up with it 3 days and 3 nights, and the rest of the job (2 months of it) is on a par with the start. Nobody will read the book.

You will not care to hear about my sorrows, and I have not many joys at present, so this letter is just an interim report to say that I will write to you properly later.

When was that damned godson born? I shall never succeed in remembering, and think of having his names and date tatoo'd on my chest.

> Love from
> Timothy

The following two letters, both to Mary Potts, were written during White's convalescence. Possibly distressed by his star-crossed passion for Stella, White pours out the ambivalent self-pity produced by his conflicting desires to be alone and to be comforted.

[November 25(?) 1936]
The Hospital, Buckingham.

Dear Mary,

I am so fuddled nowadays that I can't remember whether I answered your kind letter or not. I think not. They have been cutting out my appendix. It is not particularly nice, and you don't even get a baby as a consolation prize at the end of it, but no doubt a lot of benefits will accrue. I find that my brain will not work now

82

any more, but they say it will come back. It is a slow business writing letters, so, with love to Pottës, I will stop. I will write later.

Best love from
Timothy

[December 4, 1936]
The Hospital, Buckingham.

My dear Mary,

I feel such a miserable wreck and they are turning me out of here next Tuesday. They say I must go away for a week or two to convalesce and keep urging that I should stay with friends at the sea, and things like that. But I have no friends—I have never considered other people, so why should they consider me?—and don't know what to do. A very nice acquaintance will harbour me for two or three days, say Tuesday to Thursday, and then I wondered if (should you still be widowed from Potts) there might be any room *for a P.G.* (we know each other well enough to make no bones about *that*, I think) in Cambridge for a week? I do so need to stay *with* somebody, instead of just an hotel, because if alone I should merely gravitate to the bar for company. I cannot face the loneliness of my cottage yet, and I thought it might be good for me to have you to talk to. I am all ends about my psycho-analysis, as well as the other things, and have nobody to tell about it, because, except you and my mother and Tilly, I have told nobody. I realise that whether you can fit me in or not will depend upon when Pottës ends his term, but I don't know when that is. I thought at any rate there would be no harm in asking. I know you *would* have me if you could.

Dear Mary, I find my life such a burden—not because I am any longer *inclined* to take notice only of myself, but because I *must*. I should like to, and should be in a position to, think of other people entirely, 33% of the times: but it is useless to do this before I have

83

begun my charity at home. The trouble with me is that I do not love outside myself enough (I can only pour it out on guns and fish, etc) but until I have put *myself* in order for loving I can do nothing about it. So it is a vicious circle, a lonely egoistical one.

I write all this because you must be warned. How on earth I can even ask you to love and help me, when you will be busy all the time doing it for your children and Pottës I don't know: it is unfair. But you are so full of love that I suspect you of being able to manage it. How men do prey upon women! But I have never had one to prey on.

Shew this letter to Pottës. It will make him furious, for he will see how basely I am wheedling. But what am I to do? Anyway it is not stoico-laconic, damn him.

Love from
TimΘ

Out of the hospital and well along the road to recovery, White appears to have shifted moods considerably, and appears in this letter as the gracious host/suitor and master of the revels.

[January 1, 1937]
The Cottage, Stowe Ridings, Buckingham.

Beloved Mary, noble Potts,

Indivisable twin deities, I shall henceforth always write to both of you at once and each of you will have to answer separately and that will be a Good Thing.

I am having a stately party in 20 minutes, a party of six persons (The Allisons, 2 friends of theirs and the dreaded night nurse) whom I am taking to the Hospital Ball—excuse me while the soup boils over—after ceremonies so high, banqueting so rare, that scarcely such were ever heard of. The study has been turned into the dining room, because it is the only room with a table in it, and I broke one leg off the table during the preparations, so now the venetian goblets and unpurchaseable dinner ware stand rather nervously on three, like drunk men expecting a hiccough, and there is no table cloth, so I used a golden bedspread, which looks magnificent, and all the candles drop their grease on it. There are also two bottles of champagne, and we shall all be in tails, and Admiral Purefoy and General Widrington will be in velvet knee breeches—there goes the soup again—and the rest in pink tail coats, if they have got them, and I have hors d'oeuvres, soup (well, some soup), chicken, plum pudding and mince pies—*all* out of tins.

Will the terrible nurse like it? *Both* of you were wrong about her in your letters, but I am going to try and do what you say. I feel like some sort of depressed conscripted Chinese coolie being urged into battle by rival generals who will sit far behind the firing line and little I'll reck if they let me sleep on in a grave where a soldier has laid him. Little will you reck either, you remorseless Mussolinis. It is not *you* who have to go down with the ship and be eaten by crabs. However, I'll nail my silk pants to the mast and risk the dénouement somehow. Or will I?

Anyway, there goes the soup again and
Here comes the Bride.

TimΘ

Tuesday [January 1937?]
Stowe Ridings, Buckingham.

Dear Pottës,

Could you find time to make a small research[2] for me? I want (a) the *earliest* text of lines 98 and 99, First Part of *Henry IV*, Act IV, Sc. 1.; (b) The first folio text of these lines, if that may be considered the most authentic, Shakespearian or un-buggered-about; (c) Dr. Johnson's emendation of these lines, with his note on them if any.

All my miserable little editions have different readings, and I am anxious to establish in an article for the Field newspaper that the reading

> "All plumed like *ostriches* that *wing* the wind
> Or *like* young eagles having lately bathed"

is perfectly good falconry—in spite of the fact that Johnson (I have a vague recollection of this) got laughed at for it. They pointed out that ostriches don't fly. But "wing the wind" means "puff out their feathers and flap their wings to and fro in the effort to dry them after bathing."

I am only writing the article because I have such splendid photographs of my Estridge doing this (by the way, a Keeper of hawks is called an Austringer, Ostringer or Astringer, the root of the word being exactly the same as the root of ostrich—use your own Greek for this) and *The Field* will not care a fig about Shakespeare criticism, but for conscience sake I should just like to get my facts accurate.

Don't trouble if you are maddened with examinations or anything.

> love from
> Tim⊖

F1 "All plum'd like Estridges, that with the Winde
Baited like Eagles, having lately bath'd
Glittering in Golden Coats, like Images,
As full of spirit as the moneth of May,
And gorgeous as the Sunne at Mid-summer,
Wanton as youthful Goates, wilde as young Bull."

"Wing" is an emendation made by *Rowe*.

Bate—to beat, because she beats herself with Unquiet fluttering.

Dear Pottës,

You will see by the enclosed what I think of your theories. But you know what I am. I know I am right in principle, even if all my facts are wrong, and I wonder if you could just cast your crafty eye over the latter? I *don't* know, for instance, whether Rowe gave ostrich for estridge and whether he was the person who got laughed at or even whether anybody laughed. Only, I have a dim recollection of Attwater lecturing on. somebody being laughed at for flying ostriches, and I *thought* that somebody was Dr. Johnson. Also I can't verify the folio spelling of *Taming of Shrew* IV.1.199.

Certainly we will edit a porcelain Shakespeare, but why can't it be china or just enamelled tin?

I am teeming with other ideas about hawking in Shakespeare. *Henry V*, III.7.127 is *not* the hawking bate (though the hood part comes from falconry alright). The bate there used is simply *abate*, give in, withdraw, collapse or yield—the very opposite of the tempestuous battle of the hawk's "bate." This man, says he, is displaying valour against things which he can't see (he is hooded) but when he does see them (is unhooded) all that valour will *evaporate*. Nothing to do with bateing at all. You carpet critics ought to go out into the live world and *do* the things, as Shakespeare did until James cut his head off.

I am trying to get up to London to see the Raleigh play— apparently just what I was going to write. But why didn't they call it *Shepherd of the Ocean?*

love from
Tim

Dear Mary,

When I got back to Buckingham I found that the Allison child was on the way to recovery. The poor little thing looks very run down, a tiny, mute, solemn invalid, but it does not seem to be diphtheria. He was up and out of bed.

Both Allisons came with me and the night nurse to a cinema. The nurse is no good at all—too young and terrified by even my bourgeois class of people. She had painted herself all over and drenched herself in cheap scent. She was quite baffled by being treated as an equal. I do not like this kind of pathos, but suppose it inevitable in the young. However, now I've got her on my hands I am in the usual foul position of having to do something about it. I wonder if she would prefer to be seduced or dropped.

My cottage was cold, damp and untidy, but I have set it pretty well to rights.

They tell me at the hospital that they have just sent all my letters off to Cambridge—too stupid of them, for they knew I was coming back on Friday.

Thank you, Mary, for being so sweet to me. I felt quite sane when I left, but it is already wearing off. My lovely venitian glasses are by my right hand and I think of you through them. And indeed of all your dear family.

Lots of love from
TimΘ

My dearest Mary,

For some reason I don't feel quite like adding "and darling Potts." I am writing to you because that damned little brat has not written to me, a selfish action which I hope you won't resent. I don't care a FIG for her, but God help her when I get my hands on her, that's all I can say.

We had a *lovely* dance, and I have written to her since (a *perfect* letter, beginning austerely "Dear Stella" and going on with the tenderest doubles-entendres of an *outragious* nature) and the little beast has not answered in two days. She ought to have written to me *at once*, even before she got my letter, to thank me for being so sweet to her at the dance. Well, she shall rue it.

She hasn't answered, although I asked her to *another* dance next Tuesday. It is the Grafton Hunt ball and there is no room on the dance floor. This means that if she comes it will be largely a case of sitting out, and *then* let her see the consequence of not being a prompt and devoted correspondent. I shall strip her naked in the car park, spank her with the inner tube of the spare-tyre and go to sleep with her in the largest Rolls-Royce on the premises.

To hell with the whole sex.

Damned impertinence.

Did I tell you I had bought a car exactly like yours? I went to see David Garnett in it yesterday, and stayed the night. The fish-cast which he made is lovely. [Garnett had made a cast in plaster of Paris of the 30 lb. salmon White had caught and sent him.] When I told him that Pottës had been so nervous of coming to see him, he said "I suppose I shall have to go and call on Pottës, then." Next time I am in your direction (I nearly called to-day, but thought you might have had enough of me) we really shall have to effect the meeting. I am not frightened of David Garnett any more, *and have made friends with his wife*. It is quite easy. You simply speak to her kindly, as with any other wild animal. [White was thinking of Garnett's *Lady Into Fox* (London: Chatto and Windus, 1923).] She can speak (though with great difficulty) and the result is that she *never* says anything stupid. She is *very* nice.

Love from your
distracted [crossed out] furious
TimΘ

The Cottage, Stowe Ridings, Buckingham.

Dear Mary,

I have been lost in Wales, where your letter was not sent on to me, and I am sorry if I have kept you waiting for an answer. I went away to fish for salmon in the Wye with David Garnett. At breakfast one morning I saw a carrion crow sitting on the top of a tree in the garden. One of my farmer friends here always maintains that this is a certain herald of death. I said to David: "One of us will have a death in the family today," and we got into a ghoulish conversation during which I quoted the Twa Corbies ballad and David defined at length what should be the attitude of bereaved persons towards the departed. We set out to fish and within the hour a telegram arrived to say that his father had died suddenly, without any previous illness. He was quite unusually fond of his father—witness *Beaney Eye*[3]—and had been talking about him a lot. He died in 5 minutes, between eight and nine o'clock, while we were talking about the crows.

The hospital nurse was a dreadful failure. It turned out that we were perfect strangers to one another. She gave me only one happy memory. She was sitting on my knee when poor Brownie [White's red setter], madly jealous, tried to sit there too. The nurse then said in sour and Cockney accent: "quite a fam'ly party, ain't it."

I am not going to Bennet at present, because 1) I am not so miserable as usual, 2) I have no money left at all. I don't know whether I am heterosexual or homosexual at the moment, and don't much care. I got quite fond of a girl in Wales, and stayed a fortnight after David had to leave, so as to talk to her. She was 16. I have sent her a ring with an opal in it. She was a Xtian Scientist and kept telling me that I ought not to drink or smoke, because it was an error. She was an only child. Her eyes were green, her fair hair was cut short, and she had a good figure. I think we should have made a good pair, as we should have fought like cats, but I was stronger than she was and should have ended in the satisfactory position of having a good excuse for slapping her. But I really liked her, particularly when she defied and bossed me, and so I was frightened of her when she showed signs of giving in. I may go back to see her, if I can scrape up any money or if she re-acts well to the ring. But it will have to be in the summer, when I can get her out of doors away from her parents.

I like Betsy's "Never'd you?" much the best.[4] There is a certain sarcastic comment on the veracity of Weg's assertion about it.

If you will put me up for a few days when I arrive (is Potts away?) I will (a) help you to spring clean, (b) add another chapter to the white whale.[5] But perhaps you are too busy.

Love from
TimΘ

[March 1937?]

Dear Mary,

I found David away, as might have been expected when one remembers that he must be spending most of his time cataloguing the dead father's library in Chelsea. [Edward Garnett died on February 19, 1937.] So I went to a pub for bread and cheese. The publican's wife, who had just recovered from 'flu, invited me into the parlour to eat by the fire. Then, with all the windows tight shut, I found the publican prone upon a sofa, suffering from (1) T.B. (2) influenza (3) an ulcer in the middle of his back. His daughter, bearing him company, was subject to epileptic fits and had just broken her arm having one in the earth closet. She had influenza too.

We talked about death for some time, while I gobbled my food in a perfect palsy, and then I drove away in a snowstorm to Bedford, where I have been busy having a temperature of 103° ever since, and this is why I have not been able to write a bread-and-butter letter before.[6]

It all comes of changing my shirt so as to look clean for David Garnett.

I am still too angry to write letters.
Or did I catch it from your disgraced children?

> Love and curses
> from
> Tim

White's deepening interest in falconry resulted in the purchase of a hawk, as described in the next letter. The hawk, called Gos, eventually had the bad manners to fly away from White.

[April 22, 1937]
The Cottage, Stowe Ridings, Buckingham.

My dearest Mary,

I think your new handwriting is absolutely splendid. It is the most important contribution you have made towards world peace since William. I shall have to give you a fountain pen with a fine nib.

Yes, I have been consistenly ill, and miserable, lonely, unable to write as a result, ever since I left Cambridge—but in my case there has not even been the relief of ultra violet rays. Nor has my hawk arrived yet. I got a letter three weeks ago saying I was to expect her, went into an extasy, hired a man to help me, rebuilt my mews and got another letter last week saying that she was so damaged in plumage as to be not worth sending.

I do not know when I can go to Scotland. I don't think I have got enough money in the first place, and in the second place all must depend upon the arrival of the hawk. I doubt if I should be able to travel in less than a month after the hawk's arrival. If she does not arrive at all, what about my driving you up to Scotland during Coronation week? My car will not go more than 50 m.p.h. as you know, and is perfectly safe. We could break our journey at a nice expensive hotel I know, near Scots Corner, and give Pottës grounds for divorce.

Let me know again, nearer the date, about your plans.

Love from
TimΘ

Although he may not consciously have known it, White had finally evolved a project that would bring him the results, both literary and financial, that Potts had always predicted for him—the first of the Arthurian books, *The Sword in the Stone*.

[January 14, 1938]
Crown Hotel, Wells, Norfolk.

Dear Pottës,

No, I am not married, divorced, in gaol or dead. I have £41 in the bank. No books have been published since the last you heard of—*England H.M.B.*—but there is one in the press. I think it is one of my better books, so probably nobody else will. It is a preface to Malory. Do you remember I once wrote a thesis on the *Morte d'Arthur*? Naturally I did not read Malory when writing the thesis on him, but one time last autumn I got desperate among my books and picked him up in lack of anything else. Then I was thrilled and astonished to find that (a) The thing was a perfect tragedy, with a beginning, a middle and an end implicit in the beginning and (b) the characters were real people with recognisable reactions which could be forecast. Mordred was hateful; Kay a decent chap with an inferiority complex; Gawaine that rarest of literary productions, a swine with a streak of solid decency. He was a sterling fellow to his own clan. Arthur, Lancelot and even Galahad were really glorious people—not pre-raphaelite prigs. Anyway, I somehow started writing a book. It is not a satire. Indeed, I am afraid it is rather

93

warm-hearted—mainly about birds and beasts. It seems impossible to determine whether it is for grown-ups or children. I will send a copy for my godson's birthday, if out in time, and you must try it on him when he is about twelve. It is more or less a kind [of] wish-fulfillment of the kind of things I should like to have happened to me when I was a boy. But you can't tell whether you have written a good book or a bad one till long after. You are too close, and it is like having your nose touching a big picture or your mouth full of lots of dough. So far as I can make out, Macmillans are going to refuse to take it up in America, so perhaps it is a bad book after all. Their refusal will incidentally land me in queer street financially, as I have gambled on them taking it. What I fear is that it has feeble traces of A. A. Milne. I should have liked it to be like Masefield's *Midnight Folk*, a book which I love this side idolatry. It is called *The Sword in the Stone*.

I did a lot of research into the 14th–15th centuries, in a mild way.

I have also written a book called *Burke's Steerage* or *the Amateur Gentleman's Introduction to Noble Sports and Pastimes*. It is a short, cheap thing, doing for sport what Cornford's *Microcosmographia Academica*[7] did for your damned university. But it is not good.

Also I wrote a book called "A Sort of Mania" [this became *The Goshawk*]. It is about my hawks and living as a hermit. Unfortunately I believe I shall have to re-write it entirely, as it has faint traces of value.

Writing books is a heart breaking job. When I write a good one it is too good for the public and I starve, when a bad one you and Mary are rude about it. This *Sword in the Stone* (forgive my reverting to it and probably boring you sick—I have nobody to tell things to) *may* fail financially through being too good for the swine. It has (I fear) its swinish Milneish parts (but, my God, I'd gladly be a Milne for the Milne money) but it is packed with accurate historical knowledge and good allusive criticism of chivalry (I make the fox-huntin' comparison with some glee) which nobody but you will notice.

As for your news (a) if you are the Senior Tutor, it is time that you got me a fellowship. If your college does not offer me one within the next ten years, I shall refuse it with a copy of Johnson's letter to Chesterfield, when they do.[8] I shall also refuse the Chancellorship of your University, but take Oxford instead. (b) I advise you to remain £1385.16.8 in debt, but retain all three houses. They will be worth much more than the overdraft. All the people round here have made money out of real estate. Why not buy a few pubs as well? (c) I think 26 years of tenancy is just a nice time. (d) what fun you will have with 5 W.C.s It is almost a register.

I am beginning to run out of reasons for writing to you, and that reminds me that it is very decent of me to write at all. For you told me a direct lie during our late correspondence about falconry in Shakespeare, and to find that you were ready to falsify your academic conscience so upset me that I never wrote the article and determined never to have anything more to do with you. BAIT *does* mean to refresh, *is* utterly different in derivation and everything else from BATE. I looked it up in N.E.D. for myself. When I found your treachery I tried to tell myself that it was just at the end of term with you, you were probably very tired, not responsible etc. Still, it was a shock. And the Porcelain Shakespeare is off.

What I mean is that you did not like to be told anything new about Shakespeare by a mere pupil of yours, so you subconsciously proceeded to think yourself into a state, out of which state you were able to convince yourself that one of my facts was shaky when it wasn't. I wouldn't have minded if you hadn't lied to yourself.

I seem only to be making it worse by explaining. Please assume that I am not trying to be rude—only offensive. The best way to get the tone of it would be to read it out loud, with a kind of broken laugh.

Yes, and why haven't you confessed about your beard?

How is Mary's sister? I specially want to know this.

It was odd that our notes should have crossed. Did you like the story? I thought the end was a bit banal, but the middle part about the old gentleman in Knickers and the whole father-son relationship struck me as exquisitely comic.

I am staying in Norfolk to shoot wild geese—the latest craze. God knows what I shall think of next.

Love and forgiveness to you.
Best love to Mary.
A look of confused benevolence for my godson.

Tim

I did get Mary's photograph of the infant. It seems a healthy one. She may go on with it as before.
David Garnett is editing T. E. Lawrence's letters. I stayed there a month ago and he read me lots of them. I feel very proud of this.

Sir Sydney Cockerell, mentioned in the following letter, was to become one of White's friends and correspondents. Some of White's letters to him were published in *The Best of Friends: Letters to Sydney Carlyle Cockerell* (London: R. H. Davis, 1956). The controversy White mentions involved an unsigned article in the *Saturday Review*, in which White had bitterly expressed his dislike for the Fitzwilliam Museum extension; Sir Sydney Cockerell had answered the "Cambridge Correspondent" in the same paper and shown that the latter was far from the facts.

[August 30, 1938]
Stowe Ridings, Buckingham.

Dear Pottës,
I wonder what you and Mary have been thinking of my supposed birthday present to the Godson. Well, out of sight but not out of mind. I had to tear up the whole Collins page proofs, they had done them so badly, and the result is that the book [*The Sword in the Stone*] is only out this week. They have still left out some of the tailpieces.
The book is being published in America by Putnam's, and has

there been chosen (but the month not yet fixed) as a dual choice (this means it is bracketed with another) by the Book of the Month Club. It will help me financially a great deal.

Pray apologise to my godson for the "fine-art" condition of his copy. It is a result of staying with Sir Sydney Cockerell (who is going, I hope, to collect me along with Rossetti and co) and the proper thing for you to do is to affix this letter to the title-page, when the whole concern immediately becomes worth millions. Sydney Cockerell is a charmer. Whenever he meets a genius he immediately takes down all their particulars and makes them turn out their pockets. I met him at Sassoon's in Wiltshire and fell in love with him at once. Do you remember when I was having a controversy with him in the *Saturday Review* about the Fitzwilliam? I haven't dared to confess that I was his anonymous persecutor.

Some time next week I may be going through Cambridge. If only I could remember your new address (plural) I should see what could be done about it.

Are all of you dead, cross with me, or elevated to the peerage? I cannot suppose that you can have all died at once. Why does nobody ever write to me? How is Weg's leg (twice)? How the harpsichord? Has Mary preserved that musical-pictorial-allegory? Tell her to put it in an air-proof tin box. Now that I am a book-of-the-month man, you will be able to dower all your children with it. I drive about in a large grey sort of Rolls-Royce called a Jaguar, with a cigar sticking out of the window. It is the kind of car that the Maharanee of Sarawak drives in. I think I am going to come out of my wilderness soon, and explain things to people, or get crucified. Fortunately, as you see, I had the wit to accept the principalities etc. when offered them on the pinnacle or wherever it was.

What price another war, you moralist? I am going to fight in the wretched thing after all, partly because I don't consider my own life particularly worth fussing about, partly because I think it might be good for me, and partly because I think one ought to do what other people are doing. That fellow Huxley (so Hester Sassoon [Siegfried Sassoon's wife] told me—I can't vouch for it) has cleared off to America in anticipation. [9] He always was a bloodless fellow, and let's hope this will result in his dropping all that loving-the-fellow-men stuff. Better for him to run away and be a satirist than stick it out and blither. It's more in his nature.

Sassoon's new book will be good. A high-spot chapter is the re-visit to a rectory of his holiday childhood, with the war-memorial lych-gate new. He is a queer, good man. He looks 30. Is 52. A noble, red-indian face. Very nervous and a bit selfish. But enough, or too much.

Write to poor   Tim

The Sword in the Stone had been bought by the Walt Disney organization for an animated film, and White, for the first time, was entering the world of media success. It was not until 1963, however, that the full-length cartoon *The Sword in the Stone* was released.

[February 14, 1939]
Ostrich House, Wells-next-sea, Norfolk

Dear Mary,

Thank you for your kind congratulations. The Disney business means nothing, I'm afraid. He may only use it for a short cartoon, in which case I get about £100, and if he does it feature length (like *Snow White*) it will be about £500. However, the motion picture industry seems to have taken a fancy to me in general, as a Mr. Lewin of Paramount wants me to go to Hollywood as technical adviser to a perfectly super-awful film they are doing about King Arthur. I have been sent the script (a thing which has apparently never been done before). It was delivered in a platinum casket, under guard of forty mounted camelmen, ten elephants, and 200 motor cycling policemen who bicycled slowly on either side of it, blowing syrens! It was carried at a foot pace. Shall I go or not? I should like to ask Potts' opinion on this subject, as I know it will be sternly moral. In the film, the wicked villain Mordred (a slightly older man than the hero, Arthur) magnifies a *platonic* affair between Guenever and Lancelot and, with the aid of his Lady-love, Morgan, brings all to ruin. The remainder ride off into the remote future, with Arthur's ghost beside them. (In actual life, Mordred was Arthur's son and Morgan was his aunt!)

Will you send me a p.c., telegram or phone call, saying whether you can give me *luncheon* on Saturday next, 18th? It is my only possible date, what with rushing off to America etc. Could Potts be persuaded to drop in for it?

Love from
Timothy

CHAPTER 4

Doolistown

In February 1939, David Garnett invited White to Ireland for some salmon fishing in the rivers Dee and Boyne. Garnett had a good day's fishing and White, who had not been as lucky, decided to stay in Ireland a little longer. Garnett's wife, Ray, asked the nearest farm if they could put him up: the farmers were Mr. and Mrs. McDonagh. The McDonaghs, as it turned out, would be White's hosts in the Irish village of Doolistown for the next six and a half years.

War was declared while White was in Ireland, and although he spent all the war years away from England, he could never quite reconcile his absence with his patriotic need to serve. Having had tuberculosis when he was twenty-one, and being a resident in Ireland, he had no fear of being conscripted, yet he frequently wrote to his friends in England, offering his services in the fight against fascism.

Still, in the last analysis, White could not dream of leaving his beloved setter and companion, Brownie, and was quite happy not to be needed in England. Finally he decided that his own contribution to the war effort was to do what he did best, to write, and on December 6, 1940, he told L. J. Potts that he was planning to add a fifth volume to his projected Arthurian tetralogy. Indeed, he had changed his mind about the whole theme of the *Morte d'Arthur*, and the purpose of the books had become the search for an antidote to war. As he wrote to David Garnett, "The last book, is, I hope, the crown of the whole. The epic theme is War and how to stop it . . . You see, the Round Table was an anti-Hitler measure."

But White not only wished to write a fifth book, he also wanted to modify the first three, which were already in print. This began a long argument with his publisher, who was concerned by the idea of a fivefold Arthur in the middle of the wartime paper shortage. Finally, however, a compromise was effected and White gave up the hope of seeing his fifth volume in print. It was published as *The Book of Merlyn* after his death.

Volume two of the Arthurian series, *The Witch in the Wood*, was rewritten several times from beginning to end, with Mary and L. J. Potts blue-penciling the passages that were not in keeping with the rest of the book.

The main problem with the book was that he had put too much of his hatred for his mother into the character of Morgause. White and the Pottses realized that this problem had to be overcome before the novel would be successful.

While in Ireland, White attempted to go native—even proclaiming himself Irish, since his father had been born there. Combining his boundless desire to learn with an equally passionate desire to fit in, he studied Gaelic, said the rosary every night with the McDonaghs, and seriously toyed with converting to Roman Catholicism. In fact, he had gone so far as to schedule a baptism, but before it could take place he said to the priest who was instructing him, "You don't really expect me to believe that, do you?"

In Ireland, White also found the perfect context in which to indulge one of his less beneficial avocations, drinking. Although he was aware that he could not write when drunk and could, as he said, go on "the water-waggon" for extended periods, he always treated the abstinences as temporary, sometimes even planning the exact date when he would start drinking again. The desire to live life on as intense a level as possible was at least partially responsible for his drinking. Loneliness, the desire for solitude, and the need to belong clashed constantly in the course of a lifelong effort to sustain as high a version of any state as possible.

As divided about Ireland as he was about every other aspect of his life, White eventually produced a book about the Irish, *The Elephant and the Kangaroo*, which offended as large number of people. Chief among them were his loving hosts, the McDonaghs, who were so deeply hurt by his portrayal of them that they permanently terminated their friendship with White. As for Irish readers in general, they greeted the book's publication with rage.

From 1939 through the end of the war, there are several gaps in the Potts-White correspondence. Potts, extremely busy as senior tutor of Queens' College, was in a "reserved occupation" that he was not allowed to leave, for he was seeing companies of air-force lads through the college every six months as well as doing his share of fire-watching and air-raid service. Mary had three young children to feed and educate under difficult conditions. As for White, he used to say that "getting letters out of an author is like getting a farmer to dig your garden in his spare time!" What few letters there were came either from Doolistown or from Sheskin Lodge, in County Mayo, where White went shooting and fishing, sometimes in the company of David Garnett and his wife.

On November 25, 1944, White went through one of the most painful ordeals of his life: Brownie's death. His red setter had been "more perfect than anything else in all my life . . . she was wife, mother, mistress and child . . . she was all I had."

[March 24, 1939]
G.V.J. Maxted, Chopman & Rowe, 85 London Wall, E.C.2.
c/o Mrs. McDonagh, Doolistown, Trim, Co. Meath, Eire

Dear Pottës,

As usual I am writing to you when in trouble. The fact is, I have one or two thousand pounds: a distressing circumstance to which I

102

am by no means accustomed; and I don't know what to do with the stuff. I believe one has to "invest" it, but I don't know how to do this, nor what in. It is in the bank at present, in the current account. This is not very paying! Will you please find time to write and tell me about money? I am absolutely unable to imagine how to begin, even, as all the stockbrokers in the books I read always take it away from people like me at once, and spend it on cigars. I am reading Trollope's *Prime Minister* at present, in which there is a shady character called Lopez, who I am sure would not allow me to keep it for a moment. This is why I am writing to you—the only honest man I can think of—instead of to Sir Sydney Cockerell (who would make me put it in 3% consols) or Ronny [McNair] Scott (who would buy cigars with it, I fear) or the Headmaster of Stowe, who would use it to purchase himself a baronetcy. I don't want to go to my bank manager, as he is the one who always advises me to put it in the current account, out of which I am sure he abstracts it to buy himself beer. Besides, I am quite sure the current account is not the place for thousands of pounds. What I want to know is, how does one set about investing money—if by going to a stockbroker or some such personage, do you know of an honest one—and what sort of investments does a person make anyway, when the world is to be blown up at any moment? Perhaps I had better have it in gold and bury it in a bog near here. I am thinking of staying in Ireland for another month at any rate, for if you people rush into war as soon as you look like doing it, I may be able to skulk about under the shamrock until the first few bombardments are over. What a world! How is your beard? Mine is much more formidable than when you saw it, but unfortunately it won't grow thickly—only long. I think of tying ribbons in it.

> love from
> TimΘ

White settles in Ireland, cultivates the Merlynesque beard with which he would come to be identified and, with Potts's constant aid and criticism, continues with *The Witch in the Wood*, which will become part of *The Once and Future King*.

[postcard]

[July 2, 1939]
Doolistown, Trim, Co. Meath, Eire

It is splendid news that you are free and I hope the M.S. will have arrived by now. I feel that there is considerable truth in the charges of cheap anachronism and "determined facetiousness," so please don't hesitate to blue-pencil whatever offends you. Indeed, you can help me most by doing this. The thing is *meant* to be farce, so I can't alter the main theme, but I could cut the worse blemishes of detail and perhaps add several "nature bits" at the beginnings of chapters, thus bringing it more into line with the tone of *The S. in the S.* I hope all are well in your tribe? I am learning Irish seriously—pretty good at my age, don't you think? I still wear my whiskers. A maiden lady who keeps a shop in Trim said fervently "O my God!" on seeing me for the first time. I hadn't the presence of mind to say I was only S. Joseph.

[July 18, 1939]
Doolistown, Trim, Co. Meath, Eire

Dear Pottës,

Thank you very much indeed for your most helpful letter. I am sending a copy of it to Collins, and I hope you don't mind. If they will only give me time (the trouble is that these Americans have a most complicated system of advertisement, which, once launched, can hardly be arrested, like a war) if they will only give me time, I will do more or less what you say. There is a splendid critic in America, who helps me on these things as you do, and I shall steer a middle course between you. Instead of making the village the hero of the story, I shall bring in Arthur himself, as a parallel plot in Camelot. All you wanted was to *have* a hero, because the Queen was so nasty, and Arthur will make quite as good a hero as the village would have done. I need not tell you how grateful I am, Pottës, for your help. You will have to guess it from the fact that I value it at the hellish cost of rewriting half a book. No time to write more in these circumstances. See attached reference to genius in Tutors.

Love from,
Tim

[July 19, 1939]
Doolistown, Trim, Co. Meath, Eire

Dear Pottës—You can't think what agony it is to re-write a book. The old part rises up like Banquo and stands between you and the page. However, I am struggling manfully, and I have begun with the village instead of the Queen. She and her family come in at the *end* of chapter one (a long chapter)¹ and then we go off to Camelot, where Arthur is inventing his Might for Right idea (instead of Right to Might). I had hoped to keep this side of the story for Book 3, because it really belongs to the Launcelot part, but I have decided to sacrifice it towards sweetening the present work. Then Chapter 3 goes back to Lothian, half the school-room part is cut, and we get a scene in Mother Morlan's house in the village. This is as far as I have got so far, but I am working on the principle of suppressing as much as possible of the early bits about Morgause. I shall leave her to the chapters on her which you mention. I shall visit Camelot, for conversations between Arthur & Merlin, 3 times, at intervals throughout the book. When I get half way through the book, I shall begin to leave it alone. My books always gather momentum, and sail themselves towards the end.

I wish you could see the holocaust of pages already thrown out. I have half a mind to send them to you as ashes, in an urn.

105

Now, Pottës, the reason why you couldn't use your blue pencil on the first draft was because it was wrong structurally. You would have needed scissors and paste. In the present draft I am recreating the structure according to your ideas, and you *could* use the pencil. Is there any hope of reaching you with a typescript again, if you are enough interested, or will you be here, there and everywhere? I am worried about this Point Counter Point criticism (which I interpret to mean: habit of switching from one place to another in the course of a chapter, with a line space between them). I can't seem to rectify it, and have a drowning man's hope that you could. I have a vision of you inserting a conjunction or something with your blue pencil, scratching out the line space (which is a trick I hate anyway) and leaving all serene. There may also be a few errors of *tone*. It is very difficult to write a book all in one tone, because no author ever is in the same tone for months together. It is like singing a very long song unaccompanied, and you get off the note. You might be able to pencil the margins of these false bits, and then I could write them over. (That Morgause scene on the cliffs with Pellinore was such a tonal error: I have destroyed it in toto.) Could you think of doing this? Oh my God, how I *hate* writing.

love from
Tim

[July 25, 1939]
Doolistown, Trim, Co. Meath, Eire

Dear Mary,

I keep writing to Pottës (like launching troops into battle—you don't know what has become of them) so now I shall write to you. It is just this, a brilliant suggestion, but I suppose nobody will take it seriously except myself. Why don't you and Pottës and the three brats (good for mothers to be told their babes are brats, even if they aren't) come to stay with me in Ireland for the last fortnight in September? I have taken a shooting Lodge in Co. Mayo (look at the atlas) which has plenty of room for all, and 2 maids. Advantages: no housework for you, nothing to see except a bog ten miles square and some mountains, nearest neighbour 5 miles off, lake for children to bathe in, sea in vicinity. I firmly purpose to fish, shoot, hawk nearly all the time. You might not know I was there. So long as you brought a car, I really think you could be happy. Pottës can walk and quarrel with his children and so can you, just as well in ould Oireland as anywhere else. Free grub should nearly cover expenses in coming over, which are *very small. Two* people *and* a car can get return ticket for £7.10.0 If you felt like making a month of it, I know of a place where they only charge £2 a week for single people, and you could come over for all meals. Unfortunately I have David Garnett and his wife and family the first fortnight, and that is why I can't ask you then.

N.B. A man fishing can be talked to all day, and if he is an equanimous fisherman like myself he does not mind how often Weg falls in or Betsy(?) gets caught. Don't you think the children would enjoy it? It is fine air, free country and all men equal.

P.S. I have been on the water-waggon for 5 weeks. Now think

    Love from
    Tim

I will borrow you a piano accordeon, and Potts must bring some books. But the car is the vital factor, so that both factions may have mobility. The place is a Sahara.

[August 1, 1939]
Doolistown, Trim, Co. Meath, Eire

Dear Mary—unless you *want* to have a holiday away from the children, why don't you keep them away from school? I expect Pottës is being old-fashioned about this. If they miss a fortnight of school it will put them back about 3 days once they get to school again (experentia docet—don't forget I was a schoolmaster) not more. Schools teach with frightful deliberation and any bright scholar can catch up a fortnight in 3 days. And if they are not bright scholars, schools are no good to them anyway. Against this 3 day set back you can put the experience of crossing the sea, an invaluable service to their geography and general knowledge! And if it should happen to be good weather, won't they get health running o'er the bogs so free, shouting Potts aboo? Think of all the absence from school which happens through mumps, chicken pox etc. School curriculums are invented for just such emergencies. Tell Pottës to stop being a pedant, or I won't re-write any more novels for him.

Dia is Maire duit agus Pádraig

A cara

Toirdealbac Ó Zealazáin

[August 21, 1939]
Doolistown, Trim, Co. Meath, Eire

Dear Pottës—Thank you for your charming letter, with its beautiful compliment about being your best friend, taking it all round. I have always wanted to be somebody's best friend, but never succeeded. I have no friends, only acquaintances: You have no idea how curious it is to live one's whole life like a cat: or have you? I forget how old you were when you married. [Potts had been 32.] Anyway, you never but once wanted to be married, until you suddenly took it into your head and got married at once. I don't think you noticed you were lonely before. I have noticed it in my own case and it grieves me. This paragraph is like being sick. I shall stop.

Dont worry about Morgause. I only wanted your help because,

once you have written a book and corrected its various scripts a dozen times, you get to know it by heart. The result is that you lose all sense with regard to it. It becomes worse than trying to re-write. To Be or Not to Be. It even becomes meaningless, like when you say your own name to yourself hundreds of times. It is not that I am at all humble, or even that I value other people's criticism more than my own. It is merely that for me the words have lost all reality, and it is as if I had gone deaf and dumb. In these circumstances the only thing I can do is to see that the M. S. is read by somebody whose judgement I respect. I would not re-write for anybody except you & Mary.

Well, I suddenly realised that you two had been reading the book nearly as closely as I had, so that presumably you would be in or near the same affliction. So it would be stupid to rely on you any more. If I had sent you the book for a second go, you might have been deaf and dumb as well. It went off to America a fortnight ago.

I rewrote the first chapter, mainly about the village, introduced an Irish saint called St. Toirdeálbac, cut more of Morgause, did much more on the children, and put in six chapters about Arthur himself, fighting Bedegraine from the saxon end. In fact, I did what you told me, except that I thought of the Arthur chapters for myself. There is a great deal more about the village—St. Toirdeálbac marries Mother Morlan, so that it is a double wedding at the end—and I cleared up the Q. Beast, according to directions. Almost every word of your advice seemed diamond, and I did nearly all of it. Whether I did it successfully or not, I can't say. It is still just a mass of words to me. When I see it in print they will *look* different. I am hoping to hold up the English edition till next spring, by which time I may have recovered my sight and hearing enough to revise what was printed in America. In any case, I shall not regard *any* of the books as finally composed until I re-write the whole thing and publish all four in one volume as The Doom of Arthur. We are still in the work-shop. I send out my artist's proofs unfinished, in order to have something to live on meanwhile.

I am deep in vol. 3, and already have finished vol. 4, except that I shall have to re-write it wholly. In these circumstances I am simply taking no notice of all your war business across the sea. I am trying to write quickly, as this is only fair, but until I have the work completed I am afraid I shall be too busy to fight. It will be peculiar to have to tell the Examiners in Conscientious Objection that No, I am not a conscientious objector, but at the moment I am too busy, but I will come as soon as I can.

Yes, it was a great pity about your visit to Eire. It would have been nice for me not to have been alone in that big house. (This sentence inserted so as to make you feel a cad, and come next time.) I am convinced that we could have enjoyed ourselves, whether you brought the kids or not. What a good word "kids" is. There is a stage when children just are kids. Yours are just about entering it. I am beginning to drivvel now. I am not going to invite anybody for my second fortnight. For me it is Aut Something, Aut Nihil. Can't remember what the Something was, but in this case it is you.

> love from
> Tim

White expresses his ambivalences about his place in the war effort, and presses onward with the Arthurian books. Potts's letter to White is one of the few to have survived intact in Garnett's leaking shed, where White's correspondence and notebooks had been stored.

> [November 8, 1939]
> Doolistown, Trim, Co. Meath, Eire

My dear Pottës,
I told my agents to send you a copy of the *Witch in the Wood* when it arrived from America last week. The postal arrangements are such a nuisance nowadays that it seemed better to have it sent direct, even if it arrived without my signature. Otherwise we should have been bandying the thing to and fro across the Irish channel for ages, and it did not seem worth it.

What do you think of our combined job? Personally I think it is pretty frightful still, but it will nearly do. This volume can only hope to be a necessary link between the other parts of the story, and, if it succeeds in that, I shall have to be content.

Have you, or has Mary, the strength of mind to go through it once again with a blue pencil? This is only the American edition, and I could alter it quite a lot before publishing it in England, and finally it could still be changed before all the four books come out in one volume. So it would be an immense help to me if you can suggest improvements. One way of improving it, which still remains, is to cut out some more bits about the queen. Also those tedious knights.

Perhaps you would prefer to wait until you have read volume three, which will be about the Lancelot-Guenever imbroglio. The first three volumes will be written in prose, in order, as it were, to fix the background of the three main sets of characters, and then the fourth volume will be in the form of a straightforward play or tragedy, showing how they finally clash together.

It is terribly difficult to get hold of books in Ireland, and I badly want a copy of the *Misfortune of Arthur*, by Thomas Hughes. If you could be able to get me a copy of this in Cambridge, I should be very grateful for it.

How is the family, and how are you all enjoying the war? Write and tell me as much as you think will please the censor. I am trying to buy the place which I invited you to visit last September [Sheskin Lodge, County Mayo], and, if I do get it, and if the war will only shut up, I am expecting you and your whole family to spend at least one month with me every year. It is a lovely place, and if you don't fall in with this plan it will mean that you are abandoning a great creative artist to intellectual isolation. This will mean that I have to stop writing, and it will be your fault. There are 40 acres of wild garden for the children to play in. It is made for children.

What else can I say? I have offered my services to the Ministry of Information, but those worthies don't seem to have noticed it. Until there really is a shortage of cannon-fodder, I shall stay here. When the war broke out I had David Garnett and all his family staying with me. We had a peculiar sort of time, like something in Tchekov. I asked myself what I should be fighting for, if I fought, and the only answer I could invent was Civilisation. I then decided that I could do more for Civilisation at present than fight for it, since I could make it. So until either the Ministry of Information wakes up, or else there comes the cannon-fodder shortage, I am staying here and spending eight hours a day on finishing Arthur.

Love from,
Tim

[April 7, 1940]
Lower Farm, Hadstock nr. Linton, Camb.

Dear Tim,

This is an attempt to emerge from the partial insanity in which the war potted me. It is part of a general campaign of writing to my various friends to say how do you do? (though I have had news from Tilly). Has the enclosed anything to do with you? I fear not. But I think you ought to meet the author (if it isn't you); at least do something generous. It is important to treat one's name with courtly respect.

I am re-reading all of your letters I haven't put away. The first was written when you had first written *The Sword and the Stone*. Mary and I are just reading Malory, which I can't have read for ages; because I find the various knights *are* very distinct characters (as, I find, you say in the afore-mentioned letter). I agree about Gawaine, possibly Kay. I do not like Lancelot, so far—he is rather too "head of the house." Tristram is extremely interesting: a rather comic figure I think—for instance, his forgetting about La Belle Isoude till he suddenly remembered her when he got into bed with the other Isoude, and then being dreadfully upset. And being nearly murdered in his bath by the Queen of Ireland. I agree that Arthur is very fine. But what *does* surprise me is the novel-interest in Malory, which no one (except you) seems to have noticed.

I find that all the other letters are about *The Witch in the Wood* and I think I did answer some of them after a fashion. I must have said to you that we thought *the W in the W* pretty good in the end. I am sorry always to say "we," but I never read anything (except in a hurry because I have set an essay on it or something) now except aloud with Mary. There are a number of things I don't much like; but it would be a long business to note them down, and I haven't time to do it now, but perhaps will in the summer. But I don't know why you shouldn't do this yourself, after you've finished the whole saga.

The kids are all well. William is 4. He is very well, but at present his chief characteristic is a steady whine (punctuated by louder manifestations varying from a bellow to a scream). This is very tiresome; fortunately my mother says that I was just the same at his age, which though it isn't much comfort at least forces me to be less angry.

I am getting to dislike Cambridge quite a lot: but I think it's quite a healthy dislike, that the money I get makes it worth while. I also dislike the war: but I think it was fated to happen and nothing could have stopped it. But what with war, and all this communism among the young, and the almost complete disappearance of gentlemanliness as I understand it, what is a poor middle class man to do? We seem to be in a period like the period when Malory wrote. When you have finished your Tetralogy, you had better turn your hand to writing an *equivalent* of the *Morte d'Arthur*—because your book is not quite that.

Well Well

Mary sends her love.

Make what you can of this letter, and when you edit my literary remains, you need not include it among them.

Love to you. And write and tell me all your news, if you can find time to. How you are living and what is happening in your history.

Pottës

My beard is getting redder daily, and it insists on taking an Edward VII shape, which was not what I intended. The village children shout Ginger after me, I am sorry to say. I am determined to live it down. But I think it prevents undergraduates from taking me too seriously.

You had better have this letter of Collins' back. I very much liked Collins.

White's opinion on women, and the effect of that attitude on the female characters in *The Once and Future King*, is described with an extraordinary amount of self-awareness in the following letters.

[April 9, 1940]
Healion's Hotel, Belmullet, Co. Mayo

Dear Pottès—How right you are about Tristram. Unfortunately I have an incurably middle-class mind and I never see the real jokes until they are pointed out to me. Hitherto I have been treating Tristram as a mere cad—he is foul to Mark, and I am sure he was always bullying Palomides because he was a "nigger." I used to attribute his extraordinary conduct towards his two lady friends to simple caddishness. Now I see that he is a great comic figure. He only comes into my Tetralogy by report and reference—very rarely—but I shall alter these references a little, to fit your obviously inspired interpretation. You are quite wrong about Lancelot. He was an intensely *ugly* man, quite startling to look at, and he was distressed about this. When he took a *nomme de guerre*, he called himself Le Chevalier Mal Fait. He was also a sadist and very much muddled up psychologically. This was why he always had to be merciful etc. He was a romantic, and wanted to "do miracles." His Guenever trouble was not Arthur, but the miracles. But you will have to read my third volume, before you understand him. (Little boys still believe that they won't be able to bowl well in the 1st XI match tomorrow, if they abuse themselves today, and Lancelot was

114

captain of the 1st XI. Guenever, whom he couldn't stop, was stopping his two main things—his bowling (feats of arms) and his miracles.) He was top of the batting averages—Tristram & Lamorak were second and third—and he did manage to perform 2 miracles. The second ends my third volume, with him in tears. In the end, he died in the odour of sanctity—literally. I mean literally literally. But you will just have to wait for vol. 3. I am still miserable about vol. 2 (Witch in Wood) and may have to scrap the whole thing. Have you found what a remarkable person Guenever was? She is an Anna Karenina, but her trouble is that she has no children. Arthur had 2 illegitimate ones, and Lancelot had Galahad. (I have had great fun with Galahad: as a little boy I made him play with dolls all the time, and the chief doll was called The Holy Holy.) But Guenever is terrific. "Fie on your weeping" says Bors to her (Bors was a mysoginist like myself, so Guenever irritated him particularly), "for you weep never but when there is no boot." Guenever is one of the realest *women* in literature: not a Dresden shepherdess or any stereotyped figure, but somebody with a frightful temper, enormous reality etc. etc. She lives on a different plane—the female plane. I treat her with the greatest respect, like somebody handling a cobra. But I like and admire cobras. I hold her tightly by the head and unfold the coils with respectful wonder, studying their firm markings and wonderful strangeness. Read her intense scene with Elaine, just after they have driven Lancelot mad. It is a great piece of feeling and dignity on both sides. What a wonderful man Malory was, to do the Dostoievsky in four or five sentences, instead of taking a hundred thousand words for it.

What a selfish man you are, not to write to me more often. I have been stuck, without being able to write a word of the Tetralogy for 3 weeks, just for want of such stimulus as your letter has given me. Now I shall be able to write away. Don't you think you could manage to drop me a few crumbs more often? Particularly any speculations which may strike you while you are reading Malory? However, I suppose I am selfish too, to want your letters.

I am sorry that the village children call you Ginger. Here they call me Santa Claus, and I answer to it. You had better try answering to Ginger. It seems to mollify them. Are you finding great uses for your beaver, as I am for mine? I keep pencils, pens etc. in it, and frequently forget them, which scares the maids.

Love to Mary

from
Tim

When I find that one of the maids is looking at me like a rabbit at a ferret, I put my hand to my beard and find a pipe cleaner or a paper knife, which I had left there by mistake.

P.S. I have written nearly or more than 70,000 words of Vol. 3 (The Ugly Man) and I am just at Lancelot's affair with the second Elaine. There are two troubles at this point, which the Pottës family may eventually have to clear up. The first trouble is Guenever, who, at this point, is at her change of life. I have never had a change of life and I don't like asking strange women about it. Indeed, I don't like asking women at all: those who have passed it seem to prefer to pretend there wasn't one, and those who have not passed it don't seem to like to face it either. Is Mary bold enough to read this part of Vol. 3 with attention, and see if I have gone wrong? To tell you the truth, I am having some trouble with *all* the characters just now. One of the things which Malory chooses to ignore is that his Great Lovers (!) were increasingly older than 30. At the present moment (imbroglio of Elaine 2) Guenever & Lancelot are about 46 and Arthur about 54! I feel shy about ascribing sentiments of passionate love to such people, and yet I am having to peg away at it as best I can. If either you or Mary have heard anything about what love feels like at 50, or about whether a man of 50 can go on loving a mistress of the same age, with whom he has been sleeping for 30 years, I should be glad to hear it? And what about love-making during the change of life? Has Mary some famous book on this, or will she write me a brief monograph on the subject (and will it get past the censor?)?

Trouble number 2 keeps my heart in my mouth, but I have made my choice and I shall have to brave it out. To confess it in one word, I have run the two Elaines together into one person. In my reading of the matter, the maid who floats down to Camelot is the same as the one who gave birth to Galahad: a fat old matron, pathetic and abandoned: her son dead: no lily maid. In one way this is a sensible, economical step (almost the only place at which I have wandered from Malory) but in others it is a mistake. I did it largely because I thought that M. may have himself been muddling his sources in this matter—for Lancelot's mother was herself called Elaine, and it seemed really too pathological to give him *two* mistresses of the same name. Also it keeps the plot neater to have a single Elaine as one of the main figures of its eternal quadrangle.

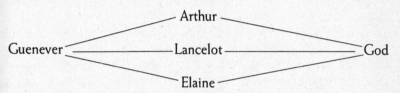

The objection is that Malory's *psychology* is better than my plot, when you reflect that most of the characters are about forty-five. It is just the age at which Lancelot would seek a young girl, instead of the ageing Guenever. And, by turning the 2 Elaines into one, I am eliminating the young girl. It is a nasty problem.

[April 22, 1940]

I wrote all this immediately on receiving your letter, and now send it off, as I daren't re-read it.

[April 25, 1940]
From Mr. L. J. Potts, Senior Tutor, Queens' College, Cambridge

Dear Tim,
I hasten to answer your letter before postage goes up. As Tilly says, it is important to be careful in small things. But also your letter

is the kind that needs a quick answer. We have got a bit further with Malory since I wrote. I am not so sure about Tristram after all. The important thing seems to be that he is Cornish: The Round Table seem to view the Corns with a mixture of contempt, suspicion and patronizing good nature—rather like the 18th Century Londoners' attitude to the Irish. But Tristram was taken up by them—Lancelot scolded him about La Belle Isoud, and Arthur patronized him, and he had a very good batting average. At the moment he is a sort of mixture of Oliver Goldsmith and Ranjitsinjhi. But we haven't got to the end of him.

I reserve judgement of Lancelot—I shouldn't have judged him, because I haven't got up to his real stuff. Nor can I say much about the Elaine business. I have only got up to the place where Lancelot is beginning to be a bit of a scandal with Guenever, and Arthur is being sensible about it. But your idea of Guenever is right—She is obviously a most formidable woman. A sort of Queen Victoria. We shall see. Do you get Sir Dinadan in? He is a most delightful character—perhaps the one really nice person in the whole business. For you know they are a grim lot, like real people. What swine the Lot family are (except Gareth). Look here, I supose it's your doing, but how odd it is that I should only now have realized what a novel the *Morte d'Arthur* is. Academic people are pretty bad, but how on earth *have* they managed to read this book and not be fascinated by the character. And how could I read it and not see *anything* in it—I mean anything that *is* in it. I wasn't such a fool. But I think one must be very chastened to see with Malory's eyes. Perhaps one must be living in a world like Malory's and ours, where civilization is just about dead.

I am sure Mary will give you her views on change of life. I don't think you need be worried about the age problem. I am pretty sure that passionate love can last for decades, and with the medieval system by which you didn't live with your mistress and were brought up to clothe the business in religious emotions it must have been particularly easy. *Our* love convention is based on the Italianate Elizabethan precocious boy and girl romances, which Malory expressly repudiates. See "How true love is likened to Summer."

I daresay you may be right about the two Elaines. Can't you get hold of some scholar in Dublin (say at Trinity College) who has got up the medieval stuff and ask him. Anyway, the two Isouds are clearly the same woman, and that sort of thing is supposed to be always happening in legends. But that of course doesn't affect the story as *Malory* saw it.

I must stop this now. By the way, I *do* answer to "Ginger." But the horrible thing is, I have a natural antipathy to boys. William will probably cure me of it, homœopathically.

Love
Pottës

[December 6, 1940]
Doolistown, Trim, Co. Meath, Eire

Dear Pottës. I like getting a good excuse to write to you. Today I have written to my London agents, telling them to send you a copy of the American edition of the Lancelot book *[The Ill-Made Knight]*. It is for the collection, *not* for you to read. I should prefer you to read the English edition when it comes out—spring, I suppose—as it is somewhat improved, compared with the American one, and really I don't see how I can force you to read all my books twice. Let Mary read it, if she likes, and if there is any trouble about Guenever's sex problems she must just send me a booklet about the facts of life. You will be amused to find your own comments on Tristram in this vol. verbatim. I am hoping two things very much—that I have not made Lancelot into the prig you think him, and that Guenever is a little real. I have just let her do her things, without much comment. The next volume is going to be called *The Candle in the Wind* (one has to add D.V. nowadays) and is about the final clash, worked by Mordred. It will end on the night before the last battle, with Arthur absolutely wretched. And after that I am going to add a new 5th volume, in which Arthur rejoins Merlin underground (it turns out to be the badger's sett of vol. 1) and the animals come back again, mainly ants and wild geese.[2] Dont squirm. The inspiration is god-sent. You see, I have suddenly discovered that (1) the central theme of Morte d'Arthur is to find an antidote for War, (2) that the best way to examine the politics of Man is to observe him, with Aristotle, as a political *animal*. I don't want to go into all this now, as it will spoil the freshness of the future book, but I have been thinking a great deal, in a Sam Butlerish way, about Man as an animal among animals—his cerebrum etc. I think I can really make a comment on all these futile-isms (communism, fascism, conservatism etc.) by stepping back—right back into the other mammals. So, to put my "moral" across (but I shan't state it) I shall have the marvellous opportunity of bringing the wheel full circle, and ending on an animal note like the one I began on. This will turn my completed epic into a perfect fruit, "rounded off and bright and done."

My trouble still is that cursed second book. I hate Morgause so much that I can't write about her. Will you believe it that I have already re-written it, *since* the time I re-wrote it for you, and it is still hopeless. I am thinking (for it will have to be done again before the end) of tearing it up wholly, and re-doing it with Morgause as a straight witch, no farce, and lashings of celtic twilight. Have you an opinion on the subject, or did I stun you too much with all the times you had to toil through it?

Dont forget that this is *The Matter of Britain!* Look at this short list, my lad: Nennius, Geoffrey, Malory, Purcell, Hughes, (Milton), Tennyson, T. H. White. You could treble it, but I am mentioning the *important* ones. This is a letter from a man they will be putting in the literary histories, Pottës: yes, willy-nilly. The subject does it. A man who wrote out the *Morte d'Arthur* in Morse Code would still have to be mentioned in literary histories, because it is the *Morte d'Arthur*. So look on my works, you Pottës, and despair.

love to all from Tim

Dear Tim,

I do like your Celtic "T"—much better than your capital R in the middle of words. Oddly enough I did that once for a bit and got in a fearful row for it from George Townsend Warner[3] (the greatest schoolmaster there has ever been, and a man of unerring judgement [and when I say the greatest schoolmaster, I don't mean the greatest man who is now or has been a schoolmaster (that is of course you)]). That sentence is like the sentences Empson used to write when he was doing examinations here. I suppose he still writes them.

Well, it was nice to hear from you. We were wondering about you last week-end. Thank you for the Lancelot book. I don't think I shall be able to hold off till the English edition comes out, which I should like to do since "the latest edition is always the best, unless the editor is a blockhead." It's a pity that word blockhead has rather gone out: it's more poetical than moron.

We are sure to read Lancelot over Christmas. Mary will no doubt send you some words of wisdom about Guenevere, if you have got her wrong. I can't say what I think about the projected fifth book—everything depends on what you make of it, since there is no particular theoretical reason for it, though of course you can easily find one if you want to. (My brain is stupid and my style all in a mess this morning—either because the weather is quite unbearable, or because I've got diarrhoea, a complaint I so seldom have that it always slightly demoralizes, or because I'm invigilating a lot of scholarship candidates from schools doing an "applied mathematics" paper in the stinks section of the examination and the dreary cerebration going on all about me is sending all the virtue out of the air. I have had to "leave the room" once already, and after wandering about the purlieus of St. John's and finding a Lady's Cloakroom, which need would have forced me to violate if it hadn't been proprietously locked, I threw myself on the mercy of a bedmaker and was directed to the right place. By the way *how* can two particles of equal mass (particles, forsooth) connected by a string (of length 1) be placed on a table (however smooth) with the string *perpendicular* to the edge of the table. It beats me, but I suppose it's all right—at any rate the schoolboys are all taking it lying down. One of them almost literally—he has his head on the table and is rubbing his chin gently to and fro over the paper with a vacant and mildly sensuous expression on his face. But the question about the particles is question 10 out of 10; and as scientists never have the gumption to do anything but work straight ahead, they probably never get up to question 10, which is very likely a mere dummy. Anyway the previous one is exciting enough—for it has a car ascending a spherical hill at a velocity of V in a vertical plane through the centre of the hill; and if they can escape that with their lives I expect they will be mere gibbering idiots and will push the particles about on the smooth surface of the table with broad smiles but no particular object. The whole thing suggests to me the fate of that man who went mad during the English Tripos a little before your time I think. And didn't he afterwards change his name to Baron Bravo or something, and get a job at Stowe?

The trouble about book 2 of Arthur is really that you never published the *pirate* book ["Rather Rum"] or *You can't keep a good man down*. Between them they got rid of a good deal of waste matter projected in your mind by Morgause. Also the pirate book is the most uproarious thing you have done, and so good that you need to get some of that sort of high jinks into your collected works. Could you possibly find up the pirates and make Collins publish them—if possible *now*. Tell him it's getting in your way and you can't get Arthur really right till you've got it published. I can't think what you're to do with Morgause, except keep her right out of the book (except for hints in the thoughts and conversation of the boys and villagers—and perhaps the single scene on the ice),[4] or of course leave her as she is. My trouble is that I can't quite reconcile myself to doing without Morgause, unless you gave me Lady Madge Calcutta [a character in "Rather Rum"] in exchange; and yet there is too much of her—she is too much exposed in all her vulgarity—for the final scene of the book—it sickens one. As you say, of course Arthur was tired out, and one falls for women before one knows them. What is *true* in the book is the contrast between the genuineness of the village, and even in their childish way of the three foolish knights, and the meretriciousness of the great lady; and this is superbly brought out in the scene on the ice, which is in its way as good as Bottom and Titania (the moral of which is the same). I think the quarrels between Mark and Morgause are much too crude: quarrels between such people are ridiculous, like Oberon's and Titania's, but they are really for me double and tigerish—as you see them in Strindberg. Not on the prep school level. But you *are* quite right in saying you hate M. too much to do any good with her; and if you re-write the book I don't see what you can do but cut out almost all of her, leaving in things like the remark about the butterfly. ["She juist cotched his flutter-bye in her hond, ye ken, and pullit him asunder. . . . She hauled off the wings, yin after anither." *The Witch in the Wood*, New York: Putnam's, 1940, p. 70.] Don't actually show her in her bath—but do it somehow indirectly. And I don't think you should describe her flirtations with Grummore and Pellinore; but leave them to tell each other something of her frightful nature. As for the farce, it is holy and sublime, and right at the root of what you are trying to say. If it went, nothing would be left of this book. The whole of the Saint [Toirdeálbach], which you added is good; and all the village is lovely. However, don't be too much influenced by what I say. I couldn't *write* the book, so I don't feel very confident about telling you how to. Only I see the difficulty, throw out suggestions in case they might set you off.

I think I will keep this till to-morrow, when I go home for a couple of nights. We now live at Balsham (West Cottage, Balsham, Cambs), three bedrooms, a sitting room, a kitchen, a chemical latrine, and a dug-out with six bunks in which the whole family plus one can sleep as easily as anything. Unfortunately I have to be here too much to get really countrified. We have let the Bateman Street house to a posse of Roman Catholic nuns who run a nursing home. The Tillyards are in sole possession of Lower Farm Hadstock. Our family are getting on with their lessons.

Love from all
Pottës

123

* * *

The themes of the Arthurian books were still evolving. Here we see White working on introducing the anti-war theme and animal symbolism. As the war dragged on, both White and Potts were feeling its difficult and seemingly endless pressures.

[January 8, 1941]

In consideration of the signature, I had better add as a P.S.

From T. H. White,

Doolistown, Trim, Co. Meath, Eire

Dear Pottës—Thanks for your helpful letter. As a matter of fact you suggested the very alterations to *The Witch in the Wood* which I had already carried out in my 3rd (?) draft. As I told you, even that turned out to be a failure, so I am re-doing the whole thing with a different woman altogether as Morgause. I have chucked overboard all idea of building her on my mother, Lady Calcutta, the publican's wife or etc. Instead, she is now a pure melodramatic WITCH (rather fun) who goes about boiling black cats alive and so forth. Housman wrote a poem about her. (Her strong enchantments failing, Her towers of fear in wreck, Her limbecks dried of poison etc.)[5] I shall make her wildly seductive. Circe? Anyway, black hair and a whiff of incense, or is it assafoetida? Haggard's *She*. Much easier than trying in vain to keep my temper about people like my mother. You will think that I never write to you except when I want to get something out of you, and you will be quite right, because I restrain myself from writing without occasion, for fear of growing a bore. This time I am writing for information which I can't put my hands on in Ireland, and, as you are a member of the most learned foundation in the world (my God, how I still wish I could be a don) you will e'en have to help, if you can. It is this last volume, or Harlequinade, to my Arthur. Do you remember how the doctor in *The Way of All Flesh* prescribed "a corpse of the larger mammals"?[6] I have been thinking along these lines ever since the war broke out, and I am coming to certain conclusions which I believe might be

124

salutary in regard to the next Peace. The main hypothesis is, that Man is a mammal, surrounded by about 25,000 species of backboneless ones. Instead of approaching the future politics of Man from a Marxian, Fascist, Conservative or other ideological basis, I suggest that it may be as well to approach him from a "naturalist's" point of view. Animals have politics, and most interesting ones. I think I can show that a certain form of politic is inherent in man's structure physiologically. Obviously I can't explain the thesis to you in a letter, when it is going to take a whole book to expose it, but one of the main pillars is this suggestion that we might be a little humble for a change. The monstrous hubris of the 19th and 20th centuries, which assumed that this one mammal (out of 2,850 mammals) was the only one worth considering makes me sick. And they even condescended to their own ancestors, Scott & Co. writing about them in a sort of Olde Tea Shoppe nursery jargon. With Hitler & Co. we now find (as would have been obvious to any but a blockhead) that man has not progressed a bit since the (sic) "Dark" Ages. Why would he? It takes a species several million years to modify itself, not a couple of centuries. Naturally this line of thought, which I am trying briefly to *suggest* for you instead of outlining it, took one back to the question: What is right or wrong (for a species)? Well, I can only suppose that it is Right for a species to progress in doing whatever it does. It would be quite wrong for a tortoise to attempt flight. It has no wings. In the end, you come down to the idea that a species must specialise in its own speciality. Follow that up, and you find that what is right for man depends upon his speciality, his wings, tail, beak, backbone, fins, antennae or whatever his most special speciality may be. And you will find that his most s.s. is his cerebrum. This (not the cerebellum) is as much overdeveloped in Man, as a species as, for instance, the nose of an elephant is overdeveloped from my nose. Well, that is as far as I have got at present (except that there are the most interesting political conclusions, if true, which I here omit) but I can't rush baldly into my conclusions until I have polished up my animal physiology to see where the leaks are. Keep on reading right ahead, and you will eventually arrive at what I want you to do for me, but before that we must go back to the beginning of the hypothesis. I said that animals have politics, and so they have. Aristotle's only known mistake was to define Man as the political animal. Think of ants, bees, wasps, wild geese, elephants—in fact, think of any animal you like. Nearly all have politics, and some have politics very close to the great nostrums of our century. Many insects are fascists, many birds communists. In the course of far too tedious speculations for a letter, I have dredged up ants, wasps, elephants and wild geese as those whose politics are of the greatest present interest. Before I begin to draw conclusions about the future of human politics, from a humiliating comparison with *their* politics, I must obviously know more about the cerebra of these animals. At least we draw towards my humble petition. Can you find a respectable biologist, physiologist or natural historian in all your noble university who happens to know of a published work which deals with *the comparative anatomy of the brains of all animals*. I want a book in which I can look up the anatomy of the brain of an ant, an elephant, a wild goose and a man. I don't mind how "learned" the book is, though, in point of fact, I only want to know two things about the various species: (a) how large the total brain is in comparison with the body, and (b) how large the cerebrum is in comparison with the cerebellum.

If no such book is published, can you by any means persuade some respectable person to give me this information in a letter? All I want is four little diagrams, like the following imaginary ones:

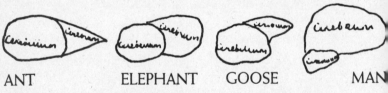

ANT ELEPHANT GOOSE MAN

together with a simple little table like the following one:

WEIGHTS OF BRAIN IN PROPORTION TO BRAWN

	Brain		Brawn
Man	56 oz.	in	2,688 oz.
Elephant	x oz.	in	y oz.
Goose	z oz.	in	a oz.
Ant	b oz.	in	c oz.

Mind you, I am not set on the Ant. There are several other insects, such as wasps, which might be of equal interest as fascists. If you can't get the name of a book for me to buy, but are reduced to asking a savant for the answers to my queries, it may be as well for you to shew him a page or two of this letter, rather than try to explain the problem to him yourself. Everything depends upon the difference between cerebrum and cerebellum, as I know from my association with hawks, and, indeed, it might be wiser to ask for a table *shewing the relation in weight of cerebrum to cerebellum*, rather than the relation of brain to body, though I could do with both. If you knew anything about Ireland, you would know what a hopeless task it is to trace these data on this side of the Irish Channel, and so you would forgive me for bothering you with all this verbiage. If you can help, please do. If not, you know quite well that I shall be your grateful pupil till dead, and pupils are not allowed to feel anything but gratitude to their Okain. (Irish word—don't worry.) Pottës, what do you mean by talking about my "capital R" in the middle of words? If that highly inferior Harrow dominie of yours had known anything about hand writing, he would have known that the "capital R" in the middle of words was just as celtic as the famous "Celtic   " which you seem to approve of. The change in my handwriting is probably due to my learning Irish. The Irish produced in the middle (dark) ages the most beautiful minuscule script which has ever been perfected, and they still use it, so I shall sign this letter to your and the censor's horrible mystification with my full name.

Corbealbai Ó Zealagáin

P.S. The whole of this letter could have been rendered unnecessary if only I had been in England, with access to the B.M. Reading Room, but note that I am not, and forgive it.

P.P.S. Ask Mary why my godson writes backwards? Has he been

reading *The Sword in the Stone?* [Merlyn lives backwards: he knows
what is going to happen, but not what *has* happened.]

Dear Tim,

Your request is modest, but embarrassing for I confess to an
antipathy for scientists in general. One of the few scientists I love is
a world-wide authority on the human brain; unfortunately he is in
Australia. I assume there is not time to put you in correspondence
with him; but you may as well have his address—Professor Frank
Goldby, University of Adelaide.

I am going to send your letter to a well-wisher of both of us,
Angus Bellaris. He has become rather successful in medical
sciences, and a good academic anatomist and zoologist; and he will
certainly know or be able to find out, what you want. I think he can
be trusted to do your job honestly. I haven't got his address this
evening, but expect to have it to-morrow. And I shall ask him to
send you the book you want or if there isn't a suitable one to send
you the information.

I will write at length some time—Meanwhile: I think your
proposal about Morgause is the best possible. By all means make
her a witch proper. The idea of cosmetic witchcraft in itself was
good, but in the interest of the book as a whole I don't mind your
sacrificing it.

We thoroughly enjoyed the *Ill-Made-Knight*—Mary has written
about women. I told her I consider myself much more ignorant
about women than I thought I was a few years ago. One is not
married for nothing: at least I now know I know nothing about that
difficult subject.

I agree with her that Guenever will do, on the whole. Am I right
in saying you have concealed, even partly *conquered* your dislike o
her very creditably. I think her convincing throughout. As for
Elaine Mary thinks you in as a psychologist. I think the defect is

artistic: though only a small defect. I think Elaine was mad. In most respects sane, but on the point of Galahad megalomaniac. A sort of Joana Southcote. Her father had told her the prophecy, and she got it into her head that she was the Virgin Mary. Hence she allowed herself to connive at the conception of Galahad in an exalted spiritual mood, as I really think a devout girl might, for God's sake. But then nature retaliated on her, and after the act she fell suddenly and hopelessly in love—and with the illogicality of women thereafter religious exaltation and sensuality were fused into a single emotion. But not so Lancelot. The other small point is I wish you had followed Malory in making Lancelot's shame be for having threatened to kill Elaine rather than for having begotten Galahad. This lifts him above Guenever, where he ought to be. If you make any alterations this need only be very small. All the men are excellent, esp. Lancelot. Arthur is splendid.

Yours
Pottës

[December 21, 1941]
As from Queens'

Dear Timothy,

I put my address as above, though I am at home, because I am at home so seldom. And this is only a note, because my intellect, if not dead, sleepeth. The lot of an adult civilian in this war is not yet materially bad, but it doesn't conduce to any but the crudest social exchanges. It is just a matter of trying to keep one's feet from being swept away, and one's self-respect from receiving the death blow from any of the buffets it daily receives. Cambridge is surprisingly busy, trying to continue higher education while contributing to the war effort. The young men seem to appreciate our efforts, but they are inadequate to the demand and still more to the ideal. Tom Henn is a Major in the Army, Tilly has just become a Senior Tutor

129

(which makes me feel like Wordsworth's child who is father to the man).

I look forward to visiting you some day, if you stay in Ireland.

Pottës

[May 8, 1942]
Doolistown, Trim, Co. Meath, Eire

Dear Mary,

I suppose you have blotted me out of the Family Bible, but I can't help it. Getting letters out of an author is like getting a farmer to dig your garden in his spare time, and also I have been having some kind of internal poisoning which has made me melancholic, plus a mass of worry about what my duty is in this war and all that. I have had to drop all my English correspondents—I scarcely get a letter a month—for fear of their disapproving of me. I have lost your letter, but I remember it in full. My godson is a cypher to me because I have met him so little, and I am too afraid of Betsy to say anything about her. God save the man she decides to marry, for he hasn't a chance of escape. I don't suppose you ever thought of a Nell Gwynn carreer for her, did you? She could send you and Pottës plenty of champagne, and end up as a duchess with plenty of little Fitz-es, if you thought it suitable. But don't let me influence you, even if anybody could influence Betty. It is Weg that am worried about, for I detected in your letter a misunderstanding about her. Why shouldn't she like snails if she wants to?[7] Darwin did. I would rather have the education of Weg than either of the others, and I would overwhelm her with gasteropods, hymenoptera and worms. There is nothing nasty about snails and (I am serious) you and Pottës are perhaps in this one particular not suitable parents for Weg. You are both of you townees, or at all events rather imperfect naturalists, and you don't understand that the first qualification for being a good biologist, which is what Weg ought to be, is to be unsuperstitious about the supposedly dirty animals. If I were

130

bringing Weg up, she should take toads to bed with her. If she is still on snails, why don't you get her some books on them unless I have written about it too late? Or you could try her with Ants—Unless I have misread between the lines of your letter, you are discouraging her because she is experimenting in a line you don't understand.

My Arthur book drags miserably along. I thought I had finished it 6 months ago, but have had to re-write the last volume. I keep telling myself that it is more important to get it done than to compete in the war as a disabled seaman, but I have relapses when it is too hard to wade against the stream. I tried at the outbreak to get some intelligent employment from Ministry of Information or British Council, but naturally they don't want intelligent people in such employment. Then on the collapse of France I joined our redoubtable Irish Home Guard, but was chucked out again almost at once, on suspicion of being a 5th column. More lately I have sent in my papers for a commission in the R.A.F.V.R., but they kept me waiting 2 months and turned me down. I suppose it is all for the best, as it really is more sensible to finish Arthur properly.

Here is a story. I was sitting on the bog this afternoon with an old man of 80. He said: "Did you ever hear tell of the Wicklow Hills?"—"Yes, I did"—"I was passing by one time in a train and a man in the train was after telling me there does be a big lake on the top of them. Would you believe that?"—"Yes"—"I was asking about it afterwards and another man told me there does be a mighty serpent in this lake, as big as a tree, with eyes on him as big as a cow. Every seven years that serpent puts his head out of the lake and bawls out: 'Did tomorrow come back yet?' And that's the year the tinants don't have to be paying any rint. Would you believe that?"

Try it on Weg.

I wish I could hear your harpsichord again. We have a lovely looking Broadwood piano here—a funny looking thing, neither upright nor grand, very beautiful, quite ruined, and of course always mute. I am sad when I think of your music. Do you remember what they found in the Countess's bed?

It will be fun when you come to visit us here, after the war. Later

131

on, when Pottës is the President of Queen's, you will have to invite
me to the Lodge and pretend I am a lion. I am in *Who's Who* already!
By the way, tell Pottës that my predecessor in the Arthur business,
Richard Hughes, was a fellow of Queens'.

The ink is running out.

Love from
Tim

Thank the brats for Xmas cards. Betsy will be a slick artist but Weg
has imagination. How I wish I knew more about William.

White had begun translating a medieval work of natural history that
had been given to him in the original Latin by Sir Sydney Cockerell. It would be published as *The Book of Beasts*.

[November 19, 1943]
Doolistown, Trim, Co. Meath, Eire

Dear Pottës,

I am engaged on a work of real scholarship at last. That is, I am
translating a 12th century Bestiary out of illegible, abbreviated,
dog-latin, into English, with notes about 3 times longer than the
work itself.

The history of Natural History is shortly as follows: 1. There is
the continuous body of country tradition running parallel the whole
way i.e. what peasants talk about in pubs. 2. Presumably several
Egyptians, Assyrians, Persians and the like wrote works of Natural
History, but, so far as my knowledge extends, we have been
rescued from these by the fire of Alexandria etc. 3. Your friends
Aristotle (as a serious student) and Herodotus (as a raconteur) next
enter the field. (Please excuse all this lecture: you will see why
presently.) 4. The landmarks after them are Pliny and Solinus—if

you know of any other important ones, I would be glad to hear of them. 5. Several early Fathers of the Church produced Greek, Syriac or Latin texts about animals, and, so far as I know at present, these were S. Isidore, Ambrose (who wrote a Hexameron) and an anonymous person known as Physiologus. 6. Round about the beginning of the 12th Century another anonymous collector, a monk, probably in an English monastery (the English have always been the prime movers of natural history—generally inaccurate) digested the works of Isidore, Ambrose, Solinus, Physiologus (and some shreds of parallel public house tradition) into the first extensive Bestiary, and this is what I am translating. 7. The tradition of the Bestiary extends to the present day, through Aldrovandus, Sir Thomas Browne's Vulgar Errors (which is only a commentary on Bestiaries) and a large number of more famous modern people like Buffon, Linnaeus, Geo. Edwards, Gilbert White, T. H. Huxley and so forth, but I need not trouble you with these. (They include Hilaire Belloc.)

I shall have to be acquainted with all these people in my notes.

I am acquainted with all of them except Aristotle. I have been to various book shops to order Loeb editions, but always defeated, because we did not know which works to buy. More than one of them had titles which could have been applicable to Biology, and I did not want to waste my money.

This is why I am writing to ask if you are able to send me *a list* of the works of Aristotle which dealt with *Men, Beasts, Birds, Fish or Plants?*

I shall have to get them with translations into English or Latin, as I don't intend to learn Greek.

That is number one question. Number two is, if you know of any other classical natural historians of importance, ye are to declare it. Number three is about the Cambridge University Library. Do you know any efficient mediaevalist there, well enough to introduce me to him? (There are certain readings in a M. S. at Cambridge which I shall need verified, as they seem to have been rubbed out in the reproduction I possess, and there are other little problems.) Also, is there any sense in my proceeding M. A. of your University, in order to get books from the library? Would they send them away (to

Ireland) and at what stage does a book become too precious to send away to anybody? e.g. I dont kid myself that they would trust a Bestiary itself to the M'est of A's. Or would they? I believe old Sydney Cockerell would put a word in for me, if that was any help.

Why not send some news of your family?

love from Tim

To Mary Potts he describes at length and in ambivalent detail his life in Ireland. Much of this material would go into *The Elephant and the Kangaroo* (here called "After You, Deluge"), a book about Ireland that would insult his friends, the McDonaghs, and arouse general Irish indignation. The little girl's book that White mentions, "Black Maria," was published in 1947 as *Mistress Masham's Repose*, and was dedicated to Amaryllis Virginia Garnett. The third book White mentions working on, "The Insolence of Man," was never published.

[December 22, 1943]
Doolistown, Trim, Co. Meath, Eire
From T. H. White:

Dear Mary,

William's first rate calendar has arrived safely this year. If he made it by himself he is a clever boy. I feel despicable about him and you and several other things, but what can I do about him? In the present state of commerce between the two islands there is nothing I can send him—except another calendar—not even money—and I'm damn sure he does not want a calendar. Nor does he want a letter from a useless godfather who can't stump up, so the best thing seems to be to leave him alone until the war is over and I can send the rational ten bob which is all he cares about, if he has any sense. It is like what they used to say when the Germans were winning the war at the beginning: Better to start badly and end well, rather than the other way about. It will be a pleasant surprise for him to find he has a godfather at all, if the war ever ends. He can't have any recollection of me, so I am determined not to start one until it can be a pleasant one.

And then there is owing you a letter for 12 months. I have no excuses at all, but I shall make a penance of it by writing at least 5,000 words in this. And I shall write them small and neat and legible, and after every ten words, I shall stop and kick myself in the small of the back. So you can see how I will be meditating on my crimes.

Well, Mary, in the course of an innocent life the only thing I have discovered about women is they like to have letters about *people*. I will try to tell you about the people on this farm, as you and Pottës and the whole bloody brood of you have promised to visit it for a holiday when the war is over. (Unless you bring camp beds for the cubs, you will all have to sleep in one double bed. The bedroom is enormous—about as big as your house—but there is only one bed in it. However, all that will manage itself later, and we may be able to sleep somebody in the company rooms.) Well then, first of all, the farmhouse itself is a sort of semi-genteel structure of the eighteenth century—the sort of place which once belonged to a "squireen" who whored and hunted beagles and drank far too much claret (which he could not afford) and was invited to Dublin Castle once a year. No English person knows anything about Irish history, so I don't know if it is any good my telling you that Major Sirr once used to dine here. He was one of the numerous traitors who stud the simple annals of this country i.e. one of the people who were loyal to the established form of government. It was he who arrested Edward Fitz Gerald, one of the numerous heros who etc. i.e. one of the people who were not. Anyway, the house is a square pink box with lovely windows and a nice fanlight. Everything else is unutterably horrible. The walls are made of a sweating stone so that all the rooms are full of mildew: the company rooms face North: not a single window faces south: the furniture is late Victorian: everything is falling to bits. Everything in Ireland always does fall to bits, partly owing to the frightful climate, which must be the wettest and heaviest in Europe, partly owing to the fact that the Irish are an ancient race with rather less mechanical aptitude than Hottentots (with whom they are contemporary) and consequently they are unable to keep anything in repair. There is no bathroom at all, and the sanitation is out door, with accommodation for two, side by side.

Now this house used to belong, about half a century ago—together with some 500 English acres of good farm land—to an old lady who was too fond of entertaining priests to dinner, the catholic priesthood is the ruling body in Ireland, and she thought it grand to entertain them with champagne. The farm could not stand it, and she got into debt. Eventually she lost all but 100 acres of the land. When she died, it was inherited by one of her sons who had asthma, the others having mostly skipped to America, after having robbed her of the few remaining cattle. The asthmatic son inherited, among other encumbrances, the support of a nephew (a son of one of the robbers who had skipped) and this nephew was called Paddy McDonagh. He was brought up in the kitchen, finally inherited from the asthmatic uncle, and is the present owner of the farm. He is about sixty years of age.

Paddy McDonagh has a nose like the Duke of Wellington, a neck like a tortoise and clammy hands. He is a darling. He adores and reveres me as a super human being and I am always cross with him. He cannot tell the time by the minute hand of his watch, cannot recognise photographs—which he holds upside down—and, although he is supposed to be a farmer, cannot plough, sow or work horses. He is terrified of all the animals on the farm, including the turkeys. He does not know his own second name, nor his age, and, in fact, if I tell you any more about him, I shall begin to gibber. But he is as kind as could be, cries with enormous teardrops if one of the dogs dies, does not drink excessively, and only steals small articles. He is hopeless.

So is his wife—Lena McDonagh is about 55. She comes of a large family, the deceased father being a fairly wealthy cattle dealer. She seems to have been the idiot of the family, whom all the rest "put upon," and finally, when she was 35, the cattle-dealer married her to Paddy in desperation. She is tall and thin and perpetually harassed. She has twice been gravid, but dropped the babies prematurely each time—a part of the general inefficiency in Doolistown. I love and pity her very much indeed, much more than Paddy, and if she were to die I would not stay longer. It is absolutely impossible to give you the faintest idea of the contents of her mind. It is what I would call a catholic mind. She believes the kind of things which were considered to be outworn superstitions in the 12th century. She is utterly un-bigoted about these beliefs, and never gets angry with me for not sharing them. As a housewife she is wholly incompetent, as she cannot think of more than one thing at a time, and very little about that. Consequently she always stops whatever she is doing half way through, and does something else, also half way. If I tell you any more about her either, I shall also begin to gibber.

Neither of them makes the faintest attempt to think about the future of the farm, but they are both adepts at thinking about the past i.e. nobody cares a damn whether we ought to be ploughing for next year but both are blaming each other because the ploughing was done wrong last year. In the end, meeting a mutual impasse, they adopt a policy of "whip the cat." The farm labourer gets blamed for whatever goes wrong i.e. for everything.

Perhaps you have grown to be a better farmer since you took to living on the land, so I will just tell you our situation at present. If you don't understand it, your farmer's wife will explain (but not believe).

(1)—Last August we were still doing the *previous* year's ploughing.

(2)—Our sugar beet is still in the ground, and the hay still cocked in the fields.

(3)—We threshed this week—the ricks were not on stilts.

(4)—We have not ploughed a single acre for next year, and won't for 3 months.

The farm is of course at a dead loss, and I am in the precarious position of having adopted these two poor creatures, like a tit trying to feed a pair of cuckoos. I have to do the ploughing myself, as Paddy can't and won't and the hired labour is always being dismissed (on the "whip the cat" policy), and I have to earn enough money to keep them going. Before he died, it was Papa-Cattle-

137

Dealer who kept them on their feet: now it is me. I never thought I should adopt people who were nearly twice my age, but had hoped to adopt some children, that I could spank.

I adore them both, and they both adore me. We have never spoken a cross word. I sometimes feel as if I could scream my head off.

Dear Mary, is this rather like being married?

Don't think that these people are naturals. They are slightly more incompetent than their neighbours, but it is mainly just that they are Irish. The thing partly comes from the race, but it is more from the climate. I sleep two hours more a night than I used to do in England, and my brain has become a sort of gas-mask—the part you breathe through.

Do you study races? It is fashionable in England at present to say that there is nothing in it—to spite Hitler—but there is. There is a kind of racial volcano, either in Germany or Russia or further east, and this is constantly welling up with new races, who have new weapons. They push the older races out-wards, like lava from a volcano, until they spread to the sea rims and can't go further. All the prehistoric cultures of Europe are on the rims of Europe, pushed out from behind—Lapps in North, Celts in Brittany and Sicily, Minoan bull-fighters in Spain, etc. Well, we are the last rim of all over here, and here we have the débris of every inefficient pre-historic culture which has been smashed by the volcano in four thousand years. The interesting thing is that, now we have better communications, the sea rims no longer hold us, and we get pushed over to America.

The climate is the other thing. This comes to us on the prevalent S.W. winds, uninterrupted over the whole 3,000 miles of wet Atlantic. Every cloud that reaches Ireland has been sopping up the sea since it left America. Consequently it is like supporting a succession of water-logged cushions. We are practically forced to hands and knees.

Well, Mary, you can't say I have not warned you what to expect when you come. There will be nobody to talk to in words of more than one syllable: it will rain throughout your visit: I shall crave the satisfaction of sitting beside you in the necessary house. There will be nothing to see or do. This is why all Irishmen are forced to be drunkards, and why they murder each other when drunk. Naturally they can't stand the sight of one another. But if you do come for all that, I can promise you that it will be an experience worth having. The way to experience Ireland is not to expect anything in particular, but just let it happen. Five years later, you say: "That was Irish."

So far as the children are concerned, they should love it. I have a pet bog in which I intend to immerse my Weg—probably she has a more grand name now—and Eliza will of course be busy washing. Poor William, what can I say for him? I only remember christening him and listening to him bawl at a later date. Does he like birds or anything? He is an enigma, and must work out his own destiny. Pottës is to be intoxicated, whether he likes it or not, at an orgy of Irish whisky with the local schoolmaster. He must pretend he is in Sweden. Nobody needs to amuse you.

Would you like to broadcast from Radio Eireann while you are over here, on the harpsichord? I have been boasting about you for four years to all my friends, so you will rather let me down if you don't. Did you know that I have been elected the Chief Bard of Erin? We have poetry competitions on our potty little wireless, and I win them all.

Mary, it is half past midnight, but I will bloody will fill this sheet or bust. My darling Brownie, now grey-haired, is looking at me reproachfully, saying, For God's sake, Master, why don't we go to bed? But I am going to do my penance properly, although there is a horrid bruise already in the small of my back. Even the pen is giving out.

I am writing four separate books at the same time, apart from the farm work. They are (1) A book about the McDonaghs, which will probably be called AFTER YOU, DELUGE; (2) A book for a little girl, a daughter of David Garnett's, on the lines of *Gulliver's Travels*, called BLACK MARIA; (3) a book about the causes of warfare which I finished two years ago but am still fiddling with (because it is too good) called THE INSOLENCE OF MAN; and (4) a translation of a 12th century Bestiary, which I wrote to Pottës about some weeks ago, but he does not answer. Shame on Pottës. All these books will eventually penetrate to the Pottesian Library, as you know.

According to William's callendar, the date is now as above, and this letter has narrowly escaped the fate of some of its predecessors, i.e., to be put aside and finally dropped as not worth reading. However, I heard from Pottës today, and this has revived the subject. I think I had better answer him at Queen's, as I no longer remember when your terms begin or end. He tells me in this letter that William recollects me, and, if this is the case, I must write to him. I will enclose a letter for William with this, but I still think that if he does not recollect me (Pottës could easily be flattering) it would be better not to give it him. It must be left to you to decide.

Did I ever post the letter in which I rated you for not treating my Weg properly? You had written that she had horrid habits and enjoyed playing with toads or snails. If you and Pottës will kindly make a will at once leaving Weg to me, and get killed by a bomb, I will see that the child gets as many snails as she likes, to take to bed with her, and she will end up as a great biologist with a name more famous than Curie. Weg is far the nicest of your children—parents never appreciate their first—and I defy you not to give her toads. They are excellent beasts. So is Weg.

I must write about a million words for William, a bow at a venture.

Love from Tim

On second thoughts I'll enclose Pottës.
He must surely be at home sometimes.

Upon the setter, Brownie, his intimate companion, White lavished the love he could not successfully give to another person. The sacrifices he made for her—such as living without cosmopolitan comforts (including not going to libraries)—are apparent from the following correspondence.

* * *

Dear Pottës,

I am sorry that my letter arrived at a tactless time. The fact is that I have completely forgotten what anybody does in the civilised world, and know no more than a Hottentot whether your terms are likely to be beginning or ending. To tell you the truth, I am a bit surprised to hear that they have a middle either, in these days.

Thank you for your most efficient assistance with the Bestiary. No wonder they force you to be Senior Tutor. Most of the additional works suggested by Cook[8] will be helpful, but I really can't learn German at my time of life, for Otto Keller. The only one I knew of previously was Aldrovandus, for which I have been advertising for four years in vain. What a splendid old man Cook must be, to be so useful at his age. Do you know, I like old men. I wish you would hurry up and get old, Pottës. They tell me that by 1965 there will be hardly anybody left in England except dotards, and I promise myself to have great times then, talking sense with people who are old enough to be sensible.

I have two very bad handicaps at present, about being a scholar. One is what you will consider an ignoble one, and it is my dog Brownie. She and I are the only things we have to love, between ourselves, and consequently I am not able to leave her for more than a few minutes every day, as she disapproves of this. I don't resent never seeing cinemas, theatres, dances, etc., but I do regret being unable to visit libraries. However, I have to put up with it, and it means buying what I really need. This is where the second handicap comes in, for I have little money left and am not subsidised by any learned body. It is easy enough to write an *Anatomy of Melancholy* when you are wholly supported by Christ Church, but not so easy when you have to earn your living meanwhile, and earn a thumping one too, in order to afford Aldrovandus etc. I am not complaining, of course, as we value our freedom more than any money, but it does make it difficult to be an authority on Bestiaries.

141

I will not write to Dr. Basil Atkinson yet, as I had better get my translation finished before doing so, and am writing 3 other books concurrently (for cash). The translating goes very slowly for this reason, and also because I find latin difficult, particularly in mediaeval shorthand. How I wish you were here to help! It is useless looking anything up in Lewis & Shortt. You need Du Cange, and sometimes even he does not help. I am in a toil at present with a word called TRYPHARIUM and have partly run it to earth in an appendix to Du Cange, but still without being much the wiser. It meant either "trefoliated" or "tripartite" (like a clover leaf). The sentence, which refers to lions, is: CUJUS GENUS TRYPHARIUM DICITUR. (I write without abbreviations.) Now the snag is that there follows in the text a description of various kinds of lions (but not 3 kinds) so that it might mean that lions, like Gaul, are divided into three parts. On the other hand, the illustration shews a lion with a trefoil tuft on the end of his tail. If only I could find a word which meant *both*, I should be very relieved, as I begin to think that ambiguity is the greatest talent of a translator.

By the way, about being poor and that, I will accept your kind offer of a Christmas M.A., as I am not allowed to send money out of this country. Please tell me what I ought to do, and we will hope to settle it if the world ever comes to rights.

I have been engaged in writing to your family for most of my spare time this week, so I won't say anything about them. You must borrow the other letters for such gossip. I am sorry the other godfather [Mary Potts's brother, a naval officer] was killed. Nearly all the people I valued when I was teaching at Stowe have also been. It is what happens in wars, they say.

The Librarian of the National Library here informs me that nobody has ever yet translated a Bestiary, which is one comfort anyway. I suppose you would not let me dedicate it to you? Or to Queens'? Which would be correct? To me, they are synonymous. I doubt those y's.

love from   Tim

142

FROM   T I M

DEAR WILLIAM,

THANK you very much for the handsome and cheering *CALENDAR* which you have sent to me for Christmas. I shall now be able, for the first time in my life, to put the proper date on all my letters for a year, and I have been very careful to put the right one on this letter, in red ink, as you see.

I do not know what kind of letters you generally like to get, and so I am going to write to you about my DOG. Her picture is on the outside of this letter, so that you will know what she looks like. Her name is BROWNIE, but that is only her pet name, for she was born of noble parents who christened her BROWN MAID OF TINGEWICK at the Kennel Club. As I was your godfather when you were christened, would you like to be hers? It is a bit late, but could still be done.

Now the house in which Brownie was born was a public house in which I used to live. It belonged to an innkeeper and his wife called Mr. and Mrs. Blaize, and Brownie's mother belonged to them too. The mother was very fond of having puppies, and her husband, Brownie's father, was a member of the Highest Canine Aristocracy. He had won so many prizes for the blueness of his blood, and other accomplishments, that he had the right to write the letters CH. before his name. It stands for CHAMPION, and is for dogs the same as being a Duke. Naturally all his puppies were of the utmost value, for this reason, and Mr. Blaize used to sell them to the Stately Homes of England, where they lived happily ever afterwards. Sometimes he kept one or two himself, to train them, or when he could not get a buyer, and therefore the public house generally had about half a dozen puppies in it, owing to the fondness which Brownie's mother had for having them. Sometimes Mr. Blaize used to take the puppies to dog shews, where they also won prizes for their aristocratic principles. They used to get brushed and combed twice a day for the month before they went,

and CHAMPION BROWN MAID OF TINGEWICK won no less than ten prizes in her first year at dog shews which were as far apart as Bedford and Aberystwyth. Sometimes she won FIVE POUND at a time.

Now there was always a good deal of a scrum at bed-time in the kitchen of the public house where all these puppies lived. Naturally there were some beds which were more popular than others, and the brothers and sisters could never agree who was to have them. The Duke and his Duchess often went up to bed with Mr. and Mrs. Blaize, leaving their children to fight it out. I am sorry to say that some of the brothers were rather cads, in spite or perhaps because of their birth, and one of them was actually a drunkard. He once drank a whole pint of bitter which I had left on the floor beside my chair in the kitchen, and this made him feel so ill that he put his head into my coat pocket without my noticing, and sicked it all up again in the pocket. He felt very ashamed after that. All the puppies were always trying to sit on my lap, and, although I was kind to them in a thoughtless way, I never knew one from another.

Now, although Brownie was little, she used to think a good deal, and one day she thought that she was getting about fed up with drunken brothers and having to fight for beds. She also thought what a handsome and interesting man I was. I used to let Mr. Blaize bring her out when I had a shooting party, to train her for the gun, and she had been in my motor car, which she adored, and she knew quite well that these things belonged to me and not to Mr. Blaize. She also knew that I had a bedroom of my own, with no brothers or sisters in it.

In short, Brownie fell in love with me. She was modest at first, and did not like to mention it, but she tried to tell me as well as she could, with soft looks and so on, and I was such a fool that I did not notice. In the end, she had to declare herself. I had gone up to bed and was brushing my teeth, and the usual battle had started in the kitchen, when Brownie tapped rather shyly on my door and said: "Please, sir, can I sleep with you?" I didn't mind, one way or the other, so she came in, and there she was on the foot of the bed in the morning, looking as pleased as Punch. She thought she had got off.

Poor darling, she had only flattered my vanity. I still did not really think about her a bit. Mr. Blaize noticed it long before I did, and he insisted on giving her to me as a present. She went everywhere that I went, was very beautiful and famous, behaved most lovingly, and so I accepted her as a present—just as if she was a lampshade, or anything else without a soul.

I was kind, if you see what I mean, but I did not love her for herself alone, and, however much she tried to tell me about these things with her eyes, I was too stupid to listen.

Then, when we had been together for about two years, without my ever realising what a lovely person she was, I got interested in hawks and falcons, which I used to train to catch rabbits and grouse. They are very difficult to train, and you have to think about them constantly, and poor Brownie was always getting in the way as she asked me to love her, so it was always: "Oh, GO away, Brownie" or "Now DO leave me in peace for a MINUTE" or even "Oh, you NAUGHTY girl, now you've frightened the hawk." I hardly said a word to her except these, because I was so busy.

Brownie had tried to tell me about her love for two years in vain, and now she saw that she would never succeed. She saw that I did not love her, but only hawks, and it broke her poor heart. One day, she trod on a thorn, and I took it out for her and patted her for a few seconds, and after that she trod on thorns every day for a week, or pretended to if she could not find them, but all in vain. I just told her that she was shamming, and would not pat at all. She saw then that all her life and hopes were wrecked, and that there was nothing left but death.

There is a horrible disease which dogs have, which is called DISTEMPER. If they get it before they are a year old, they often get over it. If they get it when they are older, they nearly always die. It is terrible to see it. Brownie decided, on purpose, to have it, as she could not bear to live any longer without love. She decided to die.

She had had it for a day before I noticed, but, when I did notice, the miracle happened all at once in my heart. Something in her dying look at last penetrated my thick skull, and things began to happen. I shut up those ridiculous hawks in their barn, telling her that they could starve for all I cared; I wrapped her up in the best eiderdown; I bought bottles of brandy and port and stuff to make junket; I had a veterinary surgeon every day, and even a human doctor twice; and I sat up beside her, day and night, with hot-water-bottles, for a week. She got rennet every two hours, with a teaspoon of brandy, and I told her over and over again that if she would not die I would never keep hawks any more, or go to cinemas or to dances or to any place where she could not come as well. I promised that she should be my real wife, not a lampshade, and I told God that if he let her die I would kill him.

But I couldn't stop her. She got weaker and weaker, and it was awful to hear her breathe, and the doctors and the vet were useless, and you could hardly feel her heart. At last there came a minute when I said: "In a quarter of an hour she will be dead."

Then I said: "Well, there is nobody left in it but Me and Death. We will fight it out. I can't possibly make her any worse, so at least I will do something to see if I can make her better." So I went upstairs for the *Encyclopaedia Britannica*, and read the article on DISTEMPER. It was vague and cautious, which most of the articles in that book are, and the only ray of light I could get out of it was something like this: "It has been claimed by some writers on the subject that quinine is a specific of some merit . . ." Well, there was a bottle of quinine in my cottage. I gave her a half human dose, which burned her weak throat but she was too feeble to cough it up, and sat down to stroke her. When the quarter of an hour was up, she stood up on her shaky legs, and was sick. The next time the rennet came round (I mean WEY—the juice of the junket) she actually drank it, instead of having to have it poured down her throat. That night she suddenly ran out into the darkness, or rather tottered out, and vanished. It was pitch dark. I stayed for hours calling her and walking about in the wood with candles, but I could not find her and she did not come back. At last I knew that she had died in a ditch, so I went back and cried myself to sleep, but I got up again at dawn, and went to look for her body. I was calling and looking when she staggered out of the wood, not quite sure who she was or who I was, and I carried her home in floods of tears, but they were quite needless. She was cured. She soon got raw eggs and port wine; then she got fish; then she got rice puddings and

147

soups; then she got roast beef, turkey, caviare, plum puddings, pate de foie gras and gallons of champagne.

If you think this is a sad story, WILLIAM, you must think again, for it has a happy ending. However wicked I had been before, I kept my promises after. I never went to cinemas or dances or libraries any more; I asked her advice whenever I went near a hawk, and soon dropped them altogether; I fed her on my own dinner every day; she slept, and still sleeps, not on my bed but in it, with our arms round each other's necks; she had every possible excitement that could be suitable to her rank, including going in trains, motors, aeroplanes and crossing the Irish Sea in a ship (when I slept in the boiler room with her, because they would not let her sleep in the cabin with me); she had a special grouse moor taken for her, of ten thousand acres, and on this she learned to exercise her own trade as a setter, which she did to perfection; she was never smacked for anything whatever; she had pets of her own, just like my hawks, which she used to carry up to bed with her in her mouth, and these included baby hares, baby rabbits, baby chickens and some moor hens (she never hurt any of them, carrying); she was endowed with property of her own, including a rubber ball, several daffodil bulbs, some bits of wood, and two collars, all of which she keeps under the dining room table (one of the collars, the sunday one, is of plaited silk with a real gold clasp); she goes shooting every day for two hours, because this is her favourite occupation, and she has become the most wonderful of all gun dogs, and the rarest (because it is so difficult to be it) that is to say A RETRIEVING SETTER.

Perhaps the best of all is that she is still alive, and fat, and healthy, with no bad consequences of her distemper, and, although she is about SEVENTY years old by human standards, she is as cheerful and merry as a baby. We have both agreed that she is to live to ONE HUNDRED AND FIFTY by human measure, and then we will both die together, so that neither of us can live to be sad for the other.

You have seen her yourself. Do you remember?

When you see her again, you must be very polite and gentle, because of her noble blood and impressive marriage. She is a

LITTLE grand, on account of these qualities—not snobbish, but dignified, you understand, and it is no good taking liberties. If you pulled her tail, or hugged her without being asked, she would never dream of biting you, but she would think the worse of you in consequence. Nobody will be cross with you, however much you pull her tail, but it is only that a loving person like yourself would hardly like to do so. Besides, if you were her Godfather, it would scarcely be the thing.

WITH LOVE FROM
T I M.

ALL THE ABOVE IS ABSOLUTELY TRUE, TO WHICH WE GIVE OUR SIGN AND SEAL AT OUR CASTLE OF DOOLIS-TOWN, ON THE TWENTY-EIGHTH DAY OF DECEMBER 1943, ACCORDING TO WILLIAM'S CALENDAR.

(CH. MRS. BROWNIE WHITE OF TINGEWICK)
(Her Paw)

White had fallen off "the water-waggon," and the next few letters indicate the subsequent rise in spirits and bonhomie.

February [16?], 1944
Doolistown, Trim, Co. Meath, Eire

Dear Pottës,

I have written to you so often for help that I don't see why I shouldn't write to you once in a while for friendship's sake. I am in what Browne calls "a sober incalescence and regulated aestuation from wine." That means I am slightly tight; how slightly, you can judge from the handwriting, which will deteriorate as the letter goes on, and I get tighter. Anyway, it seems an excellent time to write.

The first thing to tell you is that I am in the seventh heaven with my Bestiary etc. I was always intended to be a scholar—thwarted by buggers like you—and now I am being one at last, off my own bat. I never read anything now except Pomponius Mela, and never do anything except make bibliographies of Sir Thomas Browne, Alexander Ross, etc. My preface to my Bestiary is going to put Sir James Frazer in the ice box, and will quote from 43 authorities beginning with the letter A alone. (This is true. They begin: "a Costa, ab Horto, Aber-Ezra (Hispanus), Absyrtus, Acius, Aegineta, Aelian, Aesop etc.," ending with "Ausonius, Austin, Augustinus, Averroes and Avicen.") If anybody in the world knows more about whether a Camel copulates backwards, I should be glad of an introduction. The fact is that I have got so far into the subject that I really and truly know the name of the only other living person I need consider, and that is a man called G.C. Druce. But I am stalking up on him fast, and soon he will be saying "That's Tim, that was" as I whistle past into a knighthood and the Order of Merit. The only other was Dr. James (the Ghost-story Provost of Eton), but he is dead. I have even caught him out in a misprint. (I mean James.)

Dear Pottës, I really must stop this drumming on my breast—you

150

know it is only in fun. Yet I am honestly delighted with it all the same. It is so nice to strike an unworked vein, worth working, and to go ahead for nothing but the nettle reputation in the bubble's mouth. It won't make money, but it is a respectable occupation. My incentive will be only that one day Pottës will say "I taught him."

The extraordinary thing about being an Authority, is that you make money. Of course, if you are an Authority on poison gas or French Letters or the Stock Exchange, you make much more, but even an authority on the history of natural history can't escape making a penny or two. Last week I went to a local sale, where there were six professional book dealers from Dublin, and bought a 1st edition of Sir T. Browne, a 1st edition of A. Ross, a 1st (English) edition of Buffon, together with about 20 other rubbishy books of the 17th century (but 3 were signed on the fly leaf by the Rowan Hamilton who invented Quaterrious) and all for less than £9. The thing was that the dealers were bidding madly for things like Newton's *Principia* (editis princeps) but they simply had not noticed what I was after. The auctioneers themselves had of course not even listed them in the catalogue.

I am having wonderful fun with my 1st edition of the *Vulgar Errors*. I dare not (am too respectable to) make any mark on the pages of the book itself (except small ticks in pencil, which I need, as I am using it as a working edition for the Bestiary notes) but the book was rebound at the beginning of this century (apart from that, it is perfectly clean) and the binder inserted half a dozen blank fly-leaves. On these, in my best handwriting, like this: I am inserting an appendix and bibliography, hoping that somebody, three hundred years hence, will admire the pains of me, as I admire those of the scribe in my Bestiary—end of handwriting. It means listing all Browne's sources, alphabeticizing them, and numbering their pages, before writing them in—a pure labour of love.

One day I shall have two volumes in the Everyman Library: (1) A Bestiary with notes, (2) *Pseudodoxia Epidemica*, with notes.

I think this ends my paen, and so I will now ask you whether you are dead yet, and if not why you don't write to me, and whether the Censors let my Brownie Story penetrate to William (they are hot on pictures, as these may be conceived to be diagrams of Dublin Castle), and to what extent you are exasperated with making lists of useless undergraduates? Pottës, don't tell me about your activities as a tutor. They are unworthy of you. What I want to know is how your book on Byron is going, or your commonplace book? Believe a poor old sage who lives among the Gaelic Hottentots, and who is catching up on you, hand over fist, simply because you will go on being a tutor, or even a proctor for all he knows: believe him, though you taught him, that you are murdering your own real genius with office work. You sent me out into the wide world, instead of letting me have a fellowship (which probably was not in your gift) and I am really grateful for this. Now, before you petrify, it is time for you to take your own medecine yourself. Wake up: if necessary, resign: leave Mary and all your brood to starve (they won't, and it will be very good for them too): come out of all that bloody tutoring and enjoy the mountain air of Parnassus.

As Browne also says, I have now reached "demention, Sopition of reason, and the diviner particle from drinke," but the handwriting seems decent to the last. The page is done.

    love from
    Tim

P.S. How are your whiskers? Mine are luxuriant.

[February 18, 1944]
Doolistown, Trim, Co. Meath, Eire

Dear Pottës,
    Today there has come a grand sort of unilluminated address, which informs me that I have grown up and become an M.A. of Cambridge University. I feel quite different already—more portly. I waddle a bit as I walk, and have decided to wear boots in future instead of shoes. Well, it was very kind of you to take the trouble,

but I don't think I can very well let you give it to me for Christmas, as I have an idea that it costs several pounds. Also I am working out a scheme for getting money from here to England, by means of a fish with waterproof bag tied to its tail and directed by wireless. I shall use an electric eel. So will you tell me how much it costs to be an Artis Magister, in case I can perfect this invention? I shall feel just as grateful if you let me pay for it, as I had rather not sponge on people until I have to, when I intend to do so with a vengeance. It's just that I'd rather save you up for a rainy day.

I wrote you a tipsy letter two nights ago, and only hope there was nothing offensive in it. Old Sydney Cockerell once shewed me a 13th century bible of his, in which some repentant and evidently experienced ecclesiastic had written in a 14th century hand:

proprietates ebrü
$$\begin{cases} \text{Primo letus et gaudens} \\ \text{Secundo sanctus et sapiens} \\ \text{Tercio tristis et amens} \\ \text{Quarto debilis— Fine stultus} \\ \text{et moriens, et omni sensus et} \\ \text{bono carens.} \end{cases}$$

I don't remember all I put in the letter, but I hope it did not go beyond *sanctus et sapiens*.

Do you know, it strikes me that we have lost touch too much? There you are in an enormous sort of office at Queens', lined with card indices of all the Christian names of all the little boys of 19 since the days of Erasmus, and I suppose you shuffle them about, and play Happy Families with them, and wonder whether it would be better to buy two asps or open your veins in a bath. Here am I, sitting in a vast barrack with a leaking roof and nobody to talk to who can pronounce words of more than one syllable, and wondering whether it is not an expensive form of suicide to do it with Irish whisky. Can't you put aside the bundles of *exeat, nihil obstat, sciant presentes et futuri, excommunico, nolle prosequi* etc., and write to me sometimes? It would be a charity to me at any rate, if we could only work up a correspondence about something that wasn't

153

just gossip. What are you thinking about? Would it bore you to hear what I am thinking about? I sometimes feel like putting a message in a bottle and floating it down the Boyne: "I am alive. T. White. 1944. Is anybody else?" How are your ethics, for instance? Mine have changed out of all knowledge. Are you doing any research or anything, and if not why not? Everybody ought to have some hobby (not gardening). Do you know I have become an expert gardener and carpenter? What a come down. But I intend to reform. Are you the mayor of Cambridge yet? How many more houses have you bought? What is the tone in the University like, I mean does anybody know anything about anything, or care?

Avicenna says that everybody should get drunk once a week, for their health's sake. Will you do so and write to me on that night? I will keep sober once a week, for my health's sake, and answer on that night. In fact, I am sober now, as becomes an M.A.

    love from   Timothy

Always the teacher, like Merlyn, White is at his most engaging in his relationships with children, as evidenced by his charming correspondence with William Potts.

[February 23, 1944]
Doolistown, Trim, Co. Meath, Eire

Dear William,

I hear you have been ill, and have had a birthday. I hope you are now better, and older. They do not seem to like us sending things out of Ireland, because of the war, but I will try to get you a birthday present when it is over. It is very sensible indeed of you to have a thinking when you go to bed. I have just the same thing myself, and at present it is a plan for making an enormous round

154

glass town, like a tennis ball, on top of the Matterhorn. They say that the Matterhorn is a high mountain in the Alps, like this:

and when I have built my town on it, it will look like this:

The Globe will be made entirely of plastic glass, and will have a population of 10,000. It will grow its own vegetables and fruit in plastic glass jars, on a system of hydroponics. It will be divided into 500 storeys inside, and even the floors will be of glass, so that if you are in your hydroponic garden on the first floor you will be able to see the ladies on the second floor from underneath. They will have to wear thick, black pants.

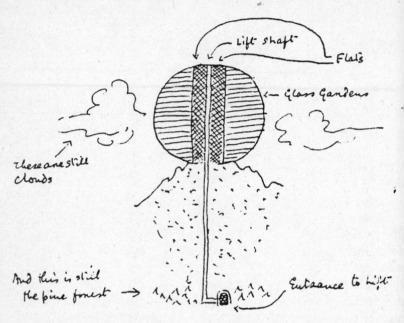

There will be a central lift shaft, for going up and down in, and the people will live in flats built round the shaft.

The advantages of living in this town are: —1 On cloudless days the view of Switzerland will be extensive. 2 On days of low cloud, there will be a wonderful view over the top of them: it will be like floating in a bubble on a sea of thick soapsuds. 3 It will look nice from down below, a glittering opal in the sunset sky.

In case the temperature may be coolish on top of the Matterhorn, or the air thin, the globe will be air conditioned inside.

At present I am rather worried about the snow, as it seems possible that there will never be any view at all, owing to the glass getting iced up, or misted like a shop window. Perhaps I will have a glycerine fountain at the top of the lift shaft, to pour glycerine over the globe. There will be a channel at the bottom, so that it can be collected to use again.

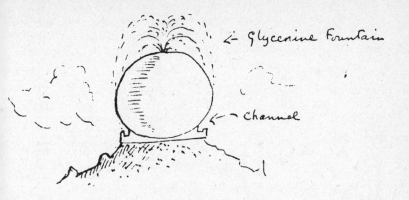

Or else we can have thousands of wind-screen wipers outside, worked by electricity, like on cars.

I have not got any further with this thinking.

Some of my other ideas at bedtime have been: 1 A Plan for preserving Mr. Winston Churchill to the Nation (after death). They made a very bad job of preserving a person called Lenin. I want to have Mr. Churchill painted with silver nitrate and then silver plated, like the radiator of a motor car. When he has been in the electrolytic tank for 15 minutes, we will raise him slightly, until his face is clear of the solution. This is because, if we plated him ¼" thick all over, it would blur the features of his face, so that part must be plated more thinly. And you would have to give the rest of him at least ¼", for fear that he might snap when lifted. 2 A Plan for rebuilding London in the shape of a pyramid, six miles high, over the river Severn:

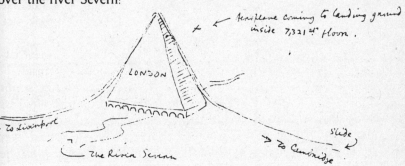

The town will be made of plastic glass, in all respects like the Matterhorn one, including gardens, and the river will carry away the drains. But the whole point of it is the *slides*. All you have to do, if you want to go to Cambridge, is to go up six miles in the control lift, sit down on a special mat made of ice (to prevent heating by friction), and slide. You can see the slides in the picture. It is on the Severn to be closer to America. There are aerodromes on every floor.

I have several other plans, but I will not mention them this time. If you can think of any ways to improve the inventions mentioned above, I would be glad to hear of them.

Will you please thank your mother for the letter I have just received and tell her it was certainly a Roland for my Oliver. It was a splendid letter, which I shall keep to read once a month, when I feel lonely.

She says you do not remember what I look like. I look like this

It is mainly because I have to cut my own hair, which is difficult at the back.

Brownie is in great form and has just fallen in love with a small black pug dog about six inches high, who returns her affections.

158

am not at all jealous, as I know that it is only a passing craze. I do not make any scenes about it.

This is all I can think of to tell you, except that I thought your plan for converting a 'bus into a farm was a very good one. I am writing a book about converting a Dutch Barn into an Ark, which I will send you some day. [*The Elephant and the Kangaroo.*]

Please give my love to Margaret, Elizabeth, your mummy and your daddy.

Love from,
Tim

That White and Potts were aware of the Merlyn/Arthur nature of their relationship is evidenced by the following exchange of letters.

Dear Tim,

The splendid isolation of Eire will perhaps stop this letter before it gets written if I am not quick. But your loss will not be great: even the remarkable windfall of two letters from you delivered by the same post cannot galvanise so inert a lump as I am in these days into anything more than a sort of grinning and posturing. However, let see what your letters will galvanise me into. Perhaps the experiment will succeed.

I do think with you that learning is a noble thing. Virtue is no doubt superior to learning, but then you never can be sure of virtue, she is a faithless jade. I have been pursuing her all my life, owing to my upbringing, and she keeps changing her shape. Also every virtue so soon as you grasp it firmly turns out after all to be a vice. "Intoxication Heavenly Maid" is no doubt also noble; and she is as faithless as virtue and in the same sort of way; you remember the second stage of inebriation—*Sanctus et sapiens*, and in short the general tendency of moralists to take to drinks, and drunkards to moralise. However, I have not pursued drink as strenuously as ought to have: we were, in the village of which my father was a Rector, on good terms with the Landlord of the Wheat Sheaf (who, now I come to think of it was also the village plumber, an extraordinary combination of trades which I used to think was the regular thing), but it was not thought to be proper for us to drink on his premises, or even to carry the wherewithal away from the pub to the Rectory. This dissociation of alcohol from virtue has, fear left its mark on me. However I will amend my ways—but (as think St. Augustine said, *not yet*). After the war is over I will come and stay with you and sit at your feet. I am now in my ninth year as a tutor, ⅔ of the way through it, and I have only got to do ten to complete the sentence, so please let me. I am taking active steps to retire into learned obscurity as soon as the war is over. All this i very unsatisfactory, but I hope to amend. My plans are now: (1) A book on Comedy, (2) a new translation of Aristotle's *Poetics*, the existing ones being all done by *classics* and therefore very inaccu rate, (3) a detailed commentary on *Piers Plowman*. The first will be a work of fiction, but the second and third will force me to acquire a lot of learning.[9]

I was amused by your qualms about letting me give you an M.A. degree (or rather, the wherewithal to buy it), you have in fact exposed me: though with your usual tact, only implicitly, not openly. I had a plot by which when I have lost all my respectable reputation and all my money I was to sponge on *you*. I think this is called making friends with the Mammon of Unrighteousness. I should be rather a nuisance, because I have been so over-done with responsibility that I shall surely go to the bad very completely. So perhaps you *had* better pay for your own M.A. so that when I do try to lay myself at your door you can say: "I know you not, old man." Still I shall be rather disappointed. In any case, you had better wait till after the war.

I shall have to stop for now. This is meant to be a start. If my resolution holds and your isolation doesn't get more splendid, I will write again. This is largely nonsense. I shall see whether I have any ideas in my head. William is enchanted with the Brownie biography. I think he wrote to you. Betsy has got mumps. All the family have had chicken-pox since Christmas.

    Write again
    Pottës

[April 2, 1944]
Doolistown, Trim, Co. Meath

Dear Pottës,

Good to hear from you again, and that you are going to commence scholar so soon, after all that administration. The book on comedy will be what you were born for: you were mumbling it twenty years ago. As for the Aristotle, better you than me, is what we say here. I suspect that you will find that if you stick to the lecture notes you will be making no better headway than the

161

classical translators, while if you try a literary rendering you will get attacks of conscience, about whether Aristotle really said that or not. However, you know about it and I don't. I am sad about the *Piers Plowman*. Two years ago I tried to write a book about Richard 2, the nicest English king, the most unfortunate in his biographers, particularly Shakespeare, and got to know a good deal about his contemporaries and problems. I did not come to love Langland. I thought he was an impossible, ranting little demagogue, who spoke ill of nearly everybody that was nice—John of Ghent, Richard, Anne, Burley etc. He liked the horrible ones like the Arundels and all the foul uncles, and he put an unerring finger on the wrong reason for everything that went wrong. In fact, I hate the swine, and shall write a book denouncing your book, as soon as it appears. Incidentally, have you ever tried to write alliterative verses? I have, and was surprised to find that it was much more difficult than rhymed verse. These artificial frameworks have a leading-astray-effect on the poet i.e. he sets out with the idea of saying something definitive, but the rhymes tend to make him say something else. Once I have written "How are you, Pottès, today?" the mere existence of the "today" at the end of the line tends to make me add "And how is Mary, pray?" even if I had originally intended to make some remark about the weather. Thus the poet is always slightly tugged aside by his rhymes: sometimes he yields to the tug, when it has unexpectedly suggested a good thing, but mostly he tries to keep to his intentions. Well, in rhyme it is only once per line that he gets this oblique pull: in the *Piers Plowman* style, he gets it three times per line (at each aliteration: I think I will try one "l" for a change, then they can't both be wrong) and this is upsetting. I also found that it was difficult to control the length of line and the variation of the Caesura, to avoid monotony. I don't think Langland did avoid monotony.

It is all very well your talking to me about morals. What you don't seem to realise is that you poisoned my defenseless adolescent mind with them 20 years ago. It was during Lent, and you had given up smoking, and you explained that you did so not for any ecclesiastical reason, but because you liked to know that you were running your own life i.e. that you were smoking the cigarettes, not

162

they you. Ever since, my life has been blasted by the same ambition, and I am particularly sore about it today, because it is April 2nd. My next drink of alcohol will be on October 1st., and please God it will be a deep one. For six months since yesterday you will hear from a sober correspondent, and it will be your own fault. Do you pedagogues ever reflect on the damage you are doing?

The only thing that was wrong with your giving up the cigarettes, was that you did it in association with a church season. If you had ever lived in a Catholic country, which I suppose Sweden is not, you would know that no respectable person can associate with Christian customs without being defiled. That's why I go on drinking till April 1st., just to shew I am only an April Fool, not Lenten idiot. I only invented this way of annoying myself last year, when it worked perfectly, but before that I had plenty of other ways.

End of page

> Love from
> Tim

White's ability to turn any experience into a creative opportunity is clearly shown in this long letter to Mary Potts, in which he describes the artistic nature of the anesthesia-inspired visions he experienced during a tonsilectomy, followed by a discursive note in which he continues to develop the McDonaghs as fictional characters.

[August 29, 1944]
Doolistown, Trim, Co. Meith, Eire

Dear Mary,

I wonder why I shouldn't write to you in August, even if it isn't Christmas nor William's birthday? It will be rather a good precedent for not writing on the latter occasions, as I usually don't. Come, we will try it.

How are you? are you still teaching all day and cooking all night and getting up at 3 a.m. to write letters? If so, you will have to get up at two to answer this. Your last is kept on my desk permanently, and I read twenty or thirty pages of it whenever I feel lonely. I suppose you are not in the flying bomb area, are you? Did William get my last letter, which was about building glass houses on top of the Matterhorn? It had some pictures in it, and may have been confiscated by the censors for fear of being a secret map of Dublin Castle. I really am getting about to the end of my patience with the stupidity and hypocrisy of this war. They said that whatever else it victimised they would not let it victimise the arts. What cant! My books are unpublishable because of the paper shortage: I can't even get paper to write them on hardly: and, as for painting, every kind of canvas and colour is unobtainable. To cap all, I can't get microfilms from the great English libraries, because the censors forbid them. I think I told you that I am doing a terrific edition of a 12th century Bestiary, and I have a sort of magic lantern which enlarges microfilm photographs, so that, when I want to consult some priceless manuscript, I only have to write to the library it lives in and they send me for 3 d. or so a microphotograph of the page I need. Well, the censors won't allow it. Good God, what do they suspect? Do the bloody fools think that the Cambridge University Library and the British Museum and great and glorious institutions like that are going to join a spy ring and send blueprints of the latest jet-propelled stink bomb to me, under cover of 12th century manuscripts? It was actually the C. U. Library who made the application to the Censorship Department, and were refused permission i.e. it was not me that was forbidden to import microfilms, but a world-famous seat of learning which was forbidden to export them. Christ, I wonder what these censors are? Grocers' Assistants, I suppose.

So I enquire whether William's birthday letter arrived?

As usual, I have no particular news about myself. I had one of my tonsils cut out a few days ago, which has done me good, for I had been poisoned to the point of melancholia for the past two years. Consequently I can talk of nothing but tonsils. I don't suppose you are particularly keen on them, but it's really all I can offer. Two things about them. The reason why I had it out was this. I began painting a picture of Hell, which I drew as a red passage-way, leading back and down into the canvas. In this cave sat two gloomy demons and myself in a cauldron of molten metal. As we had been there for several million years, which was nothing to Eternity, the whole affair had lost all interest for all concerned, and I was yawning in my cauldron. In the roof there were two inverted, oystershaped, mucous objects, which I supposed to be boulders in the roof of the cavern. Now I painted this picture without conscious ideas about it—it was one of a series of four oils which dealt with the Resurrection. But I happened to know from past experience that I frequently gave myself tips in my paintings. I mean, that my unconscious mind was liable to express itself in them. When finished, I looked at the picture to see what it was trying to tell me. (I had once before painted a picture of Hell which turned out to be an auto-analysis, and that was why it occurred to me to look at this one: I don't generally bother.)

I saw at once that I was holding my mouth open (yawning) as a hint to myself: that the cavern was my own throat: that I had painted Hell because I was feeling hellish: and that the two boulders were my tonsils. So I went straight to a throat specialist, who confirmed the diagnosis, and was home again in two days! Now the most amazing part of this story is that I had never seen a tonsil in my life, but I came round in the operating theatre and was shewn the removed specimen, and that it was exactly like the boulder I had painted!

The other story is less interesting. When I began to go off with the gas, the surgeon said to the anaesthetist: "How did that picture turn out?" the anaesthetist said: "It was a failure." "Why?" At this point it all began to repeat. "How did that picture?" "A failure."

"Why?" "How picture?" "Failure" "Why?" "Picture?" "Failure" "Why?" "Pic—Fay—Why?" "Pic—Fay—Why?" etc., etc. This then turned to "Pit into this" "Pit into this" "Pitt into this" "Spit into this." The lights went on again, and I sat up saying "*Very* interesting. It's a question of thousandths of a second." They treated me as a drunk or imbecile, saying "Yes, of course" etc, but had no idea what was interesting nor why I was talking about thousandths of a second.

But I was meaning what I said, and had been observing my reactions to the gas, while under it, *and had been thinking about them while unconscious.* This is interesting, because it shews that a part of one's "mind" does continue to function when external stimuli are out. I had noticed that the time taken between the surgeon's saying "How did etc." and "Why?" was evidently equivalent to the time taken to knock out my brain (because that section of external stimuli was repeated again and again by the brain) and consequently I had reasoned (while unconscious) that the time to lose consciousness, *or to perform the act of death,* could probably be measured by measuring the time between "How" and "Why?" This was why was babbling about thousandths of a second, and I think it is fairly interesting to note that one can actually observe and reason while the "brain" is off. Evidently it goes on working even after the messages from outside have ceased to come in, and I can believe that people whose heads have been cut off still try to talk. I think one probably retains some mental processes after death, for some time. Dim, slow and not for long, but there.

[September 7, 1944

Most of this year I have been painting pictures without pausing for breath. I have got to a stage when I stick glass eyes on them with putty, and silver tinsel for eyelashes, and they look horrible. They are oils. I have done two of 35" × 25". One of them is an OVIPAROUS CREEPER. It crawls about on its hands, in a poisonous Prussian blue light and has laid an egg. It has leaves like a castor oil plant. The other is a NEVERGREEN. It flies about on mercurial feet, with red leaves straying between flamingo and beetroot, and its flowers have feathered wings.

If I had the courage to switch over, I would stop writing books and try to earn a living as a painter.

I have been puzzling about people like Graham Sutherland—you ought to buy the three Penguin books of Sutherland, Moore and Duncan Grant. All I know is that I can paint imitations of people like Grant, but I can't paint imitations of Sutherland. So I think he is a good painter.

My glass eyes etc. are only a trick, but he is really and essentially doing what he does because he has something.

[September 8, 1944]

You must tell Potts, with whom I am furious because he won't write to me, that I suspect he ought to read Horace Walpole's book on Comedy. I haven't, but it was Horry who said that life was a comedy to those who thought, a tragedy to those who felt.

Tell Potts that personally I think Aristotle's rules for tragedy are correct for Comedy also, only the Nemesis must be bathetic. This is the only difference.

For instance:

There was an old person of Dover
    (high station—we sympathise and identify selves with—
    he is venerable, English and comes from an excellent
    locality)
Who walked through a field of blue clover
    (no crime to walk through clover, but an error or
    frailty, considering the insect season is at its peak
    and probably the field has been put up for hay)
Till some wasps and some bees
Stung his nose and his knees
    (recognition of situation—the sudden burning pang
    identified—the unwisdom of walking in clover—
    instantly there follows the simultaneous reversal of
    situation—an actual reversal for he now proceeds *to*
    Dover instead of *from* Dover)
Which caused him to rush back to Dover

167

(this is a comedy, because the Nemesis is bathetic. If,
however, the last line had been "Till he died, far away
from sweet Dover" the Nemesis would not have been bathetic,
and consequently it would have been a tragic poem
instead of a comic one)

But Potts doesn't deserve my messages.

[September 9, 1944]

I must stir my stumps and try to send you some news about
people, instead of ideas. My beloved Mrs. McDonagh has had a
bad year. She is one of those characters who do things first and
think about them afterwards, rather like a chicken with its head cut
off. This Spring she suddenly decided to visit the cow sheds. These
were in the usual state of filth, so she needed something to step on,
to keep herself out of the excrement. She selected a handy board
with nails in it, put it down nails uppermost, and stood on one. The
combination of rust, decayed stockings and shit, poisoned her foot
for four months, and now she has had all her teeth pulled out, so
she has been in a pickle since I last wrote. She has had the brilliant
idea of letting all our arable land. She has let it at 10/- an acre. She
rents it at £1 an acre, counting rates. She will get to suspect that
this is uneconomic round about 1946.

Paddy is also in trouble. He has what he calls the Neuralgy, and
is rubbing his head with Zam-Buck for it.

We have got a cat, which is the first cat I ever got on with. The
cat and I are both sadists, and we recognise this in each other, and
don't mind. It is a kitten, actually. I pull its tail whenever I see it,
and it bites me whenever it sees me, and we both don't care a fig. It
is the first time I have ever really liked a cat. It is neither sly nor
dignified nor selfish. In fact, a knock-about cat. It is black, which is
great for Mrs. McD.

I have got interested in bees lately, and have three hives of them,
except that one hive has been taken over by some wasps. Most of
the receptacles at Doolistown have unusual inhabitants. Apart from
the wasps in the bee-hive, we have some unusually malevolent bees

168

in the front hall, and all the chimneys but one have jackdaws living in them. The one chimney without daws has a tribe of cats which have gone to live there, and become wild. They come out at night to raid the larder, but rush up the chimney again whenever anybody comes into the room. They spend the rest of the time on the roof, and we don't know what to do about them, as they are smoke proof. Mrs McDonagh says it is the Holy Will of God.

You will think I am romancing, but we have a chicken with all its feathers on back to front. That is, such feathers as it has. It has no "covert feathers" i.e. it only has the primaries and tail feathers, and a few body feathers put on the wrong way round. It is bald. Paddy says it is a "Guinea hen."

Everything at Doolistown is like that hen. It is our symbol, like Ibsen's wild duck.

I caught 65 fleas in my bed last night. This will be an encouragement to you for visiting us when the war is over, as there will be all the fewer then.

I am shotten.

Fly, letter, to Mary Potts, and tell her that I love her, for being she.

    Love from
    Tim

P.S. Happy Xmas.

The worst, the most wrenching thing had happened: Brownie was dead, and the following exchange of letters between White and Mary Potts is a moving display of grief and friendship, of loss and consolation.

My dearest Mary,

I am so unutterably miserable and disconsolate, in fact howling like a baby, that I am sure you will forgive me if I try to howl on you. You know it's just sort of hysterical relief and are too generous not to help. The fact is that my darling of all darlings, my Brownie, died today. The awfulness of it, is that I was not here to help. In all of fourteen years of life I have only been away from her at night on three occasions: when I made a five day visit to England in desperate hurry; when I had my appendix out; when I had my tonsils out (two days). But I did go into Dublin and such places for a nine hour visit, about twice a year to buy books, and today was one of those unlucky days, it was not even a question of sleeping away from her, it only happened twice a year. I left her in perfect health in my bed where she always slept and was a splendid hot water bottle to me, when I got back they told me she was dead. I do not know what filthy witchery may have been practised upon her, even poison, or whether it was merely incompetence or whether nothing could have saved her in a sudden attack; I would not think about the worse of these things, but anyway she is dead now, without my having been able to help or save her as I have done three or four times before, and I am writing with her sweet dead face on my lap, as I am going to sit up with her tonight. When I had my tonsils out, I noticed that consciousness was liable to persist after apparent inertia and it is only for this that I want to sit up. To-morrow I must bury her. I don't know what I will do after that. She was absolutely well and in roaring form till the moment I left her. We slept comfortably tussling as usual for the best place in the bed. She was too lazy to get up and see me off as she had been in other occasions. I have come back to a dead wife who was mother, child and mistress to me for fourteen years, unprepared. I do not mind in the least bit about myself—for me it will even be a relief to be able to visit libraries; it is this cold Brownness on my lap, which I did not help to die that's breaking my heart into bits.

When I first got her, I was a very ignorant young sportsman; I often spanked her for matters which were no fault of hers. Setters are very sensitive dogs who take things to heart; I might have spoilt her entirely, making her a coward and a fool, but luckily I pulled up in time and at the end of her life she had implicit trust in me. I could have shook a whip at her and she would not have blinked—which is unusual in setters as they are timorous. She thought me the most superb of doctors as I had brought her through dreadful illnesses, but when she came to die, I was not on hand—a chance of one hundred and eighty to one. Brownie was the chief factor in my life, she was more to me than you are to Potts, because I had to look after her (fear of running over by motors and that sort of thing) which Potts does not have to do for you. She was the only perfection I have ever known, she was gentle and loving and trustful and afraid of cows, she was a superb gun-dog. I am writing all this, dry-eyed now, trying to convince myself, with the soft eyes on my lap that won't open. Don't tell Potts about it but don't either of you write about her to me for some time. It is like being in some other planet which I can't understand yet. I tried to cry on purpose and succeeded in a way, but that has nothing to do with it. Crying is only a self-indulgence and the awful feeling that it happened when I was not there to help, won't be lulled by this. She seemed to have ten years of life before her and lies as beautifully now as she ever did. All the happiness I have ever had was from her; if only I could have helped her to die. This morning before I left, she ate half my breakfast in bed. Now I am eating a cold sausage which she would have liked and stroking the cold silk head, and now again I am crying so much that it finishes the page very nicely.

From Brownie's Tim

November [30?], 1944
Mary Potts, 54, Bateman Street, Cambridge

Dear Tim,
I only got your sad, sad letter this evening, you ask too much of me not to write to you about Brownie. Tonight I must and you will

171

forgive me, and then I will never talk about her again until I see that you would like to.

Don't torment yourself Tim, don't. That you were not with her when she died was sad, but a small thing in the whole—you helped her to die, the death-bed is only a small part of dying, it is life that is preparation for death.

Nobody could have made another happier than you made Brownie, nobody could have loved more satisfyingly, or have been more dearly loved and thought for and understood and cherished than Brownie. She deserved her happiness and her reward was peace of mind. She trusted you entirely, that means she had faith in God. It is impossible that she died desolate or forlorn, she trusted you, she knew you had not left her and she was right of course, you came back to her. Perhaps too late for your peace of mind, not too late for hers.

Fourteen is a ripe old age, and she was never ailing or senile, what a desirable end, to be in perfect health at breakfast time in the morning of one's death in the fullness of years, to seem to have ten years of life in front of one, no decay, no rotting—the prizes of experience without the penalties of physical decay.

Lena and Paddy will be as good to you as they can, Paddy will understand your grief if not the full extent of it, and Lena will sympathize and accept it.

God knows what the spelling and punctuation of this letter is like, but you mustn't mind that or my pumposity, it is bad enough to say what you want to say simply when your head is hard and steady, and I am weeping like a fountain.

Love to our dear friend
    Tim   from Mary

I shall never reconcile myself to death, Tim, never.

Despite the emptiness that Brownie's death produced in White, it did allow him the freedom to travel more broadly, finally to leave Ireland and to return to England.

172

Dear Mary,

Thank you for your nice long letter. I am most delighted to hear that Margaret has over-bowled Elizabeth as a beauty. I will write again about my gossip and yours, but this is only a business letter and I am in a hurry to get it off.

David Garnett has offered to keep me as a pet for the rest of my life. I can't accept such an offer unless I have money in my pocket, so as to be able to leave him when he gets fed up. I am in slight money difficulties at present—only temporary—don't be frightened. I don't want to borrow any—and I want to sell my car. Also the McDonaghs are selling this farm and going to live in a town, which means that I shall have to leave them.

Now if I sell the car here, I will only get £200 for it, but they say I can get £400–£500 by selling it in England. I am only allowed to sell it in England if I give up my domicile in Eire and become domiciled in England. If I do so, I can bring the car over next September, sell it, and settle down as one of Bunny's domestic animals and incidentally see you. I have 2 novels being published in America and all will come right in a few more months.

But the trouble is that if I cease to be domiciled in Eire and become domiciled in England I may become liable to be taken by one of your press-gangs and sent to conquer Japan, which I don't want to conquer.

Potts is the only man I can think of who knows all these practical things instinctively, so will you ask him what my position would be if I came to live in England? I am at present an "Englishman domiciled in Eire" paying their income tax etc. If I give up my domicile in Eire, I suppose I become demoted to a plain Englishman. At what age do they conscript such persons for service? I am sure Potts will know.

They made me buy 2 more dogs when Brownie died, because they said the responsibility would be good for me, and it has kept me alive. All the same, my life is quite different now. I still have fits of tears about twice a week. It has been far the most awful thing

173

that has ever happened to me. In some ways, like all awful things, it has done me good. For instance, I am not afraid of dying myself now, and also I will never again care so dreadfully about anything, as it has sort of worn out my capacity to feel. There is a proverb that when your first wife dies she makes such a hole in your heart that all the others slip through.

Bunny has got excited about the 2 novels now in America, as he says that one of them is my chance to win *immortality!* Both were written in Brownie's lifetime. I must stop now, as it has made me think.

Love from Tim

But imagine if we could meet soon! My hutch would be quite near you, at Hilton. I do hope Potts will have good news for me.

CHAPTER 5

Duke Mary's

In July 1945, David Garnett invited White to stay in his country cottage at Duke Mary's, near Richmond in Yorkshire. As he wrote to White:

I do seriously urge you to consider whether you had not better come to England, bag and baggage, dogs and car, as soon as you can arrange for transport, and for the time being become my tenant . . . it is a good place for writing and an excellent place for the dogs as it is adjacent to a grouse moor.

White arrived in England in September 1945 with his new dogs Quince and Killie. He first spent some time with David Garnett at Ridley Stokoe, in Northumberland, where Garnett had a grouse moor. The two men had written to each other for years without actually meeting, and their long-awaited reunion was more rocky than either had anticipated. To make things worse, Quince, who had been specially bred by White for Garnett, proved to be a very poor gun-dog.

In October, Garnett accompanied White to Duke Mary's and left him there on his own. It was a long time since the writer had enjoyed a place that he could turn into a home and he thrived in this ideal setting. His diaries and letters are full of details about household activities: painting and decorating the house, scrubbing floors, sewing and mending clothes, getting food from the nearest village (eighty minutes' walk).

The modern Robinson Crusoe often took pride in the good organization of his carefully planned timetable and in the food he would cook for himself.

On his way to the village, he sometimes stopped at the "Punch Bowl," where he had a few drinks and a chat with the locals. He was very careful not to let it become a habit as he knew that he would never get any writing done if he started drinking again.

In 1946, White again saw the child he had loved, Annette. White was now forty and he felt that it was time for him to get married and have children. Although Annette was twenty-one when he proposed to her, he still pictured her as the ten-year-old Maria in *Mistress Masham's Repose*: "If I don't marry her I will never marry anybody and I am sick of the pale case of thought. I forgot to tell you that the book about Malplaquet was about her—She is Maria. . . ."

White wanted David Garnett and Mary Potts to meet Annette; he wanted some advice, which of course he had no intention of taking: "Not one single person we have met in any walk of life has approved of our marriage, so I am sure I am right in wanting to marry her."

It soon appeared that the girl was not very keen on marrying him and White wrote to her on the first day of each month asking her to change her mind and let him love her. He wrote the drafts of his love letters in a notebook. Each letter starts in a different way, in the following order: "My own darling," "Annette," "Dear Annette," "Dear brat," "Dear Love," "Angel." He offered to go to Cambridge with her, where she would study music and he would take up biology. He did not mind if she did not want to marry him as long as they could be together again. White pleaded and begged and felt miserable: "I won't ask you again for a month. I will not pester you with letters. I love you so very painfully."

But Annette got pregnant, married a cricket player, and called the baby Terence—the surest way to make White furious!

Just before the collapse of the whole affair, White had written to her: "You must choose for yourself in cold blood whether you mean to be the wife and mother of a genius, which is what I am going to be in ten more years, or whether you are to end up cackling about the L.B.W. rule in various bars."

As usual, he found his remedy in writing and put himself to work on a book based on *Troilus and Cressida*, which he never finished.

While he was at Duke Mary's, White continued his translation of *The Book of Beasts* and worked on what he used to call his "Walpole book"—*The Age of Scandal*, a study of eighteenth-century characters. He also took advantage of the seclusion of his Yorkshire cottage to read Shakespeare's plays and write long diaries and letters. He obtained many books from the London Library, bought an *Aldrovandus Historia* that came in nine parcels and a set of the *Oxford English Dictionary*.

Meanwhile, his Lilliput book, *Mistress Masham's Repose*, was chosen by the American Book-of-the-Month Club in 1946 and brought him fifteen thousand pounds. To avoid paying taxes both in England and in the States, White thought of emigrating, and it was David Garnett who once again found a suitable solution and advised him to go to the Channel Islands, where he would pay less taxes and could take his dogs without any quarantine.

[September 30, 1945]
Duke Mary's, Low Row, Richmond, Yorks.

Dear Mary,

I wrote an important letter to you five months ago, but got no answer. Am I to write to you for Xmas, or has Potts cut me off with 1/-? I know you have not.

It is called Duke Mary's because it is a 4-room cottage which belonged to a female Shepherdess whose name was Mary, and her father's name was Marmaduke.

She had 2 illegitimate children while cutting peat on this moor (altitude 1,500 ft. gradient one in 2.4) and carried them home in her apron.

I can't write until I know whether you or Potts are in the sulks.

Love from
Tim

"Full of gin and news" (*Mistress Masham's Repose* was to be chosen by the Book-of-the-Month Club), White brags, complains, disparages, sputters—in fact, behaves absolutely like White.

[January 23, 1946]
Duke Mary's, Low Row, Richmond, Yorks.

Revered Pottës,

I am full of gin and news. The American Book of the Month Club is a touchy body which does not like to have its choices revealed in advance, and if they are revealed by some chatterer it is possible that the choice will not be made. Consequently the only living person to whom T. H. White mentions that for the second time in his life he is likely to earn £9000 next summer is the debased and humiliated Pottës, once his guru but now a mere university politician who chooses nonentities to be the professor of King Edward. Mrs Pottës may be informed, but nobody else, and certainly not Tilly or Willy.

I have a perfect short story for you. Do you remember that a silly fellow called Professor Elton refused to give me a First in the English Tripos Part One? The scene changes, and I am a grizzled old gent with whiskers getting ready to leave Ireland. I have packed up all my books and am loitering in a decayed 18th century farm house, with nothing to do. There is a wireless set in the dining room, which I have not switched on, except for the news bulletin,

178

since 1939. There is absolutely no employment for the mind, so I switch it, and a voice instantly informs me that a certain Lord Elton is to give a talk on the 12 greatest books in the world, which he would take with him to a desert island. They turn out to be some assorted works by Homer, Shakespeare, Wordsworth and others. You know how I always exaggerate, but you must believe me this time when I tell you that the first eleven of them are all long dead and really do belong to the Homer, Shakespeare, Wordsworth level. It is just that I can't remember the other names. But who is the twelfth man? I fall back stunned and rigid on learning his name, but revive half an hour later and write to this mysterious Lord Elton, more astonished by the coincidence of having switched on the wireless at such a moment than flattered by the inclusion. He answers etc., and I feel highly delighted to be corresponding with a real lord. The scene changes again to a pub in Yorkshire, when I shew one of Lord Elton's letters to my literary agent, to impress him. He says: "Oh, that old fool. I was at Harrow with him. He was just a doddering Oxford don when Ramsay Macdonald came to power, but he knew Macdonald and everybody was astounded when the latter made him a peer."

Could anything be more perfect than this? I mean, to be such an idiot as to refuse me a First, and to keep on being such an idiot as to class me with Homer? I must add that he was going to take Homer in the original Greek.

Dear Mary,

I am tired of trying to impress Pottës. I am living in a sort of stone hay barn like this [see overleaf]:

Dear Pottës,

P.S. Dare I send you on an errand? If you preserve any kindly memory of me whatever, will you step across to the College library and look up BOTTOM for me in the O.E.D.?

I want all the references they give (probably 18th century) to this word in its meaning of *guts, stability, courage, well-foundedness.* e.g. Dr. Johnson said that a certain woman "had a bottom of sound sense." Wilkes, when fighting a duel with Ld. Talbot, said that he could

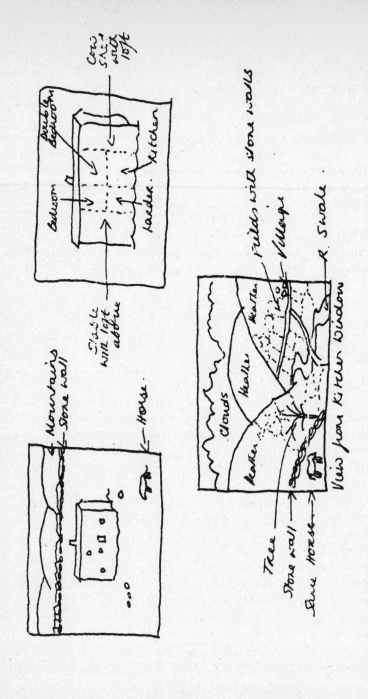

answer for his own courage, "and we shall shortly see how well bottom'd yr. lordship is."

love from
Tim.

It is for an article.

It would mean copying out the quotations they give.

White continues to engage his godson, William Potts, as Merlyn engaged Arthur, and to ply his mentor, L. Potts, with promises of gifts.

[February 1946?]
Duke Mary's

Dear Godson,
Thank you for the Xmas picture. I am coming to see you some time next April or May, whether you like it or not. I have shot a black-cock in Northumberland, the first one I have ever shot. I have 3 enormous dogs called Quince, Killie and Prudence. They are a Pointer, a Setter and a Dropper, in that order. They eat all my rations. Quince is a sentimental and timid old gentleman, Killie is a kind of pistol-packing Momma, and Prudence is only a puppy, but very big and bites my ankles. Please give my love to Weg and Betsy, who will both hate being called by these names as they are probably thinking of going to Hollywood by now. I do it to plague them. I live in the highest and loneliest cottage in Swaledale, and there are 4,000 grouse at my back door. Kiss your mother's hands for me. Do you know the charming story about Sir Edward Lutyeus, who was bald? He wrote to a lady friend: "I wash your feet with my hair. I have very little hair, but you have very little feet."

Best love to all from
Tim

P.S. It is called Duke Mary's because a female shepherd lived in it before me, and her name was Mary, and her father's name was Marmaduke. She had a baby on the fells and carried it home in her apron.

It has been lent to me by David Garnett. There is no road to it. The slope is one in two and the altitude 1,000 ft. The village is 2 or 3 miles away. I have to climb stone walls carrying my rations. I am my own housewife and do my own baking, washing, ironing etc. We are at present inches deep in snow. Until I learned of the £9000 I was actually penniless and was trying to live by selling my gold watch.

Dear Pottës,
To revert to you, I know I owe you about £20, but I can't pay till the Americans stump up. When I was in Ireland I painted a picture as a present for you, but I am having difficulty in exporting it from that country. It is called "Nebulosity in Orion." It will arrive some time at Cambridge in a very shabby home-made frame, but if you care to have it decently framed it will look much nicer. I give it to both you and Mary, so that you may have fun about who is the possessor when you come to divorce each other. Do not thank me for it till you see it.

[June 25, 1946]
White Hart Hotel, Buckingham, Bucks.

Dear Mary,
She's a farmer's daughter aged 21 and I have known her on and off since she was eleven, when she used secretly to write poems to me and bring me flowers at the cottage in Stowe Ridings. But I madly did not seduce her in those days, being under the impression that one ought not to seduce minors and that one got sent to prison for it or thrashed by her burly family. So she was seduced soon after by somebody else. In the war she joined the W.A.A.F. at the age of

182

16 and was actually given official lectures in barracks that it was "no shame to bear an airman's baby."

She thought most of her companions were prostitutes, became unhappy, owned to her real age and was discharged. Meanwhile, she says, but I never know how much she exaggerates out of bravado, she was sleeping round the shop with various Americans, aviators etc. I suppose kids do do this in time of war, like Cressida. She joined the Wrens when of military age and continued her career as a demirep. I have got her to admit what most women try to conceal, that she did not enjoy sleeping with 90% of them. She says there were about a dozen in all. After the war, when we re-met, I found I still liked her and proposed in a mad moment without being in love with her. We told her parents we were going to stay with David Garnett and removed ourselves to Duke Mary's, where for various causes she ditched me after a week and went home, but without a quarrel. Then I had the misfortune to fall in love with her. For about 2 months I was discarded, but finally have got back to good graces. We are now in the insane position that she says she won't marry me but will come to America with me as my (mistress) secretary, and her parents rather naturally say she may marry me but may not do the latter. Her indiscretions have been concealed from them and both of us are fond of them. She says that if you will give her an alibi like the Garnett one, she will come away with me again.

For that part of it we would not necessarily have to stay at Bateman street so long as we could say we were there.

But I *want* to bring her to Bateman street, for quite another reason. She is courageous, generous, honest, imitative (a good learner) and a very good pianist—scholarship standard, they tell me. Her sexual career, which she has possibly exaggerated to impress me, has not touched her innate modesty. In some ways she is a kind of bashful prostitute or juvenile delinquent. She is outwardly respectable and would not lead astray or shock your daughters, who would not know she was any different from anybody else. I am fascinated with the job of educating her, which she enjoys too and is good at, and I don't want her to spend the rest of her life with no talk but gossip. I want to get her under your wing a little, under the musical link, so that she can be with people who can talk about other things than the chat of farmers' wives—a thing she could do and wants to do, as she has brains.

What I suggest is that I bring her to see you for lunch at any rate, as soon as possible, and then you can make up your own mind whether there is anything you can do to help. In any case you would certainly have to see her and advise me not to marry her—as everybody else I know has done—out of jealousy.

I want to marry her. She at present does not want to take that high jump, partly because I am 20 years older than she is, partly because I am rather too humble in bed I suppose and partly—well, who can explain these things? She is fundamentally honest and, as you see, is no gold digger. She refuses to accept my marble balls as currency.

She will be shy of you, probably rather silent and afraid that her accent is not right.

At present, I must admit, her head is still full of her boyfriends etc., but so far as I can remember everybody's head is at 21.

Well, Mary, I will either ring you up on Thursday morning or even appear for lunch, but not to stay. Petrol is difficult. Think it over meanwhile and see how you feel.

I shall be in London most of tomorrow (Wednesday) but will be back by 11 p.m., I hope, in case you want to ring up this hotel. After that I have nowhere to lay my head and it's quite possible she will be told she can't come to Cambridge on Thursday, because it's the farmer's washing day or something. (They are big farmers.) If she can come, I will bring her on Thursday: if she can't, I will ring up. I think you said you were not going off till Friday. But if I have made a mistake, and you don't want to see us on Thursday, please ring up or *send a telegram* to this hotel, tomorrow, Wednesday, to put us off.

I have not told her that I have told you *all* her history, as it might make her feel shy on meeting you, and of course what I have told you is under the seal. Nor have I told her about my previous sexual tangles, as I don't want to do so for some reason till after we have had a baby.

Love from
Tim

184

Dearest Mary,

I have written to Cook, stating that I will take the watch to his house on August 14th. So will you leave on the harpsichord (a) the watch, (b) the article on Tears,[1] and (c) *the key of the garage?* I have the key of the house.

The reason why I have been so long about writing is that I hoped to get a letter from Annette, saying whether she was coming to Bateman Street or not. Although I have had a letter beginning "Dearest Tim," she preserves her sphinx-like silence on this subject in it. From what little I understand about her I think this means that she certainly won't come, so Potts can sleep on his drenched ground-sheet in Wales with an easy conscience, knowing that no orgies are being enacted at 54. As a matter of fact he little recks of the effect he has had upon his pupils, if he thinks that many orgies would have taken place in any case. After 3 years of morals and ethics at our most impressionable age, our orgasms are of the most respectable. We always draw the blinds.

Mary, I don't think there is anything we ought to arrange? I shall mainly eat in hotels, and make a point of leaving plenty of sugar etc. for when you come back. I do hope you will enjoy yourselves. I shall read at the libraries.

I have been making packing cases and putting books in them since I came here,[2] with one meal a day at the local pub and Killie eating all my rations, including the bread. The cases containing my books and pictures as sent over from Ireland are inextricably mixed up, and the only way one can make a remote guess at their tightly-nailed contents is by weight. I am going to make one last effort to discover which case contains Potts the Father's oil painting tomorrow, but if I fail you will understand that it means weakening good packing cases by unnailing them. I did invent a plan by which I was to send him the unique copy of my 3rd draft of *Mistress Masham's Repose,* bound in leather by the people who bound the *Codex Siniaticus,* instead, but in the rush of packing I packed it under several hundred other books, so that's a fraud also. But one or other, or both, he shall have in time, when only this wave of arrangement has passed over my head.

Mary, how am I going to see you again later on? I mean you, not Annette. Would it be a good idea if I were at Bateman Street with a hot meal ready the day you came back, if I were to make off to Hampstead, where some friends are inviting me, next morning?

Killie and I send most of our love to Potts, Weg, Betsy, William and the materfamilias.

Love from Tim

P.S. You said to come on the 8th.

CHAPTER 6

Alderney

In 1946 White went to Jersey, where he stayed for five months. He then settled in Alderney, which was to be his home until his death.

Lieutenant Commander Harry Griffiths, who served White as secretary and gardener at Alderney, remembers witnessing the arrival of White and his dog Killie by boat from Guernsey:

. . . the moment the gangway was rigged a very bedraggled and unhappy-looking red setter bitch made a joyful rush for dry land. Close behind her was a magnificent figure of a man, well over six feet, blue-eyed, and with a beard bristling in all directions. He was equally bedraggled, and a voice from the gallery said: "By God, she must have gone deep—she's fished up Father Neptune!"

White first went to a hotel, Gros Nez House, where he stayed for several nights. When he had his own house, he used often to go there for his meals and take his visitors.

After various plans to buy a castle or a fortress or a tiny cottage or a whole island, he finally chose a three-storied house in St. Anne: "I have bought a delicious little Frenchified house in the main place of Alderney . . . It has two immense greenhouses (broken) but with the vines in them. Also orchard, garage space, main drain, cobbled square—almost everything the heart could desire."[1]

The Frenchified house was progressively transformed: the greenhouse was repaired and the walls were redecorated; White's visitors still remember the crimson kitchen with its comfortable old chairs falling to bits. Mary Potts recalls the time when her son, William, aged ten, had to sleep in the cottage next to the house, which had an unfinished roof and open floors—a chivalric "ordeal" for the aspiring knight!

White built and equipped a sound studio where he could record commentaries for his films (he made several films on the puffins from the island of Burhou). He had a swimming pool and a small outdoor theater where plays were acted for his friends. He added a small temple to Hadrian and even an arch to the movie star Julie Andrews, who while playing Guenever in *Camelot* became a friend of White and visited him in Alderney.

The house has now been converted into separate flats, the swimming pool is empty, and the temple and the arch are covered with branches and leaves, but a plaster head of Hadrian was still there on the wall when I went to Alderney following the tracks of T. H. White.

White, who had always lived in rented houses or as a paying guest, felt the need to establish some permanent roots for himself. Now that he had real money to spend, he bought some antique furniture, a grandfather clock, a harmonium, a piano and several paintings of unknown people that he named his "ancestors." Each item is carefully described in the letters, including the price paid for it.

Having a house of his own and plenty of room, White could indulge his passion for being a host. In addition to the friends he made on the island, he entertained many guests from England. On one occasion, according to his secretary, Harry Griffiths, he made a list of the Alderney people who hated each other and invited them all to his domicile, hoping that he could sit back and enjoy the arguments. On the next day, when asked if he had had a good time, he replied: "Not at all, the lions lay down with the lambs and the lambs lay down with the lions!"

Among his English visitors were John Betjeman; Michael Trubshawe and his wife; his editor, Michael Howard, who came to help White with his bestiary; and David Garnett, who came in October 1948 and in May 1962. The Pottses came in May 1947 and April 1956. Mary Potts came alone in 1961 after her husband's death.

In December 1952 White went hurriedly to England, because his mother had had a heart attack. He stayed with her until she died a week later. While she was alive he had abused her roundly in his letters, but he expressed a real sympathy when she died: "I felt great compassion for the poor old soul as she came to pay her debts to life." His father had died in 1946, and White was very pleased to start a new correspondence with the remaining members of this side of his family—one of them was his cousin Mrs. Patsy Lane, whose sons, Timmy and Peter, soon joined the crowd of young people who came to stay at Alderney during their holidays.

In January 1953 White once again "fell madly in love," this time with a friend's stepdaughter, aged twenty, who came to stay at Alderney. White immediately started her education and gave her a whole set of books to read. He soon began proposing to her every day, telling her that the difference in ages did not matter, that she would come to love him and that it was a well-known fact that only prearranged marriages worked out. There were times when he would sit on the stairs outside her bedroom and write love poems on record sleeves that he would slip under her door and tear up the next morning! After six weeks, she had to run away, as she did not know how to cope, but promised she would come back in September. White wrote to her twice a day for six weeks. By July, her letters getting fewer and more stilted, he went to see her in England, but she refused to come with him. White flew back to Alderney, where he "did his best to destroy himself with liquor"[2] and even had a fight with a sailor in a pub.

A middle-aged lady, nicknamed "Puck," came to stay at Alderney in September 1956. She was the first of the many deaf and blind persons that White had invited to his house. He did all he could to entertain her, teaching her to swim and to fish, learning Braille and the deaf alphabet. Puck came to Alderney several times.

White had asked the children of a friend to meet Puck at the airport and had taught them finger-talking so that they could welcome her. There was a young boy of twelve among them, called Zed in Sylvia Townsend Warner's biography of White. He soon took all of White's affection, tenderness and love. On September 18, 1957, White wrote: "I have fallen in love with Zed . . . I love him for being happy and innocent . . . the whole situation is an impossible one."[3] This episode played an extremely important part in White's life: He was then fifty-one, and for the next four years he lived only for the rare moments when the young boy could spend his holiday at Alderney. In April 1958, they went camping together on the island of Burhou to film the colonies of puffins. Zed was one of the actors in the condensed version of Shakespeare's play, "Macbeth the Knife," that White had written for his own little theater; he also dedicated White's temple to Hadrian. When the boy and his parents decided in October 1960 to stop his visits, White was deeply wounded. On January 28, 1962, he wrote in his diary: "I sometimes begin to hope that I shall soon be able to forget about Zed. He must be 18 or 19 now, and fully committed to the rat race of his parents. Perhaps, when I haven't seen him for three years, I will reach the happy stage of not minding either way."

It is interesting to note that there are only two lines in one letter to Mary Potts about the boy who meant so much to him: "My apparent trouble was mental, like yours. I had lost the heir on whom I had pinned all my love and trust."

While he was at Alderney, White worked on the material he had in store and on the books he had already started. He continued to work on his translation of the bestiary, sometimes "nine hours day": *The Book of Beasts* was finally published in 1954. He was very proud of his appendix of forty pages and of the very long bibliography (ten pages). He knew that before him, only G. C Druce had translated a bestiary into English. *The Scandalmonger* another eighteenth-century study, was published in 1952, and th final one-volume version of the Arthur tetralogy was published in 1958 under the title of *The Once and Future King*.

The Goshawk, which came out in 1951, was based on his 1936 experience as an austringer while he was at Stowe Ridings, and *The Godstone and The Blackymor* came directly out of his Irish diaries. As early as 1941 White had started a book on a 132-year-old character named Alpha who intended to destroy the world from the island of Rockall; the character and the plot reappeared in *The Master*.

White had endless activities: writing articles for various newspapers, making films, sailing his dinghy, or trying to play the piccolo and writing to Mary Potts about it. He also spent a lot of his time painting. He used to say that writing was his profession and painting his pleasure.

When he was unhappy or lonely or trying to forget his thwarted love affairs, White continued to drink heavily. He put on weight and had trouble with one of his legs due to arterial blockage, for which he had an operation in May 1962.

White left for his American lecture tour in 1963[4] with Carol Walton as his secretary and organizer. Her brother was married to Julie Andrews, who was acting in *Camelot*, the play based on *The Once and Future King*. Carol Walton had been coming to Alderney since 1960 with the summer children who used to stay with White. She agreed to go with him, look after him, and plan his journeys on the condition that he would not drink. White kept his promise, but started again as soon as she had to go back to England. Her father, who was a surgeon, had warned her that White's physical condition suggested he might one day die suddenly of a stroke.

At the end of December 1963, White sailed from New York on a cruise that took him to Spain, Italy, Egypt, Lebanon, and Greece: "It will give me a chance to photograph some Hadrian buildings" (Warner, p. 341). On January 17, 1964, he was found dead in his cabin on board the SS *Exeter* in the port of Piraeus. He was buried in Athens, not far from Hadrian's Arch.

To young Margaret Potts, to L. J., and to Mary, White writes highly dramatically of his arrival in Jersey.

Dear Margaret,

I'm sorry I missed you at the station. You were not there when the train came in, but I did think I caught a glimpse of you out of the window, before it went out. It did both early.

Killie thinks Jersey is the finest place in all the world. We have been for an hour's walk along the sands, to a Norman Castle and back again, and all the dogs were polite to her. It is a miracle island. When you say "Could I have a drink?" or "Have you got some dog's meat?" or "Is it possible to get a taxi?", they don't say "Damn you, go and stand at the back of the queue." They say "Well, we haven't got many, dear sir, but we shall do our very utmost to do the best we can."

And have you heard the news about my crossing? I didn't even take the sleeping pills. First, at about 1:15 this morning, i.e. the midst of the night, I went aboard the lugger and drank eight large glasses of whisky. Do you remember I had lumbago? It made me limp, and what with that and my George V beard, everybody was certain that I must be a retired admiral with a wooden leg blown off at Jutland, an idea which I did nothing to discourage. So I got the most distinguished consideration and all the stewards saluted me wherever I went, standing to attention. At about 3 o'clock I buffeted my way across the boat deck through the waves to my cabin. At 3:15 Killie was sick on my chest. At 5 A.M. I was thrown right out of my bunk, a high one, by a roll, and nearly broke my leg. And who do you think was the old tar who was scoffing bacon and eggs and quaffing beakers of coffee at 7 in the morning, while the cutlery slid up and down the table in spite of the fiddles? Who but your old friend, Admiral Tim.

Tell William that Jersey is a great place for farmers. They grow tomatoes in the open field, in ridges, like potatoes, and now you can see the old stalks sticking up, exactly like haulms. Three acres is quite a decent farm, and the biggest in the island seems to be about 30 acres.

It is great granite cliffs with the sea bursting up in white fangs.

The worst part for the sea is between Jersey and Guernsey, and there the ship does not go up and down like this ∿∿∿, nor sideways like this ⌇ but corkscrew-wise like this ⟿⟿⟿

Love from
Columbus and Killie

[Written on a series of six postcards of Jersey, Channel Islands]

[November 29, 1946]
Grouville Hall Hotel, Grouville, Jersey

Dear Pottës,
   Excuse the Merry manner of correspondence, in this case perhaps justifiable. This is an odd island. Imagine what England would be if you kept it in a bath too long till it shrivelled. The cities would be villages, the villages houses and the houses equivalent to small back gardens. Except for 3 or 4 sand-dune areas used for golf courses or bathing beaches, there is nowhere on the island where one house is more than 100 yards from its neighbour. The metropolis, St. Helier, is like Brighton. On about 30,000 acres, the whole area, are 50,000 people. The cows have to be kept tethered on grass rations, because all the interior is so over-crowded. Round the rocky beach edges there is breathing room all winter, but in summer the trippers lie there like seals. All the photographs I am sending you are winter photographs. The place is good for all that. It has the sunshine record of the British Isles, and this is odd also, because it is also damp. It is a damp air with constant sunshine. It is not like your St. David's Head, though like it in the photographs, because here there is never mist, rain etc., though always this strange humidity in the air, not spoiling the sunlight. Prices are much the same as in England, except for a few exceptions. Cigarettes are cheaper. Drink about half English price. No rations for butter or milk. Meat is a little easier. Real estate costs the same. Jersey French (the old

193

Norman) is very odd. It sounds exactly like the French which Betsy speaks. When they can't think of the Norman word they use an English one, and all is in an English accent.

On the whole I think I will buy an acre or two in one of the few desolate places, and build on it. If I do not spend my money like this, I shall only spend it on drink, so one may as well lose the money one way as another. There is a plague of jews here speculating in land. They will certainly get the better of me, but perhaps better Jews than gin. PLEASE SEND ME THE ADDRESS OF *THE ARCHITECT MALLOWS* with his initials, so that I may apply to him to design my house for me. I shall be an ill-tempered client to him, as I know what I want.

I have been driving round the island for two days in a taxi. Before I fix anything I will also sail to Guernsey, Alderney etc. I have one more taxi day here, before going to the estate agents.

Everybody is startlingly polite, after England. The laws are first class. The religion is mainly Baptist. The hotel at which I am staying has no less than *four* colonels—it is a small hotel—and each colonel is worse than the other. They play golf all day and are liars and bullies and fools. I need never meet such people if I build. The genuine residents are as nice as could be.

love from
Tim

[December 14, 1946]
Grouville Hall Hotel, Grouville, Jersey

Dear Mary,

Please thank Pottës for his charming letter, and thank you for yours. I couldn't understand the latter, as it is nothing at all like Jersey French. The only Potts who would be understood here is Betsy, who would be thought an incomparable scholar. It seems to be William the Conqueror's French—I mean Betsy's and that of

194

Jersey. If they want to call you in the morning, the Boots of the hotel assured me they might say: *"Lès temps de you lever."*

I am getting happier. The Jersey pubs are open *all day*, at prices which are half those of England, so there was a time when I looked like getting the real Horrors, instead of the Glooms which I had in Cambridge. Luckily for me, I made friends with some horsey people, who offered to let me ride a point to point horse whose toes are being coddled for his approaching win in the Jersey races by sea bathing. So, as I saw it was my only hope of escaping a home for inebriates, I hoisted my old bones into his racing saddle last week, and tottered off to canter up and down the glorious beaches, pursued by whole herds of pink elephants and bits of knobbly China. We have out-distanced them. He is quite an ugly animal by English standards but I love him very much, and every afternoon I call to groom and saddle and be off with him, gradually getting soberer and more astounded to find that I don't fall off. It must be ten years since I rode a horse. His name is Michael. He is not up to my weight. He will win, I hope, in the Ladies Race. Is Margaret jealous?

I can't give Potts' love to our four colonels, as I have quarrelled with all four of them. And when I say quarrelled, if that's spelt right, I mean told them, before company, exactly what I and my pink elephants thought of retired colonels. This has had the very best results, as they now treat me with the deepest respect and make little shy efforts to interest me in the affairs of Poona. I have become the tyrant of the hotel, and respond with gracious magnanimity, patting all their old bald heads in a fatherly way and asking after the "goff." Still, I don't feel like giving them Potts' love, as it would be a bit infra dig to condescend too much.

This letter is not to ask you to do anything for me, but to tell you to do it. I think Potts' insistence on paying me formally *may* cost me several thousands, yes, thousands, of pounds, by establishing my place of business as England, just at a time when I ought to be establishing that it is not: so I have a right to be indulged. I DIRECT, and this goes for you just as if you were only a colonel, that the balance of my leavings in England, after paying Potts, shall be spent in equal quantities on my three friends, Margaret, Betsy and William, for Christmas presents chosen by them. In this fail at your peril.

Given under our New order at Grouville,
with riding switch rampant in the
dexter hand and four colonels prostrate,
repentant, upon the sinister,

Jockey of Jersey

It is meant to be a Christmas letter, with all my love to all.

White and Potts were each having their own problems, Potts with the passing of youth and White with the passing of love. The book that Potts praises, *The Elephant and the Kangaroo*, is the Irish work that raised tempers and ruptured friendships.

[June 13, 1947]
54 Bateman Street, Cambridge

Dear Tim,

I wrote a letter to you just about a month ago, but it was so discontented without reason that I didn't send it. I ought to be able at my age to write letters fit to send—or not be ashamed of sending any letter I write—one or the other; but I haven't yet reached that stage of maturity.

I have been marking Part II Tripos papers innumerable, so I didn't manage to write another letter. Now that is over, and nothing remains for a bit except end of term business and functions. Very boring because I want to write the book on Comedy: in fact I have actually started it.

I think *The Elephant and the Kangaroo* is your best book: more consistently good than the *Sword and the Stone* and better value than the last of the Arthur books. I have just discovered that a new edition of Malory has appeared, from a *manuscript,* but the wretched Oxford Press only printed a miserable number of copies and Bowes and Bowes only had *three* allotted to them, so I haven't been able to get one. Vinaver the Editor says (as far as I know) that Malory never *made* his matter into a single book, but wrote the thing in the sort of Kingsley's Heroes ways. I don't know whether this matters: I don't think it does, for Malory was never by anyone so far as I know supposed to have worked out a single sequence of events, and the unity of his book has one of atmosphere or whatever you like to call it. At any rate this justifies you in making the story *for the first time* into an Epic. However you might perhaps want to read the book in its newly published form before you issue your revised version. It may be too late and I daresay it doesn't matter. If I could have got a copy I would have sent it you.

To return to *the E. and the K.* Its unique beauty is of course your putting Mr. White in the *3rd person* (this you told us, but one couldn't quite see what the effect would be). It makes the book much more objective than your other books, because the one character you can dramatise perfectly is yourself.

I can't think of any other novelist in this country who has ever succeeded in doing this except Sterne and he didn't think of doing it in the third person. Butler made a poor job of it in *The Way of all Flesh:* Ernest is a fearful bore isn't he? Mikey and Mrs. O'Callaghan are *excellent,* but they aren't fully independent—one doesn't really see them detached from Mr. White. Mrs. O'C. is much the better of the two: you say Mikey was lovable or something of the sort—but you don't make him appear so. Mrs. O'C. you *do* make adorable: and the way you develop her into a hero is splendid. (I was however annoyed with your publisher for calling him "Repulsive" on the jacket.) ["Mr. White is also showing Mrs. Callaghan's repulsive mate . . . how to run the farm on sane principles."]

Let us know what you are doing: whether you have found a permanent home.

I am in a rather bad way: I am having my "change of life," I think—I am convinced it happens to men too, but with us it doesn't have the physical accompaniments that it has with women. I am utterly sick of Cambridge and of myself and find it a burden to deal with any human beings except my own domestic circle. I can't be bothered with any of my colleagues—with few exceptions they seem to me knaves or nitwits. This is highly senescent (senescence is very like adolescence—but gloomier because the watershed is past and one is going downhill). I got utterly worn out in the war—I never realised how much. But I really think I am getting better by degrees. I had a fright last vac, by going deaf in one ear, but apparently it is nothing worse than two great lumps of bone in my outer ear, and if the worst comes to the worst they can be chopped out, which would be a tiresome operation and may not be necessary. For the present I am all right again.

When is the Elephant coming out in England? I shall buy about as many copies as I can get hold of.

Love from us all
Pottës

[June 8, 1947][5]
Gros Nez House, Alderney

Dear Mary,

Thank you for your thrilling letter about all the freezing, flaming and operation-table ordeals of Bateman Street in the last six months. Please kiss Potts's feet for me and hope he is now quite well. If I say more, he will think I am intruding upon his proper privacy, which I dare not do. Still, I love him, which you must never on your life reveal, and honour him, and don't like to hear about operations.

IMPORTANT MATTERS:

(1) I have bought a thing like a debased sort of recorder, called a Tipperary Flute. Its really a penny whistle made of plastic. I can play four tunes perfectly. The first is called Camptown Races. You may have heard of it. After two others and a rather difficult one called There is a Tavern in the Town, I am at the end of my scores.

Please *instantly* buy for me in Cambridge a *Students Song Book* for one shilling (there is no music shop in Alderney) and post it to me at once. But first you must mark the *air* of the first *six* tunes in the book thus:

> Soh Soh Soh Me Soh Lah Soh
> Me Ray
> Me Ray
> (Campton Races, first line)

Otherwise I can't find out how to use my fingers, as I never know which blast any tune begins on.

(2) I have bought a house in Alderney, SOLELY TO ENTER-TAIN THE POTTS IN IT. I realise clearly that it will take about two years to accustom the father Potts to this idea, but I can wait. Please start now accustoming. The Summer of 1948 will be spent by them in Alderney, the finest climate in the world, without having to huddle in a lot of tents in Wales or bother about cooking and shopping. The war may have spoiled our attempt to meet in Ireland, but it won't spoil this effort. Start immediately to prevent Potts being a fuss-potts about it. Incidentally, I am also buying rather a large fortress for the same purpose. We shall sail, fish, bathe, eat, sleep, and I personally shall go on boozing. If you could see my colour now (just off Zulu) you would take up a relenting attitude to the brandy we consume in our boats. Almost any day T.H.W. is to be seen covered with tar, with a lobster in one hand, two mackerel in the other, and a bottle of Cognac at 18/- in the third. I have purposely bought a house with bedrooms for 2 married Potts, 2 young female Potts and one young male Pott, exclusive of fortresses.

(3) To revert to the Tipperary flute, I *think*, but can't be sure, that "Do" is "C"—if that makes any difference to the tunes you are going to verbalise for me. i.e.:

> Do Ray Me Fa So La Se Do Ray
> C D E F G A B C x?

I don't want to overblow at present.

In despair, I enclose my *only* score to make you see what I mean. Could you try it on a recorder or something? FOR GOD'S SAKE RETURN IT. I can do the fiddly notes, like 1. 6 × 4, without wincing.

[June 20, 1947]

Dear Pottës,

Your charming letter reached me yesterday. If you knew how much I value your letters, and how often, even in pubs, I secretly take them out to read them again, you would be more liberal.

First, I don't think it's much good my worrying more about Malory's sources or manuscripts. I've done too much of it already, for a "creative artist." I knew quite a lot about his habit of tacking sources together without caring whether they fitted (that's why there were so many different people with the same name—Elaines etc.) and I'd rather not know any more, or I shall become a "critic" instead of a "creative artist" as above.

Second, you are definitely a genius. The only wormwood pang that I got out of the blurb on THE ELEPHANT AND THE KANGAROO was the very one that hurt you—i. e. that they should describe Mikey as horrible and his farm as a stink-hole.

Third, this is a horrid confession, I have completely forgotten the right names for all your tripos candidates except Owusu, probably because the latter was black. If you could contrive to paint them different colours next time, I shall try to do better. I can only say they all seem to have got more or less what they deserved, except Owusu, who is your real triumph (and his).

Fourth, are you telling me the truth about your ears? Is it anything mastoid?

Fifth, as you will hear from Mary, I am plotting against your peace of mind for 1948. Try to swallow it in small bits at a time.

Sixth, yes, you are right that I did take the Tripos gents seriously, even if I have forgotten their names (like dismissing something agonising from your mind) and I did try with them, and they did exhaust me more than anything I can remember. How you manage to cope with the thing, I can't imagine.

Best love to all Potts of all denominations in all parts of all of Bateman St.

from Tim

P.S. (for Mary) as for Annette, I don't even know if she has died of her baby or not. I am trying to find out, under the counter.[6]

[June 24, 1947]
Gros Nez House, Alderney

Dear Mary,

I wrote for news to Annette's brother. What she has done is this. She married a well known cricketer in February or March and had a baby boy in April, which she has christened Terence, after me. So now we all know where we stand! I really must say I think she couldn't have behaved worse. It's so damned unfair on the baby. Her husband will surely have a down on it, because the name will leave him in doubt—such a cruel trick to play on him and it. Although I am furiously indignant about the ethical situation, I must confess to a horrid feeling of something like pride that there should be another Terence in the world. Unfortunately I can't write to her or send a mug to it, as this would be unfair. To make matters worse, she is living with her own parents while he's away for his cricket season. I don't see how such a marriage can possibly last. Anyway, I'm *determined* not to invite her here or write to her or do anything whatever that might make it more difficult. If she can be wicked enough to call it Terence, then her husband and the baby are getting just as raw a deal as she ever had. She is a wicked woman. She is doing it so that she can always torture him, while also keeping a lien on me. She is a bad girl. She ought to have told one lie or the other, but not both.

Love from
Tim

201

Dearest Mary,

Thank you so much for the Song Book. I play all the tunes you have marked solemnly three times a day, and am coming to have quite a repertoire. My *fingers* are beginning to live a life of their own, which is magnificent. But is there any reason why I should confine myself to this horrid plastic flute? when I blow the bottom note it goes Hoo, like somebody with asthma, instead of Too. What do you advise? Would not an ordinary penny whistle be less asthmatic?

You will have had my letter by now, about Annette's naughty trick. Tell Potts that *The Elephant and the Kangaroo* has raised a positive shriek of hatred among catholics and Irishmen in America. They are literally almost on the point of preaching the necessity of my assassination. On reading it myself in print I saw that it was more exasperated than I had intended it to be. But I'm still astonished that they couldn't see that I really loved the O'Callaghans. I am trying to arrest the English edition, to tone it down, as I really didn't want to be nasty. *The Irish Echo* of New York urges action "to put Mr. T. H. White in jail for several thousand years." The book, they say, is "just another typical English stab in the back which will only prove a boomerang" and I am to be regarded as "our common enemy." If you are ever to see me again alive you may have to hurry over to Alderney before next Summer. I also get the usual menacing letters from private persons.

I have had a letter offering to translate *Mistress Masham's Repose* into French, by the man who translates Aldous Huxley.[7] What is the position with your friend the fat lady who went to St David's? I seem to remember having put her on to my agent David Higham. I have written to Higham saying I will accept Huxley's translator unless there is any previous arrangement with the fat lady. He ought to remember whatever decision they came to. I have heard nothing in reply. It is being translated into Swedish, Norvegian,

Danish, Italian, French, but not in German. The Italian translation is *very* good, and is called *Maria Si Ribella*.

Love to all
Tim

[July 5, 1947]

I have had a second letter from you lately, saying you are just coming back from Wales. The glorious Summer has not meant a thing to me, as I spend all the time indoor with a paint bucket in each hand and a lavatory seat round my neck. I am almost too busy to drink, if you can believe that. Nobody will do anything for you—plumbers etc.—and the goods one orders don't get delivered. So I am the head paperhanger, painter, lorry driver, plasterer and everybody else. I have one man and a boy, both bone idle, also my dear old secretary, Mr. O'Dowd, who potters away at ½ a mile an hour, and an aged gardener. I really can't sit down to describe everything. Let it be a surprise for you, I hope a pleasant one. The house is TINY—you have to crawl in on hands and knees, like an igloo. But I hope it will be as beautiful as it is small. IF I can ever get any labor and materials I hope also to have built a tiny real theatre for the kids to act in, if rainy. (Out of a barn)

The square on which the house stands is a sort of *Cranford* Square, cobbled, with a faint air of being a French *place*. The vicar, the convent, the catholic priest and I are practically the four sides of it. There are 2 greenhouses which bore 2 *tons* of grapes in 1939.

I am putting in baths, wash-basins and every form of electric comfort that the mind can devise.

All the inside will be one uniform cream colour.

I have bought, for a song, some glorious furniture—mainly Regency—and intend to devote the rest of my life to behaving like Horry Walpole. But I shall drink more than he did. Unfortunately my dining room chairs cost £175, but they are perfect. (Is there anywhere in Cambridge where you can buy me a *vieux rose damask* to cover eleven Regency chairs? I have even bought myself an ancestor, for £1, almost by Hogarth. I shall call him Sir Theopompous White (d. 1775). Nearly all the furniture is period. I shall relegate my more barbaric taste and my own paintings to the theatre-cum-studio-cum-picture-gallery. The place is a sun trap. It is a cottage built any time in the Middle Ages and re-modelled about 1820, I guess.

Love to Potts and all
from Tim

Dearest Mary,

Only a very short note to thank you for buying the piccolo. Yes, I would like it *immensely*, though I don't think I shall ever be able to blow 2½ octaves on six stops. Please tell me how much I owe you for it.

I can now blow the plastic thing without going Hoo. I go Too every time.

The curse of all musical instruments is practising without enraging other people. I have to do mine on rocks far out to sea, and even then there has been a rise in the number of C. I. wrecks. The plastic thing *has* to go Hoo unless you blow boldly. It was my ashamed efforts to blow softly which produced the Hoo.

I suppose I shall have to learn musical notation, to read it easily, but I enclose the finger chart you asked for, as it is now useless to me. I only play your bits in the Students Song Book. I was playing Men of Marlach this afternoon, sitting in a rock pool ½ mile out to sea, with no clothes on, like a debauched merman. Well, well, I suppose I was born to be eccentric.

Please send me some *simple, practical* instructions on how to blow the piccolo—as if you were explaining to a child of three.

I must go to dinner.

This letter got mislaid. I shall be seriously angry with the Potts if they don't come for 6 weeks or 2 months next year. The fishing itself should be a delight—it is exactly Arthur Ransome stuff. We go in a small lifeboat with auxilliary engine and pull up lobster pots etc. Yesterday in blazing sunlight—I am the same colour as Ceteways or T'Chaka [Cetshways and Chaka were Zulu chiefs]— we got 9 lobsters, 2 dozen mackerel and 2 dozen pollack, which they call whiting here. Only it does distress me how cruel humans are to sea fish. I expostulate about boiling lobsters alive, only to be told that if you kill them first "it is like if you break a Negg" (before cooking it). Nobody troubles to knock the mackerel on the head. They are just left to suffocate in the well of the boat. They even cut off pieces of them, while alive, to use as bait.

If you happen to be talking to a biological don one of these days, will you ask him for detailed instructions how to kill a lobster instantly? And send them to me with the piccolo.

I must stop or I shall miss the post.

> Love to all
> from Tim

Say how much I owe you.

August 15, 1947
Gros Nez House, Alderney

Dearest Mary,

You must have had a baking time at St David's. We have had no rain for six weeks, so surely you are in the same boat. I am *furious* about this, because next year, when it will be just average Channel Islands weather, you will all be lecturing me about the glorious summers in Wales, quite forgetting that all the other times you have been there it has never stopped raining for a minute. Never mind, I *think* I have succeeded in buying a very small, ignoble and useless castle for the kids, as well as our town house, so that we can pic-nic, sun-bathe, explore etc. in it. It is a *horrid* castle, *not* the one I wanted, but still it is a castle. We can sleep in it, in hammocks etc.

I am underlining in honour of the Balmoral tartan on your sofa.

I must tell you about my house, which has been bought only for Potteses, and about my staff, which consequently has to be a millionaire's, but it is difficult to decide how to tell all this, so I shall go to bed and continue tomorrow or the next day.

Incidentally, a frightful thought strikes me. If I write too glowingly to you, and you read it to the kids, and they come, and find it not up to my exaggerations, won't it be a disappointment for them? Consequently, I advise you not to read this letter to any Potts under 35.

[September 27, 1947]
FROM/ Who? Alderney, Channel Islands

← BLOOD

Dear William,
This letter is BLACKMAIL of the DEEPEST DYE.
If neither of your disgraced parents will EVER write to me, I will NEVER write to them.

Steep this letter in Red Ink, if possible with Itching Powder, and stuff it down one or both their necks.

Anyway, I never cared for any of you.

Yours sincerely,
AN ILL-WISHER

[October 15, 1947]
Gros Nez House, Alderney

Dearest Mary,

So you have written to me at last! I don't feel a bit cross about the neglect. It was staying so long at Bateman Street last year which made me see what an endless struggle it was for you merely to keep all the Potts alive, without having to write to your outposts into the bargain.

Yes, any date in August will suit me.

No, I have not practiced on my penny whistle *once* in the last *six weeks*. This is because (a) I thought you had abandoned me—and still suspect it, (b) because I have been wrestling with plumbers, electricians, paper hangers etc.

My friend Rosetti, or it may have been Watts, has painted a portrait of me as a memento of this time. I am naked except for some kind of flying loin cloth, and I clasp in my arms a female plumber, with a scarf over her eyes, who clutches in one hand a lavatory seat strung with broken lute-strings, in the other some kind of trumpet made of ¾ copper piping (or 1" galvanised). She is clad in Pre-Raphaelite drapings and is evidently moribund—her face mustard-gas green. I for my part am full of vigour and am evidently declaiming the caption of the picture which is, "I will not let thee go unless thou bless me."

Others say the picture is called "Orpheus Bringing Back your W.C. from the Underworld (Under the Counter)."

Anyway, I can't practice.

The house is looking up.

I now think I *won't* have a castle ready by next August.
But everything else will be.
There may not be a boat.
Did I tell you there was a new Arthur Ransome called "Great Northern"?

Love to all from all of
Tim

[December 28, 1947]
54 Bateman Street, Cambridge, England

Dear Tim,

Many thanks. I have written to Roper [a travel agent in Alderney] (your letter exactly)—you have no idea how restful it is to have a letter written for me. What you have arranged is what we *wanted* to do, because I have got to come six days later than the others; but I must have either said the opposite of what I meant, or got into a muddle in my letter to you. This I have avoided in my letter to Roper by writing to your dictation.

Yes, it would be a good occasion to get passports for all the family. I have a recurrent travel nightmare, an invariable episode in it being that I find at the last moment that I have forgotten my passport, or lost it.

I am beginning to look forward to this visit quite indecently only I fear we shall have driven you mad before the month is out. I confess with shame that we *haven't* got our children house-trained: they really ought to be sent to the vet, but we can't find it in our hearts to do so. Their barbarity is good for me, really I think the last stage in a man's education; but for you it isn't in the contract— and you'll have to put up with the parents as well.

I shall be most interested to hear your plans for my future. I am in sight of the end of the comedy book, but the weather is very heavy.

I am sorry to say I seem to have over done it slightly in my review of *The Elephant* for the *Dial* [see Appendix C]. The young

208

men are planning a special number for the 500th anniversary of the College and they want to get contributions out of all our great men. They asked me to ask you to oblige; and I said I would [see Appendix D]. I know it will annoy you—but it would be easier than supervising Owusu. By the way, after this request was made to me I looked you up in Who's Who and found a book under your name that I didn't know of. Is it the last of the Arthur Books? —I hope you got the *Age of Scandal* safely.

Love from all and Happy New Year
L.J.P.

[December 31, 1947]
Gros Nez House, Alderney

Dear Pottses generically,

I have told you that I am far busier than L.J.P. always pretends to be. I spend my time like this: half the day mixing concrete, half the day writing books, half the day abusing plumbers, half the day writing to people in Italy or Sweden, half the day taking Killie for walks (because otherwise she gets constipated) and half the day getting drunk. You may think that there are not so many halves, but in my day there are. Now Mary Potts—I haven't tooted a toot since you wrote but I read the poacher book [*The Poacher*, by H. E. Bates] between 5 A.M. and 6 A.M. every morning (my spare time) and it annoyed me quite a lot, which meant that I was *really* enjoying it. It is just on the verge of being credible. This seems churlish, unless you understand that a Xmas present of an old boot *from you* makes me *weep* with gratitude. But still, like G. W., I can't tell a lie, about the written word—and I must affirm that your old poacher is a total humbug—but then, all poachers and gamekeepers especially are. Now William, thanks for the Xmas card. You will think me a useless sort of person not to have sent you a present, nor to Weg, nor to Betsy. I don't know quite what you would like, so I thought I would wait till you were all *here*. Now Pottës, would you and your lady wife kindly stop cringing about the future manners of your children? In the first place the house was *specially built* for them to kick to bits. In the second place, I've met them, haven't I? Do you suppose I've never seen them before? In the third place, I am already constructing a kind of barred menagerie with wire-netting, trapezes, nuts etc., where they will be quite harmless. And in the fourth place, if *only* we can get a summer anything like the last, we shall seldom be in the house at all. As for getting bored with the parents, I hope to lock Potts senior up in the library, to finish the book on comedy, when tiresome, while I scarcely hope to meet Mary Potts at all, as she will be too busy fishing her children out of the various *fatal* currents which surround this island.

Mary Potts: for some things in this house, I have paid through the nose, for instance £175 for the dining room chairs and £250 for the curtains etc. But your old pal is not such a mug as he is painted, so may he mention his two great *coups?* He has bought an original portrait by Si Godfrey Kneller and an original Herring (senior) FOR ONE POUND EACH! There is an original Adam ditto (£3). In fact, it's been fun. The little theatre or studio will be ready when you come, I *hope*, and I'm now trying to buy a grand piano for it. I will write all details about where people are to *sleep* when the mists of futurity begin to rise, but I assume that the two girls can have the same room, and the two seniors wllaf2hve to share also (separate beds). There are two things which you can help me in (I'll repeat them to you, week after week). One is, to buy me an entire parachute (like Pottses' pyjamas) for the theatre curtain and dressing up (C.O.D.). The other is more important. While reducing your baggage to its shabbiest minimum (for the airplane), can you contrive to *bring your sleeping bags* and *buy one for me.* This is because we have some desert islands hereabouts (one is pronounced BURROOO) on which it is extremely dangerous to sleep, among the puffins etc., so I thought we might try it.

54 Bateman Street, Cambridge

Dear Tim,

Thank you for your letter—or at least those parts of it addressed to me. I shall answer them as concisely as I can.

I am glad you are so busy; it always makes one feel useful. But I, unlike you, am naturally idle.

Thank you for your encouragement to me to clear out of Cambridge. All that you say is true; especially that this University has gone downhill so rapidly in the last few years as to be quite alarming; most of our physicists even seem to have gone elsewhere, and if that isn't rats leaving a sinking ship I should like to know what is. They are even *bribing* us to stay, by raising our University stipends so that I shall be making £1500 a year when the scheme goes through. If I could see my way to about £1200 in any other job I should jump at it. But I can't afford to throw away £1500 just now, with the children's education looking as though it may run to £600 a year or so. It's no use talking about Education Acts; if you want a decent education you have to *pay* for it. On the other hand, one can get on almost more comfortably without education in this bloody century; but I can't and won't reconcile myself to that sort of affairs. There is a good sentence in Jane Austen "saved *as we all are* by a comfortable sense of her own superiority she would not have exchanged etc." That's cool isn't it? I like it. I have had a fearful idea of trying to get hold of the Ministry of Education and offering to organise the teaching of English for them from the Primary schools upwards. I suppose I'm going mad, like the man in *Le Dernier Milliardaire* [a film directed by René Clair] who became a dictator.

Of course you won't be in the least interested in the book on Comedy: it is mostly humbug and nonsense of my own. But I am *enjoying* writing it. I shan't send it you until it gets into print, because two people nearer to the level of the people I fondly suppose will read it are already criticizing it chapter by chapter, and if I get any more criticisms I shall have to re-write the whole thing. I was amused that you noticed my translation of "trips." I admit that

it is improbable, but it pleased my fancy. I'm afraid it was a
frivolous note: I can't remember whether I meant it seriously or not.
In any case I ought to apologise. Oh, by the way the Comedy book
has got to be *in* by April; I've nearly finished it, and *ought* to have
quite finished it.

Love
Pottës

[May 18, 1948]
3 Connaught Square

Dear Mary,

When Potts didn't answer my last letter I began to dread that you
intended to revenge and not come, but Roper tells me he has at any
rate bought the steamship tickets, so all is well. I won't give you
any more advice about the journey, as you are grown up, and Potts
enjoys worrying for its own sake, beyond saying that the great
desideratum is to avoid spending a night in Guernsey, where the
hotel would be expensive. Instead, I'll tell you what's in store for
you here.

In the first place, I put myself firmly on the water waggon nine
weeks ago, to be in a good form by August. Then I bought a vast
radiogram and about £100 worth of records, so that your stay will
not be without music. An awful thing has happened to me since
this, for, out of sheer meaness, I have become musical! After paying
so many shillings for a record, and because I *owned* it, I began to
take an interest in playing it. I literally spend 2 hours every evening
listening carefully, not reading or thinking or doing anything else,
and for the first time in my life, I can say with my hand on my heart
that I think Beethoven was the greatest musician in the world, and
of Beethoven I choose the pathetic and the appassionata and the
pastoral symphony.

But we won't talk music till you come.

The next thing is beds. Somebody has got to sleep in a double

212

one, either you and Potts or the 2 girls. That is, if I have failed to get another bedroom ready by August. The building problem in Alderney is worse even than in England, and I am having to do nearly everything myself. Also we shall have to eat at the hotel, as I have not yet been able to move my staff in. But it is only 3 minutes away.

If you don't eventually fly here, I can lay on some air trips to Guernsey and Jersey, as it is essential to see the islands from the air, and also a speed-boat trip to France.

There is a deserted island where we can sleep a night or two (if you bring a sleeping bag for me) and for the rest of the time we must just bathe and explore and fall off cliffs.

There was a wreck here yesterday—a yacht. It had completely vanished—pounded to pieces—in 24 hours. The crew were saved but one is in hospital.

I am not organising this holiday for Potts or the children really, but for you. For one month anyway I'm determined that you shan't wash one dish or cook one egg.

When you come, I will start drinking again, but moderately, so that we may have a few cocktail parties, for you to meet our local society. It is just like living in a 20th century Cornish Cranford. There are only about 1,000 inhabitants all told. We will put the children to bed before these.

There is even a cinema—once a week!

It looks like being a perfect whirl of gaiety. One great thing is that food is really plentiful, cigarettes at 3/6 for 50, drink in proportion.

We can go fishing for lobsters, whiting (local name for pollack) and perhaps mullet. With very great luck I may be able to give you a meal of ormers. ["They taste of meat rather than fish . . . and it is well known that archangels live on them almost exclusively." (*White-Garnett Letters*, p. 232.)]

I enclose some photographs of my lares and penates. By the time you come I shall also have a grandfather clock which I am paying £250 for, and I shall be grateful to Weg if she won't slide through it. I rely on William not to smash the model schooner—which I have had valued (at £400)—and perhaps Betsy will refrain from kicking the legs off the Regency chairs. You see, Mary, I am a perfect nouveau riche, and cannot stop telling everybody what everything cost.

You cannot hope more than I do that your hateful children will behave—at any rate *in* the house. The great thing will be to keep them outside the house for as many hours as possible. The only thing I expect you to believe is that, even if they kick the whole structure to fragments, it will have been worth it, to have you and Potts and them here.

    Love from
    Tim

P.S. And you needn't worry about the children either. I have hired a field surrounded by electrified barbed wire, with a part-time Gestapo Nannie Armed with a Tommy gun.
P.P.S. Incidentally, after all the alarms and excursions about tickets have died down, you might send me a post card saying just exactly which day I am to expect which of you. That is ALL.

Wanda Landowska was the Polish-born harpsichordist who initiated the revival of the harpsichord in the twentieth century. Dr. Edith Summerskill (M.P. for West Fulham) was White's Aunt Sally: she stood for all that was wrong in England (women governing!).

            [September 1948?]

Dear Mary,
I promised I wouldn't write about music, so of course I must. I listen to it for 2 hours every night. And the awful thing is that I must also write about MEN v. WOMEN. I find that I can understand about 80% of what the men sing, even in Italian, but I can only understand 5% of what the women sing.
Why?

Obviously, because the men place some value on the *sense* of what they are singing, with their minds, but the women are only singing from their emotions or from their guts.

On my records, the women could just as well sing LA-LA-LA-LA (for their emotions) while the men have to sing NON PIU ANDRAI etc. (for the meaning).

In the end I can only say that I loathe all women indiscriminately, present company excepted, so what have you got to say in defense of that?

I *don't* think women should have the vote.

I *don't* believe in democracy (most voting coal-miners would be far better dead).

I *don't* want to pay taxes in order to keep alive the old, the futile and the inefficient.

I *don't* care a damn whether Wanda Landowska chains herself to a thousand railings, or whether some hons-frau is called "Dame" so-and-so, or whether coal-miners and wrens and nationalised bitches and female politicians (like that frightful Dr. Summerskill) get into parliament or make me give them my seat in the tube or not. All I want to say is, Dennis Noble or somebody of that sort sings me a song as if he *meant* something. While "Dame" Whibbly-Wobbly sings nothing but "Wa-Wa-Wa."

Have I insulted you enough? I feel too bitterly about it.

Love from
TIM

[September 1948?]

Dear Mary,

Don't you think it would be rather fun if I were to write you a bread-and-butter letter instead?

You know I went away quickly because I did not want to burst into tears in public.

Here is a fairly good example of peripeteia which may amuse Potts. It is in *Readers Digest*, who have never heard of peripeteia. You must understand that *Hearst* is the multi-millionaire newspaper proprietor, while *Howey* is his advertising manager.

Last year Hearst decided that his Chicago newspaper needed boosting. "Go out there and boost the circulation," he said. Arriving on his familiar battlefield, Howey looked around for a story conforming to his pet formula: "Humanity is a Wonderful Thing." Housing was a major problem in Chicago, and a little girl had written a letter to the editor of the *Herald-American* which said in effect: "Please help me find a home—I have never slept in a bed." Howey published the letter and a photo of the little girl looking wistfully into a store window in which he had arranged a display which featured a child's bed. In no time he had Chicagoans worried about the little girl. And, of course, they had to buy the Hearst paper every day to find out how she was getting along. Among those who were reading the heart-breaking stories was Hearst himself, who was so touched that he wired Howey $10,000 and said: "Please buy the little girl a home—you are breaking my heart."

It is a beautiful afternoon, and nobody to bathe. Killie feels puzzled.

So far I have not dared go upstairs at all, consequently I don't yet know what kind of crate I shall need to order, for sending back Margaret's camera, Betsy's knickers, William's telescope and Potts' review of a book by Tom Henn.

I am going now to solemnly play Jesu Joy *alone*, as a kind of dirge, if I can see the music.

> Love from
> Tim

[October 4, 1948]
3 Connaught Square, Alderney

Dear Pottës,

Your gift of Malory was quite a milestone in my life. It really is good stuff, not just vapouring, like some (not you) I could name.

I enclose a photo of a portrait of me, which I consider a masterpiece of character. You see how he [Jonathan Van Doorn] has caught me just about to contradict you on any subject under the sun.

Now you know I have only paid him £25 for this picture, although it is life size. Could you help both him and people like Tilly? When Tilly is painted, as he must in the course of nature be, he will fall into the hands of some fashionable portraitist who will charge the presentation committee about £400. But if he is done now, and with this efficiency, how much he would save?

Evidently we can't ship him off to Cambridge unless we get several commissions. What about you? (Venn has been done?) About the Vice-Chancellor?

In time I shall forward some of the *superb* photographs which Mary took and which I have been too drunk, lazy and engaged in being painted (and feeding puppies) to bother about.

Garnett and Walmsley are both coming to be painted.

love from
Tim

White the chatelain, busy and house-proud, writes to Mary Potts, while White, the burgher in spite of himself, skeptical but town-proud, writes to her husband.

[January 1, 1949]
3 Connaught Square, Alderney

Dear Mary,

As a housewife yourself I believe you are going to forgive me for not writing before. I have bought another garden, and perhaps the island of Jethou, and what with one thing and another it has been impossible to write. May I add, I am sober?

You only have to wash up and feed your family, but I have to build as well. It means twice as much work. I have quite calmly decided not to open any letters. Sheridan did this. He had to. So I have some letters from Margaret and the hunch-back girl and others. They are simply not opened or forwarded. (I will forward your pictures—but it costs me agony.) Do be forgiving, and try to imagine that I have not only to wash up but also to build.

I am much happier and better looked after than you remember. I have a butler, cook, tweeny and gardener—no less. We all get on quite cheerfully together. I don't eat at the Allens any longer.

My exhibition of the air in Jesu Joy is *smashing* and people queue up outside the front door to hear it. It bursts your heart.

Now, for the last time, Mary, don't be cross with me. As one housewife to another, let us understand that we only send each other friendly, infrequent and distracted messages. It's quite likely that I won't write to you for six months, and I'm resigned to the fact that you probably won't write to me for nine.

Now I must rush out and pull down the washing, because it has started to rain.

You see?

Love from
Tim

[January 1950]
3 Connaught Square, Alderney

Dear Pottës,

Thank you very much for your book on Comedy, which shall take a proud place on my autograph shelves—next to Henryson. It is beautifully got up and reads much better than it did in typescript. Somehow it looks much meatier. I was wondering while reading your remarks about Aristotle's "probability or necessity," what about burlesque and fantasy? What would Aristotle have made of *Animal Farm* or *Vile Bodies* or *Peter Pan*. He could hardly have crammed the last of these into satire. I must really get down to reading Ben

218

Jonson some of these days. The trouble about being educated at Cambridge was that one chose the necessary specialisations for the Tripos and seldom afterwards filled in the gaps. Unhappily I did have a try with *Every Man in his Humour*, which, as you say, is far from his best. It bored me stiff, so I have never gone on to *Volpone*, which I must do.

A very great miracle has come to pass in Alderney. A totally unpaid committee of ladies, who seemed on the face of things merely to be busybodies, got together and started a library. (I was far too haughty to have anything to do with the miserable thing, imagining a tattered collection of Ethel M. Dells.) How wrong I was. By begging in the right places—particularly in America—they have got together 3000 excellent books, with sections for Art, History, Biography, Belles Lettres, Poetry, Drama and even Reference! The largest (Fiction) section is of course the most used, but it has plenty of the very latest stuff—Bates, Shute etc. For all this not a penny has been paid, and the ladies "sit in," unpaid, from 10 to 4:30 every day, on a rota, as librarians. We, the public, pay 3d. per book—solely in order to buy new ones!

Now don't you think this is a noble and astonishing thing?

Love to all
from
Tim

White's interest in music had been encouraged by Mary Potts, and, as usual, his enthusiasm soon took flight. The "thing" mentioned in the first sentence is what he used to call his "Walpole" book—*The Age of Scandal*—a study of eighteenth-century characters.

3 Connaught Square, Alderney

Dear Pottës,

Here is this thing, which I lay as usual at your feet. If you hadn't educated me, I could have happily gone on writing rubbish for rubbishy people. But having had the disadvantage of being educated by you, I have to try to be a scholar once every ten years. It's like a seal that has to come up through the ice sometimes to breathe. This is my first breath since I left Cambridge—so please be kind to it—and I have two more gasps up my sleeve. After that, if you don't extend a helping harpoon to me, I shall simply sink back into the depths and write best sellers.

I have sent a copy to Tilly, but not to anybody else in Cambridge so far. I would have *liked* to send one to Trevelyan, as there is certainly ONE SENTENCE in the whole book not previously known to him. But I feel shy. Also I would have liked to send a copy to Dr. Raven.

You will scarcely believe it, but I am still plodding on with the Bestiary, in my intervals of sobriety, and PLEASE TELL MARY THAT I HAVE BOUGHT A *HARMONIUM*. I play her copy of the *Beggars Opera*—*imagine* the *Beggars Opera* on a harmonium—with unbelievable brio and one finger—and, may I say, with unbelievable satisfaction to myself. The point is, to pump like mad with your feet, but to snatch your finger off the ivory as quickly as possible. My harmonium (which cost me £9.10.) has 3 stops. One is Vox Humana, and you have to pedal like mad for that. The other two are simply treble-couple and bass-couple. Naturally nobody wants to listen to this wailing except me, and I have to close the doors and windows. Tell Mary also that sometimes there comes on me a kind of Holy Ghost, by which my fingers (one finger) run or runs away with itself and simply plays, without any reference to a printed note. It is something to do with the "musical (mystical?) mathematics of the city of Heaven." As a mere don, Pottës, I don't expect you to spot that quotation, says he, probably because he is afraid that you won't like his book.

love from
Tim

*   *   *

The next group of letters again displays White's always eager imagination and his unquenchable desire to learn. Here his love of animals, of history, and of the fantastical met in his work on *The Book of Beasts*.

[postcard]

[November 10, 1950]
3 Connaught Square, Alderney

Could you translate this underlined word for me? Speaking of the Parrot, Bestiary says: "Ex natura autem salutat, dicens Ave aut *Kere*." (KERE) Is it a greek word? So far I have put: "It greets people of its own accord, saying Hail or What Cheer." But it may just as well be "pretty Poll." Am having tremendous fun turning the book, which is practically finished, into less jerky simple colloquial speech.

    love from Tim

[November 1950]
3 Connaught Square, Alderney

Dear Pottës,

Thanks for the p.c. Then I will translate it "What-Cheer or Ta-Ta." After all, parrots are rather vernacular birds, and do not address each other in the language of Homer.

I am having tremendous fun with the Bestiary—doing nine hours a day on it. There is something fascinating about translating things—in my case, since I don't have to be so deadly accurate as a translator of Aristotle [Potts had translated the *Poetics*] it is the pleasure of not writing a word that I can't give chapter and verse for, while at the same time trying to give myself the utmost licence within the terms laid down (i.e. as above for "Ave et Kere").

A "devout divine" called Simon Browne (1680–1732) once happily remarked: "I am doing nothing that requires a reasonable soul: I am making a dictionary."

Just so the happy translator.

> love from
> Tim

[postcard]

3 Connaught Square, Alderney

FULL TEXT WAS:

It is only from India that one can get a PSITACUS (parrot), which is a green bird with a red collar and a large tongue. The tongue is broader than in other birds and it makes distinct sounds with it. If you did not see it, you would think it was a real man talking. It greets people of its own accord, saying What-Cheer? or Toodle-oo! It learns other words by teaching. Hence the story of the man who paid a compliment to Caesar by giving him a parrot which had been taught to say "I, a parrot, am willing to learn the names of other people from you. This I learned by myself to say—HAIL CAESAR!"

A parrot's beak is so hard that if you throw the bird down from a height on a rock, it saves itself by landing on its beak, with its mouth tight shut, using the beak as a kind of foundation for the shock. Actually its whole head is so thick that if it has to be taught anything, it needs to be admonished with blows. Although it really does try to copy what its teacher is saying, it wants an occasional crack with an iron bar. While young, and up to two years old, it learns what you point out to it quickly enough, and retains it tenaciously; but after that it begins to be distrait and unteachable.

HAPPY XMAS! (This is a Xmas Card)

DISTRAIT—OBLIVIOUS.

The death of White's mother in January 1953 actually completed their tempestuous relationship on a benign note. At the end, he cared for her, and she died holding his hand. This peaceful farewell relieved White of some long-lasting emotional burden. After his mother's death, perhaps urged by it, White must once again have contemplated marriage, for he soon embarked on another unsuccessful love affair.

[January 11, 1953]
3 Connaught Square, Alderney

Dearest Mary,

I only opened your letter when I got back to Alderney today, having been away in England at the death bed and funeral of my mother. Thank you very much indeed for the fascinating hawk book, which must have cost the earth. I had not seen it before. How I wish I could read German, to understand the hooding part. This is two recherché books you have sent me—how well chosen! The other was *The Beggars Opera*.

My mother had a heart attack. I was with her the last 7 days of her life, and she died holding my hand. She was 75 and an arresting personality. She lived the life which she chose for herself, as we all do, and was willing to abide the consequences. I felt great compassion for the poor old soul as she came to pay her debts to life.

It is good to hear that Potts's *Aristotle* has found a home. Tell him that I have at last completed the Bestiary, which will probably come out at 3 guineas, a superb volume, packed with notes. Those who have read it tell me it will be a permanent book. Some *few* people will still be reading it hundreds of years hence: i.e. the people who are interested in Bestiaries. The nearest I can compare it to is a sort

223

of Burton's *Anatomy of Melancholy*, as the notes are as copious as the text and drawn from my whole range of reading in 30 years.

Please will you remember to do the following thing for me? Ask Potts how I am to get a D. Litt. or Ph.D. or whatever it is, I can't remember. In about 3 years I shall be penniless. There is no longer room for private enterprise in the Farewell State, so I shall have to get a lecturing job somewhere, and a Dr. would help me. I seem to remember that one was allowed to submit 3 printed works to some committee or other, who then either did or did not give you this degree. I could put in *The Age of Scandal*, *The Scandalmonger* and *The Book of Beasts*. But I would rather put in the Beast Book by itself, as it really is a piece of original research, not a mere anthology like the scandal books. I am excited about it. It will have about 150 illustrations! Jonathan Cape and Putnams of America are thrilled with it, in spite of the immense cost of production and typographical difficulties. The notes are very slightly Gibbonian. Tell Potts that in the end I taught myself Latin simply by reading it. It soaked in through the pores somehow. I got to like it very much, I mean the language.

Pottës

This Bestiary of mine has an *Index* and a *Bibliography* of 20 *pages*, which is definitive—so definitive that it mentions MSS. in the possession of learned societies, which have never been published. I hope it will be a monument to all you have taught me, and that it will combine scholarship with entertainment. It can't help making a slight profit in America at any rate, as there are several billion learned libraries on that continent, who will all have to buy it at 3 guineas.

I wonder how you got on during your sabbatical year in France and to what extent you emulated the feats of Wordsworth in that country? How have you been enjoying the new Boswell book? What a darling he was! I must stop now, as I have to write letters about wills and coffins and all the usual agony.

love from
Tim.

3 Connaught Square, Alderney

Dear Pottës,

Thank you for your long, helpful letter. My mother's death provides me with a little money, which will keep the wolf from the door for another year or two, unless I get married. So, on the whole, I think I won't apply for the lectureship. Perhaps something else will turn up when the inheritance runs out.

Don't worry about buying the Bestiary. I will of course send you a copy, as I have of all my books. This time it will be quite a present, as it is coming out at 3 GUINEAS! There are about 150 illustrations: half the book is notes (very difficult to fit in): and Cape discovered that he could not possibly afford to do the thing by himself. Luckily, Putnams in America gave him an order for 3000 sets of sheets in advance, so they are going ahead. I don't think it will come out before Spring 1954. It is terribly complicated for the compositor.

It upsets me that you say I can't get a D. Litt. with it. Couldn't I put in *The Age of Scandal* and *The Scandalmonger* as well? Isn't there something lower than a D. Litt.?

Honestly, this Bestiary ought to be a winner, if anybody gives it a fair chance. I have carried the matter further than Montagu James or any of my predecessors did: there is a Bibliography of about 20 pages, a fine Index—which I completed in about one week, living on Benzedrine—and the Introduction, which I have modestly inserted as an Appendix, is more lucid than anything previously written on the subject. After 1954, anybody who wants to write about Bestiaries will have to apply to me for information, just as I used to have to apply to Sir Sydney Cockerell and Mr. G. C. Druce. In fact, after 1954, Bestiaries and White will be wedded for eternity.

It won't make me any money, but should go on selling permanently a few copies every year.

If I were not the modest fellow you wot of, I would say it is a kind of minor *Zeus* or *Golden Bough*. The notes are quotations from everybody from Aristotle to the American magazine called *Life*:

about as many quotations as in Burton's *Anatomy*, and all pertinent.

It is so learned that in one place it has to explain to the N.E.D. just where it has gone wrong in its definitions, which it does in the kindest way, without being clever, rude, or bossy, and Baxter and Johnson, the successors of Du Cange in compiling Mediaeval Latin dictionaries, have written to ask me for new words—of which I can give them six. I have also had to put the *Encyclopedia Britannica* in its place, about the derivation of the word "pheasant."

It has all been tremendous fun and great labour, one of the few books I have even enjoyed writing.

How is Aristotle going?

The film man called Crichton did not turn up, as he had been whipped off to America at a moment's notice. Please ask Mary to put in a good word with him for me, as I am thinking of breaking into the film industry.[8]

The girl did come, and I fell madly in love with her, the first since Annette. She is only 21. She has now returned to England to be presented at court, and is then off to Spain on a film job. Afterwards, she says she is coming back here in the summer, but the desperate danger is that some young Guardee, film star or toreador will snap her up in the meantime. My trouble is that being a sadist makes me far too gentle with women, and though I have no Conscience, which is merely a sense of Wrong or Guilt, I do have an Honour, which is a sense of Right. Consequently, as no women have any sense of honour, and actually like being knocked about, they never realise how kindly and decently they are being treated, and indeed feel contempt for such treatment, considering it a sign of weakness. Women are Huns. Still, I adore her. I let her go to Spain, encouraged her to go, though it was cutting out my own entrails, simply because young persons who enjoy foreign travel have to be given these happinesses while they can relish them. I suppose it was madness not to be selfish about it. I think she would have stayed if I had ordered her to. She has only written to me once since she left. But I won't write to her unless she writes to me: I won't scold or repine: I won't betray my human dignity, nor hers. An odd thing about lovers is that they seem to think that being in love with somebody gives them some sort of right to that person: that the other person *ought* to love them back. There is no ought about it, I have no rights in Rachael, and if she doesn't write, well then, she doesn't. I am just unlucky. I know this is a most impractical way of looking at things, and that it will probably be the Cressida story over again: some less scrupulous Diomed will get her. I wish I didn't always fall in love with people so much younger than myself: it puts me on my Honour, which means at a disadvantage.

When I was in England about my mother's death, I got into touch with one of my few remaining relatives, a girl cousin called Ruth with whom I had been brought up by our grandparents, during the long spells when our respective parents were serving in India. I found I liked her a lot. She is a British Israelite, a pronounced churchgoer and prayers at night sayer, and is almost everything the opposite of me. Yet she is wholesome, like some nice bread. She has married a person called Frank Day, who runs the Tunbridge Wells or the Crowborough Musical Society and is himself an excellent pianist, about as good as Mary. Has Mary ever heard of him? They have two children. The whole lot are coming in the summer.

I get more work than I can be bothered to do. What is the use of earning money to be redistributed to lavatory attendants by the Chancellor of the Exchequor? However, I am doing half a dozen broadcasts when they send the recording unit over to record me, and will do the Bestiary on television, and am at present—in March, imagine—writing one of the four stories which will constitute the Xmas number of the *Illustrated London News*.[9] A friend here is making a film script of one of my novels. [With John Wylie, White wrote the filmscript of "Dayblood and Distant Thunder."] Will Mary remember to ask her brother whether he is interested? Also, I am doing occasional reviews for *The New Statesman* and for *The Observer*.

When Alderney was occupied by the Germans, they used our church as a store and took the bells from the belfry, which was used as an observation post. The bells were sent away to be melted down. On liberation, we got them back, two broken, and now we need about £1500 to have them recast, returned, rehung. I was approached to write a poem about this, for sale in a brochure appealing for funds. I have done this, and will send you a copy when printed [see Appendix B]. John Betjeman thought of the scheme.

Do you know anybody who wants to buy my mother's house for £3000? It is in Burwash, practically on Kipling's Pook's Hill, looking down on Kipling's valley, 3 beds, 2 receps., kitchen, scullery, W.C., bath, telephone, electric light, bus route, garden and orchard of about 1 acre. Also garage and small greenhouse. It is a honey of a house, just right for retired gentleman ruined by taxation.

You never told me the history of your sabbatical year in France. Will you one day? I imagined you leading a double life in Paris, disguised as Van Gogh. But I am sure you won't answer this letter, so you must get Mary to tell me the story of it—such parts as you have revealed to her.

I have discovered that it is a very good thing never to tell women anything. It gives them something to think about, which keeps them out of mischief, like the dog which had fleas, an occupation which kept it from worrying about its immortal soul.

How is Mary? Has she stopped shedding her epidermis through worry, or are the Pottës worries still at full tide? Please give her an ample hug from me.

By the way, I got quite a compliment last month. The Secretary of the Cherubs Club at Queens' wrote to invite me as a guest to their annual or termly or whatever it is dinner, proposing to put me up for the night. I was absolutely thrilled to be remembered by this club, of which I was once the secretary myself, after twenty-five years, but I could not come. They have asked me to try and fit it in next term, which I will do if I can organise some broadcasting etc. I also have a date to talk to some literary society at Oundle, which might be made to fit with this. What are the dates of next term?

Well, Pottës, I scarcely know whether you will be pleased to have such a long letter as this or not, what with all the essays which you have to read. Don't start absentmindedly correcting it in red pencil.

love from
Tim

3 Connaught Square, Alderney

Dear Pottës,

Well, it is about 17 years work and it seems to have dropped still-born from the press. Only one big paper has reviewed it, *The T.L.S.*, in which a wretched young fellow called Green busily reviewed himself and misrepresented me. I own it seems a bit hard to work all that time without any kind of subsidy and then be overlooked. A few minor papers have given short paragraphs saying how funny the book is, in spite of my desperate efforts in the appendix to explain that it was not. Green wrote: "The text itself continually amuses. . . . The irreverent reader will find much to amuse him here." *T.L.S.*, October 29, 1954: "Creatures That On Earth Do Dwell."

Alas!

love from
Tim

[December 12, 1954]
3 Connaught Square, Alderney

Dearest Pottës,

"No, you never did send me the Aristotle, and I need it *badly*. There is a fellow on this island called John Wyllie who was a squadron leader and finally a Jap prisoner during the last war. He is trying—very successfully—to break into literature. So far, he has published 2 books—*THE GOODLY SEED*, and *RIOT*. He is technically uneducated, except at killing people, so I have to do his punctuation for him, and a good deal of criticising too, which he is splendid at accepting. Like all these expert aeronauts, he is interested in the technique or mechanics of his new trade and he *longs* to read your Aristotle, so that he may learn about recognition and reversal of situation etc. So, quite apart from the fact that you ought to send *me* a copy, do be a kind fellow and send it, suitably inscribed, so that I may lend it to *him*.

Against all expectations, *The Book of Beasts* is selling well, has reached its second edition in spite of the idiocy of the reviewers. Also I have had a few fanmail letters from famous people that I had never met. The odd thing is that the famous people *do* get the two main points, while the reviewers don't. The points are, of course, that this is a piece of original research—the very first and only latin prose bestiary ever translated into English, after 16 years work on and off—and that it is *not* a funny or credulous book. (Have you got to the Appendix yet? You really ought to read it first.) I won't name my famous fans, as one of them is a mortal enemy of yours![10] Also I am careful not to name you to her.

You ask about the illustrations. *All* are photographs from the original M.S.

Please will you and Mary and the family accept this letter as a Christmas Card? I enclose a bestiary photograph to make it seem more so. It is of the tree called the Peridexion, but the text differs from the one I used. It might amuse the librarian of Queens' College to try and puzzle it out!

love from
Tim

[April 4, 1955]
3 Connaught Square, Alderney

Dear Pottës,

Thank you very much for your splendid long letter, and for the two copies of the *Poetics*. The man I wanted the spare copy for is away in Holland, so I shall have to keep it till he comes back. I have not yet more than glanced through my own copy, as I am involved in writing a new novel [*The Master*] which keeps me busy from dawn to dark. But what I dipped into during my lunch hour seemed accurate, clear and sensible. I like the "blurb" you chose for him from great men in the Introduction. Yes, your persecutor was *Dorothy Sayers*. I heard of the correspondence and sent for copies, as I don't subscribe to that malevolent rag, and I can't help saying that you seemed to be the winner. She is an ill-mannered and pretentious woman—but then all women are, and I can't help being grateful to her for encouraging me about *The Book of Beasts*. If she hadn't suddenly flown at your throat, but done the opposite thing, you would have liked her too. You scored by being charming and humble (falsely, I expect) in your replies. Don't worry about the few mistakes. Nobody can possibly get everything right in a first edition. In *the B. of B.*, I stated that Chaucer did not read Bestiaries, and have now discovered a quotation in which he refers to Physiologus by name. We must count our triumphs not our blunders.

I am glad the children are getting on so well. The only one I can offer any advice to is Betsy, and that is to sleep with the owner of the Theatre Company. The girl I was after two years ago has pursued this course industriously and I gather is now practically the owner of Hulton's Press, with two secretaries of her own. Quaere: do male secretaries have to sleep with their female bosses? A shameful aspect of this is that though I have not seen her for two years I would still come running if she crooked her finger. It's a sort of Manon Lescault job. Anyway, I have given up my amorous propensities, like you and Dr. Johnson, and I don't much regret them. The older I get, the more I enjoy my prejudices—which are, at the moment, (a) that all women are odious and contemptible, (b) that the only decent music is percussive. I have plenty of others.

Please tell Mary that I have got a long-playing self-changing radiogram with lots and lots of Beethoven, Tchaicowsky and everybody else. Just now I have got a bee in my bonnet about Gilbert & Sullivan. Allow me to try to interest you in it. (1) Everybody knows the official attitude of the musical eggheads who sneer at them because, "it is not good music." Well, it isn't meant to be, any more than caricatures are meant to be good painting. It is satirical, and if you think yourself back into the days of bicycles and *bloomers*, it is good, decent, Victorian fun. The music is as much a leg-pull on music, as the words are a leg-pull on drama. (2) The

231

literary side provided by Gilbert is *stunning*. I would like to deliver the Clarke Lectures on Aristotle's *Poetics* with illustrations solely from Gilbert & Sullivan. Consider *H.M.S. Pinafore*. The Captain—and a right good captain too—is in a high station, but he commits the error or frailty of stating that

> "Though 'Bother It' I may
> Occasionally say
> I never use a big, big D."

("What, never?" "No, never." This is hubris.) At the climax of three love affairs, which all reach their recognition and reversal at the same moment, he learns that his daughter is in love with a foremast hand, whereupon he exclaims,

> "Why, damme, it's too bad!"

The fates have caught up with him. The First Lord of the Admiralty has overheard, and announces his tragic doom:

> "Go, ribald, get you hence
> To your cabin with celerity.
> This is the consequence
> Of ill-advised asperity."

He ends as a foremast hand.

The *construction* of these Gilbertian jokes are so frivolously, Aristotelianly perfect that they entrance me, and I contend that just as the words are a happy skit on tragedy, so is the music a pleasant skit on opera. (3) Who but an Englishman—Gilbert—could, as in *Pinafore*, make fun of England, the Navy and the upper classes? And of course, music. That is what hurts the eggheads, the musical pomposi. (You will have guessed that in the last three pages I have really been writing to Mary, not you, imploring her to give G. & S. a fair hearing. Tell her I only have two complete operas here—one is *Don Giovanni*, the other *Pinafore*, and I love them both.)

About you and the whole of your family coming to stay here in

232

the summer if possible. A. With plenty of practice I have now learned to be a first rate host, as I seldom pay any attention to the occupations or existence of my guests. Since you were last here, the house has been full every summer and I only had a row with one lot—cousins, who believed in teetotalism and British Israel. B. *But,* at the moment, I have Tommy Rose [White's flying instructor] and his wife in the cottage and I have no idea when they will go. They are decorating a house here, a slow job, and might easily not move into it before July. I will write the moment I have a certain date. Must stop. Novelists go to bed at 9:30. (and are on water waggons).

> love from
> Tim

The serious illness of his second setter, Killie, clearly upset White greatly. That White had "answered no letters, paid no bills" seems to have been literally true. White's local friend, Harry Griffiths, told me that he returned from Africa at about this time and went to see White to help him out with his accounts. He found an incredible mess of unopened letters and debit and credit notes.

[January 9, 1956]
3 Connaught Square, Alderney

Dearest Mary,

I am sorry I have been so long in answering your letter, or have I answered it? For the last 3 months I have been in the depths of misery—mentally paralysed. You know how petty troubles can add up to a log jam. First Killie comes into season—which is 3 weeks of hell for me—then the builders get in—which in Alderney is a fate worse than death—then I nearly have a libel action with *Time & Tide* —which is enough to give you jaundice—then my dearest friend Bunny Garnett sends me a presentation copy of his latest novel, *Aspects of Love,* and I hate it—which means that I don't know how to answer him—then I get ill myself with some obscure disease probably due to anxiety—then my own darling Killie, the red setter who is 12 years old, decides to sit down and die. I can't tell you what a hideous Xmas I have had. All the minus ten I.Q. inhabitants of this island spent all the time battering on my front and back doors in paper hats, carolling, revelling, boozing and falling down, howling for me to stop being silly and to come out and have a jolly, jolly drink. Meanwhile, with the doors locked and not daring to switch on a light, I was feeding the bitch at 2 hour intervals with Brands Essence and that sort of thing. I have now got a reputation for being an eccentric curmudgeon. Anyway, Killie is still alive and a little better. One of her sons, aged 7, died of the same disease ten days before Xmas.

In short, if I have or haven't answered your letter, I just don't know which way I am facing and to lift this pen is a major operation.

However, I must do the best I can.

In apologising I must tell you that I have sent out no Xmas cards or presents, answered no letters, paid no bills, and not even thanked people who sent presents to me.

One of the things which make me feel awful is that I have always sent copies of anything I wrote to the Potts family. Well, Sir Sydney Cockerell has just published a book called *The Best Of Friends*, in which I figure as a letter writer. If I can summon my vitality into my fingers I will somehow get a copy of this into your collection.

Now this is the important part of this letter.

Several months ago Pottès proposed himself as a visitor to this island. Among my lesser worries has been trying to fit in various guests. The best thing is to stop trying to be polite to them. In *theory* I have some at Easter and also during the summer, but as they are sure to let me down let's not think about them at all and let's think about the pots.

Will you or Potts or/and or/ all your children—I want to seduce Elizabeth—kindly tell me when you are coming here?

I have become the super host of all visitors, because I have at last understood that you don't have to notice who is there or who isn't.

simply pursue my own interests. My darling and aged and ill Killie only swims about during the summer months in a diving apparatus. Now this means that Pottës by himself could come here about Easter—to find out what is going on—and then, if satisfactory, the entire family could descend on me like locusts in the summer.

That photograph you sent me. Is it possible that the boy in front of Potts on the bridge is William? I remember William as a tearfull blonde. But this is a happy and athletic brunette. He will hate this description. What I mean is that in the photograph he seems quite a real person by himself.

Do please send me Potts more or less at Easter.

You will be maddened to hear that I have put out about £90 for a radiogram, and about another £90 for long playing records. In fact, I am now in the position to say to you: What Would You Like to Hear? I don't say, I have this, or I have that. I just say, what would you like? Mary, Mary, Mary—I have even got around to that idiot Brahms. I got there through the devine Beethoven—whom I possess almost all of—then through Tsiacovsky whose name I don't pretend to spell any more than "divine"—and then it got to Mozart and after that Gilbert and Sullivan (Not music).

You simply must come here and listen to my records. I have Wanda Whatsitist on a harpsichord—and she is playing Brahms— and slowly, but slowly but slowly I am beginning to listen to the calm mathematics of gentle music. It is like this and like that.

    love from
    Tim

Please, if you answer, remember that I love Killie. And get Potts to come here on a Recognisance which I can't spell.

P.S. To find out if you can come. I can fix Elizabeth.

Dearest Mary,

I wish you would not send me such warm compliments always. They make me feel quite silly and unworthy and as if you were teasing me. A little kind criticism would bring things more into perspective.

Well, since you are a woman and a mother, I suppose I must begin by dealing with your children. (This is a very bad thing really. I never expect my friends to mention Killie, who I know means nothing to them except politeness to me, yet both you and Pottës in your last 2 letters have referred to "dear Killie"! Ye generation of hypocrites, do you think I don't know that Pottës loathes dogs? However, to take a brighter view of the thing and a less biblical attitude . . . Oh Hell, what am I talking about? I thought it was your children?)

Betsy looks an absolute demon—as if Mephistophiles had dressed up as Audrey whats-Her-Name, the mermaid film star. Pottës warned me against her—at which I gave a scornful laugh—but now I shall take precious care to sup with a long spoon. Margaret, who used to be the ugly duckling, strikes me now as the prettier and probably kinder of the two. However, what does all this mean? There is no art to find the mind's construction in the photograph, and probably Betsy would prefer to be pretty while Margaret would prefer to be demonic. One thing I *can* say with certainty is that Margaret has somehow or other managed to produce a figure. The last time I saw her she looked like a bolster ill stuffed with a collection of haggis puddings. Not so now. Unless that starched thing round her waist is falsifying the outline I rather think that her proportions might correspond to the Milo Venus. Is this so? What *were* the Venus measurements? Nowadays, I'm told it is about 36.20.36? Milo was surely more like 33.24.38? And of course these *ghastly* mannequins of the present day, who all look as if they were dying of rickets and dementia, got at 15.15.15, once you've taken off the falsies and steel hoops and surgical splints and saucepan lids and bicycle spokes and rusty corkscrews with which they are held together. God preserve me from ever seeing a naked mannequin. No chance to comment on Betsy's shape as it does not appear in the picture. I suspect she is trying to make it tubular and goes to bed every night in the drain pipe or motor tyre. How nice it is to know that I am forever quite immune to both these young women. One word of sauce out of either of them, and I can describe to them the position of their birth marks and their habits on the potty. It makes one feel Olympian.

Your letter. You say that Pottës and I are good letter writers. I have news for you. It was directly and absolutely and solely the letters of Pottës to me when I was his pupil that opened my eyes to this great art. I can almost remember the day I got his first letter and the sense of discovery. I kept every single letter he wrote to me until 1945. In the course of the years, I began to colect just two other people—Bunny Garnett and Siegfried Sassoon—both *much* his inferiors. In 1945 I became homeless and left all my books and all these precious letters—nailed up so carefully in thick, wooden handmade crates—in a shed at Bunny's moorland cottage in Yorkshire for storage. It seems that a tile or something came off the roof during the next snowy winter, and when finally I had a home and could send for them, it turned out that half the crates were ruined. When I took out that long, laborious, soggy bundle, with all the letters stuck together like papier maché, I swore I would never keep another letter so long as I lived. And I never have. The *heartbreak* I could not endure again. From about 1938 to 1945 I also kept Sydney Cockerell's letters, because of the superb handwriting. They too were gone.

I had taken such *trouble* to preserve and defend these things—all in vain—that now I won't take any trouble at all. When I get a good letter from Pottës or Sydney or Siegfried or anybody else nowadays, I just pop it into the nearest book (preferably by P or S or S or etc.) and leave it at that.

Nobody will ever be able to disentangle this system of filing when I am dead, and for that matter I can't disentangle it myself.

Siegfried is quite as nice as you suspect . . . No, he is not nice. I mean he is not lovable or huggable or able to be treated with tenderness or whatever the word is. He could never have sustained

237

that warm, loyal, gentle, sensitive, mutual understanding with Dame Laurentia which Sydney kept up for 46 years. He is too temperamental and artistic for that. These words are synonyms for selfish, I suppose. Yet he *is* a fine fellow—more highly strung or "fine" than us mortals . . . Well, I can't describe it. I have the greatest esteem? veneration? affection? for him, but I could never feel tender. His wife adored him, made herself a doormat, and was herself a dear. I suppose this must have got on his nerves or something—I have no details—but now they are either separated or divorced. He himself adores in just the same way his only son George—a sort of A. A. Milne, Christopher Robin Relationship—so far as I can make out—far too possessive? As a prophet, I would suspect that he is pickling a rod for his own back. However, I am only an acquaintance and all the above may be rubbish. He was born with the golden Sassoon spoon in his mouth, and lives in the most enchanting Georgian mansion in the most enchanting village in the most enchanting county in England. All his "tastes"—none affected, all genuine—are of the most "fine." Vintage wine (little of it), chef cooking (not enough to eat), Couperin music, paintings by Cotman, poetry by Thompson . . . This makes him sound a frightful aesthete or flaneur, but he is not. He is a sort of Borzoi. They are beautiful, aloof, melancholy dogs, but not "loveable." He is as straight as a ramrod, not an ounce of fat, not a grey hair on his head. What on earth am I doing? I have not *seen* him since 1938, when he must have been about 50, though we do occasionally correspond . . . I can only answer the question in your letter by assuring you that he has *no* "horrid habits." Slightly selfish, slightly touchy, slightly possessive, slightly inaccessible—apart from this, yes, he is "a saint like person."

That seems to answer all of your letter. Except for one thing. You say that Pottës is a "very strong competitor" of mine, as a letter writer. I have never pretended, to myself or anybody else, that I was anything but a very weak competitor of his. Whenever anybody, from Bunny to Sydney, has remarked to me about letters, I have always replied, Ah, but you should see a letter from my friend Potts. It will be a crying scandal if his letters are not collected and published at some future date. Is anything being done about this? What does one do?

Would it be a good idea to tell me a bit about yourself? What happened to that skin disease? Are you still doing all the work of that vast house? Do you get more time for music? I think you told me you did, but on musical subjects I always shut my ears when you talk to me, because I know I won't understand. Once in Ireland I was driving my huge Jaguar on a road in the West, with an Irishman sitting beside me. We were lost. We drew up beside a peasant to ask the way. The *Irishman* rolled down his window and did the asking, in both languages. The peasant was utterly unable to understand a word he said! He had seen the Jaguar, made up his mind that he would not possibly be able to understand us, and so he couldn't. You are a musical Rolls-Royce, and when you talk about music to me I stand goggling with my black peasant hat in hand, not taking in a single word. By the way, I have bought a piano for you here—but of course it will be out of tune, and we have no tuner. HOW I am looking forward to your visit! Have you any idea how many are coming?

> love from
> Tim

Accident-prone as are all daring-doers, White sustained an injury that put him in the hospital, where his concern centered on Killie, who was old and sick. Perhaps remembering the heartbreak of Brownie's passing, White was attempting to prepare himself for his second loss.

[April 10, 1956]
3 Connaught Square, Alderney

Dearest Mary,

I have been having an odd time. About eight weeks ago I slipped on the ice down the granite steps in my garden, making a large hole in my head and possibly breaking my neck. Since then I have been in hospital or staying with friends—*bliss!* It was just the right time of

239

year to do it, and I shall do it again every February for the rest of my life. While you and your family were shuddering in the blizzards I was tucked up in bed with 2 hotwater bottles and a devoted nurse holding each hand and no shopping or cooking to do. But the other thing which has happened to me was worse. About a fortnight ago, *The Times Lit. Sup.* asked me to write their leading article on Winston Churchill's new book, which comes out at the end of the month. I incautiously agreed, thinking it was quite an honour, only to discover that I had let myself in for a kind of Morton's Fork—ask William what Morton's Fork was. How can a miserable little man like me set up to lecture one of the Grand Captains of the world? On the other hand, if the book is a bit childish, how can you give it an eulogy? And it is a bit childish. In one sentence, it is the work of a romantic adolescent with average ethics and supreme talents. Of course I can't say so. Also, since he is 82½ and now a dear old thing, you can't hurt or criticize him at all. Also, *as warriors and statesmen go*, he was always far the best of a bad lot. Well, I have been in the toils for a fortnight, trying to hatch up something which will please him without being actually untrue—his historical ethics are about on the level of the Harrow School Song Book, crossed with an illustrated book called *The Humours of History* which I used to read about forty years ago. If I have managed to pull this off—suppressio veri to the extent of 2,600 words is frightfully difficult—it will be the greatest tour de force I have ever attempted. I mean technically.

Killie is very well, but old and almost totally deaf. I must be ready to part with her when it comes. How I long for her to die easily and suddenly in her sleep, preferably 100 years hence. My friends took her while I was in hospital—luckily we had taught her to regard it as a second home long ago, with just such an emergency in view. I don't think she missed me a bit, and I am truly glad of this, not nose-out-of-joint. Knowing it makes it so much easier to drown in the dinghy or tumble down on the next flight of steps.

love from
Tim

* * *

Nothing that smacked of adventure was alien to White, and even in middle age he was willing, even eager, to try anything at least once. Witness his description of diving in the following letter, which reveals vividly the many and complex levels of his preoccupation with sportsmanship.

[April 18, 1956]
3 Connaught Square, Alderney

Dearest Mary,

Everything now must depend on the weather. As you know, the gulf stream for some reason misses Alderney and swimming with the fish gets frightfully cold unless the summer is good. The end of June won't have warmed the sea as much as I would like. But won't you leave your home in such a posture that *if* the weather is decent you *could* change your week into a fortnight? You will adore the under water job. You don't have to go down at all, only keep your head under and swim as slowly as a shadow. Then the fish let you swim with them and are interested and vaguely friendly. One fish that I met last summer actually *lay on its side* on the sand at the bottom, to observe me (upwards) better. It assumed the position of one of those Etruscan figures naked on a tomb at the British Museum.

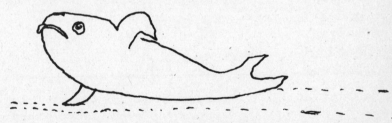

Did I tell you that last year an Admiralty diving vessel turned up to amuse itself in our harbour? It had all the now obsolete gear for the Jules Verne kind of diver, so, as this was probably the last chance ever, I got them to let me go down in the whole

241

paraphernalia. It is *agony*. You know how when you see a film of divers they always seem to move slowly, like old, old men. No wonder. They are carrying about 140 pounds of metal, extra to themselves—30 pounds of lead, for instance, on each foot and 60 lbs round their necks. Try lifting even one foot through one inch, with 30 lbs on it. The deck is strewn with ropes and tubes and to step over each one is like jumping a high hurdle. Climbing up or down vertical iron ladders is hell. As for the bottom of the sea, you can have it. It is simply a collection of mud and seaweed with a few drenched cigarette cartons here and there or worse. I mean in a harbour. The man who quacks at you through the telephone thing is unintelligible and the pressure is inclined to pop your eardrums even at six fathoms. I met another diver at the bottom and we leaned against each other like two amorous manatees, making faces through our glass plates, and when at last I dragged my dropsical body to the top of the ladder my nose was bleeding. One is too old at 50 for these low jinks. On the other hand, it is good for one's soul to put one's life *in other people's hands* once every few years. It was enchanting to be *mothered* by these tough, tender, bronze young men. The diver whom they are dressing and whose life depends on their efficiency is always addressed by his title—"Diver."

"Sit here, Diver." "Now your left foot, Diver." "Stand up, Diver."

I loved being a titled, important person—like being called "Master" or "President" at a college—a sort of knight in armour with his attendant, faithful squires . . .

Suddenly I realize that today is early closing and must instantly stop to shop.

love from   Tim

White's ability to sketch characters (either in his drawings or in his writing) with an almost Dickensian vividness is brilliantly conveyed here, first in his wonderfully ambivalent rendering of an impossibly irritating and lovably impractical do-gooder, then in the moving and wistful portrait of Puck, a deaf-and-blind older lady whom he adopted, along with animals and children, on a summer-visiting basis. White's abiding sense of charity was matched only by his natural inclination to intolerance.

Dearest Mary. Thank you for the splendid photographs, which I have stuck in my album. There were no pictures of the Popsie [T. H. W's boat] before. Plenty of Pottses, however, from the last visit, and neither of you seems to have altered much. The one of Potts smoking on a No Smoking notice is very moral. I owe you vast sums of money for those breakfast bowls, but don't know how much, so enclose £2 at a guess, as I have a vague memory of their being 6/- each. I ought to have thanked you for them, and written a long letter, long ago. Somehow I seem to have been too busy to write to anybody about anything. It must have been after your visit that Cheshire the V.C. turned up. He had hardly been here a couple of days when he announced that I had to start a Cheshire Home for him in Alderney—you know, for these Down-and-Outs—and gave me £1000 and buggered off to India, where he is presumably hopping about in a dhoti with a swami. We (the people who do the real work—I am furious with him) were left to get together a Committee, negotiate for Druitts (the big house on the square outside my windows) and find out the *practical* details as best we might, of course unpaid and unlike him unpraised. Honestly, it is all very well being a saint and going about starry-eyed, distributing cheques for £1000—he has about a dozen homes here and there, mostly in desperate financial difficulties—but the genuine workers—who never get mentioned—are the ones who stay at home and struggle with accounts, forms to fill up, etc. After long wrestling in committee and endless letters to bureaucrats we discovered that (on our cheque for £1000) it would cost £4,500 to buy Druitts, and £14,000 *a year* to keep it up with the 23 patients we expected, and that none of this money was forthcoming. We also found that we in Alderney were not assisted by National Health and could get no help from the M.O.H. in Jersey, Guernsey or S.W. Region, were cut off by sea from all services such as physiotherapy, consulting physicians, dental attention, invalid chairs, all appliances, and that the very patients would have to be expensively brought by air, and any visitors they ever had would have to charter aircraft to do it, and the cost of living itself was higher in Alderney than on the mainland. Also the patients and the nurses refused to come. The fact is that if you do have £14,000 *a year* (instead of £1000 *for ever*) the sensible place to start a home with it is bang in the middle of Piccadilly Circus, where conveniences are handy for the afflicted down-and-out, and *not* at Timbuctoo. The whole Cheshire Empire, so far as we strugglers were able to find out, was in a state of chaos—except the shew-piece at Le Court—which could hardly be embarrassed after its Carnegie grant (was it Carnegie?) but which kept all the money for itself. The V.C. meanwhile had gone Yogi or something and is still in India (no address dependable) and has written us just 3 letters since he left. Not letters, notes. Anyway, the upshot of that piece of business was that we had to disengage ourselves from Druitts—to the anger of the vendors—and return Cheese's cheque to him and advise him to try elsewhere, if he must try anywhere. It is the last time I will work for a saint. (Did you know that this is literally what he secretly or perhaps unconsciously aims to be? Having collected all the medals there are, what else can he aim for but a halo? He is a dear fellow, just as nice as he was when my pupil at Stowe, and as a person you can't help wanting to protect and serve him—but oh what a nuisance saints can be. His future is quite plain before me, if not before him. He will become a monk—probably a Carthusian—and after some years as that sort of hermit will get permission to start a new sub-order of them, who will go out to tend down-and-outs, and he will become the first Abbot of this order, the Cheesians, and in due course, about 400 years hence, will really and truly be St. Cheese. Well, good luck to him. But he *must* learn to be more businesslike, because good abbots are good business-men. It will be fun, 400 years hence, to have spent a few months doing the real work for a saint—but I shan't get a mention in the

244

hagiographies, any more than our secretary, treasurer, welfare officer or medical officer. We kept the committee small and worked well together and became friends and made the right decisions, just like the workers at his other establishments, but we don't qualify for Blessed.)

Side by side with the Cheshire chore, another thing which has interfered with writing to you has been a much more rewarding effort of my own—the thing I think I told you, about the Deaf and Blind. My first guest arrived some time in August I think it was with her guide and the whole thing was a smashing success. She was a little lioness in her late fifties, a maiden lady who had gone deaf/ blind when she was about 12, and she was ready to try anything once. A *heroine*. Can you believe it, she insisted on being taught to swim, and did swim for many minutes all by herself in the silent, dark *waves!* She would *run* on the sands—you try running with your eyes shut and cotton wool in your ears. She swarmed up the lighthouse to the platform on the very top. She went fishing in Bender's boat—the only boat out—it was quite a breeze, —and caught four pollack, the first fish she had ever touched alive. We took her to a cocktail party and met the president and the captain of a submarine and a French fisherman wrote MATELOT on the palm of her hand—which she could read—it was a thrill, as she had never been abroad, or, of course, in an aeroplane—and the grandest thing of all was that the *children* adopted her. Being deaf/ blind like that, she has to walk sort of loosely, putting her feet down like a judo expert in falls, and she carries her head slightly back, with the blind eyes half open, and children, who are inclined to fear the unusual, often shrink from and treat her as a freak. But every summer some very nice children indeed come to Alderney, among them [well-known cricket commentator] John Arlott's family, who are fond of me, and while I was learning the deaf/blind alphabet preparatory to her visit I suddenly remembered that small boys like learning secret languages, so I offered a 6d. prize to the one who would learn it first and in ten minutes the craze had swept the island. The result was, she was met by me and Killie and five kids and we dragged her into the car by all available arms and legs and began writing on her fingers at once, to see if we could, and

245

from that moment for seven days it was a riot! The last day, they arrived running at the airport just in time to see her off and had bought her a little silver brooch of a bird and they *kissed* her goodbye. It was the first time she had ever been accepted by children. Really, I have hardly ever had a happier week—it was ding-dong all the time—and almost weep to write of it, but with tears of pleasure. The children were best, but I did well too. I was taking her for a walk among the german fortifications one day when some blessed inspiration made me realise that she would like to be the leader for once, instead of always being led, so I drew her into an underground ammunition store which was quite extensive and utterly black and *how* proudly she encouraged me, saying "Just hold my hand and trust yourself to me"! As a matter of fact, it was not quite pitch dark, but I pretended it was. It is all arranged now that I am to pay for four such visits every year, and of course my lioness shall come back every time. I have taken up Braille. Imagine it, so did the kids!

These have been my major concerns, but other things have kept me from writing too. I had my publisher [Michael Howard] with wife, Nannie and 3 brats for some time (3 weeks?) and the Bailiff's wife came from Guernsey for about a fortnight and a deaf/blind guide to arrange about the next cargo of them and an old lady of 85 with her husband, unless these were before you? All the time I have been filming. There is the film about Birds & Boats, in which we finally managed to climb up the Garden Rocks (death!) to handle the baby gannets. I got pictures of eggs, young & adults of all the main birds—puffin, razorbill, guillemot, shag, gannet—also porpoises. We caught all the adult birds by hand, including a guillemot, which is not easy. Also there is a film called There Go The Ships, which is the life of our little harbour all through one year, with fishing boats, cargo boats, yachts, naval visits and the climax of the Queen Mary which gets the caption And There Is That Leviathan. It also has some aqua-lung swimming and 2 lovely dives in slow-motion by a visiting swimmer and lots of bits of local colour—siamese cats on yachts, Killie shrimping, a conger nearly 8 ft. long etc. Other films were my Visitor's Book—too little of you and Potts, we must put that right next year—and one wet afternoon we amused about a dozen children by writing, dressing, mounting and photographing a black-and-white thriller called Pong the Hateful Chinaman—very blood-curdling.

Along with all this and no doubt several other things which I have forgotten about—oh yes, of course there was always the Popsie—she is out of the water for the winter and I am partly decking her in—I have been doing my usual writing tasks. I have done the fronts for the T.L.S. three times this year, once on Julian Huxley, who squealed with rage, and twice on Winston Churchill. Also some reviewing for Time & Tide, Daily Telegraph etc.

Killie has been well—touch wood. I managed to rig up photoflood lights and a Heath Robinson system of bits of string to pull, and took 50 ft of her having her ear done at bed time, having supper in bed, and finally licking my hair grease off, as she does every evening before we go to sleep in each other's arms. I had to act in this film *and* photograph it, as she would not have behaved naturally in our private life if anybody else had been present. Very complicated strings.

I am not sending you any Xmas present except this letter, as I begin to think that presents are best for children, while letters are for those one cares for as grown-ups.

When you come next year, you must let me know *early*, as I shall have to fit it in with my 4 parties of deaf/blind. One of these is to be an unlucky youth of 21 or so, who wanted to be a journalist when he was stricken with meningitis, and now this, poor devil. Another is to be an elderly widow of 63. It turns out that I am just the job for the deaf/blind. I seize them by both hands and give them all my heart for a week—which leaves me prostrate for a fortnight. Also you have to keep it up by letter afterwards, as you can't take them up and then drop them.

    love from
    Killie
    and
    Tim

In the summer of 1959, White was fifty and Potts a few years older. Potts's heart attack must have been deeply distressing to White, if only as an omen of things to come and of the utter ending of youthful carelessness. The following letter reads almost as if White were intentionally returning to the idiom of teacher and student, to the language of youth.

[July 1, 1959]
Alderney

Dearest Pottës

I am so very sorry to hear of your heart attack, probably due to worry, but glad it was not worse. As I get older myself, bits keep falling off, like an old car, but one can't do much about it. In some ways it will be a relief to be dead—no more spare parts to fuss about, and think what a rest too!

Curse you for sending me this list of pronunciations. In the first place, the pronunciation of Gaelic varies from South to West, like Devonshire from Aberdeen. In the second place, half the names on your list are from English maps, spelt phonetically, while the other half are in proper Irish. In the third place, I never did learn gaelic properly and have forgotten what I did learn. In the fourth place, the Irish themselves are in a total muddle. In the fifth place, what phonetic system do you want me to adopt in giving you the pronunciation?

Of course, you are *quite* right about the infantilism of the Irish, but it only makes them howl louder if you tell them so.

Your letter is, as usual, absolutely splendid in its penetration and Samuel Butlerishness. I am said to be a good letter writer myself—or was, when the Sydney Cockerell letters were published—and I suppose you realize that I have learnt the whole thing from you, and that I tell everybody so? When people compliment me on my letters, I say, Ah, but you should see my teacher Potts's!

You have done a great disservice to posterity by not collecting and printing your letters.

However, you are quite right about teaching people things. Let the buggers find out for themselves.

Best love from   Tim

[September 3, 1960]
3 Connaught Square, Alderney

Dearest Mary,
I did get a verbal message from you last week, delivered by some pianist woman who was here on holiday, and was going to write as soon as there was time. But I had my usual holiday children and parents here and was in fact in France, at Cherbourg, from the 31st till today, when your letter arrived. There is nothing I can say about your bereavement. He was a *splendid* fellow and you did have a splendid marriage for thirty years or so, which is more than I have had, if that's any consolation. Anyway, God's a bugger, and that's all there is to it. [L. J. Potts died on August 30, 1960.]
The pianist lady said with every appearance of sincerity that you are a genius and probably the best harpsichordist in England. So now you will have to stay on in Cambridge, surrounded with young harpsichordists as pupils, friends and worshippers, rather like a super edition of Mrs G. (do you remember her?) and on the whole, what with that and your three children, I don't think you will be so badly off. Will it help you a little to think of me? I have no wife, no children and no harpsichord, and I manage to plod along!
Where am I to send this, and will you care to come on a visit? I can *always* fit you in on a sofa, even if the house is apparently full.
Potts had more influence on my life than anybody else has had.

love from   Tim

249

* * *

The following group of letters shows White's enthusiastic and touching multi-pronged campaign to buoy Mary Potts's spirits after the death of her husband. During this period, he was witnessing the successful Broadway musical version of *The Once and Future King*, *Camelot*, feeling a glow of major success at last, yet, during that time, his devotion to his dear friend never wavered.

[October 18, 1960]
3 Connaught Square, Alderney

Dearest Mary,

I hope to be able to call on you, if you feel like it, round about the 14th or 15th of next month, on my way to America. No need to put me up, as I can sleep at the University dorms and spend the day time with you. I am feeling just as ill and miserable as you are, and loathe the idea and the bother of going to New York, so we certainly look like cheering each other up! Nevertheless, I have to go, partly because I adore Julie Andrews and partly because it is good for business. If somebody doesn't snatch the money out of my mouth, which seems all too probable, I look like being a rich man.

Will you just drop me a post card, saying whether you will be in Cambridge round about the 15th? I can't be certain of dates, as I have to rush about a good deal looking for visas etc. and the musical itself keeps getting put off.

love from
Tim

[November 18, 1960.]
Royal Court Hotel, Sloane Square

My own dear Mary

I hope you won't think this a very eccentric bread-and-butter letter, and I know you won't be offended when I explain that it is exactly what my teacher Pottës would have done. I am merely repaying, now that I can well afford it, the exact sum which Pottës gave me anonymously, as an undergraduate, to save my life, when he couldn't afford it. To his dying day he never admitted it, and the money was handed to me by Laffan—"on behalf of donors who did not want their names to be known."[11]

When I see you again, soon I hope, perhaps the actual physical gap in your left breast will have filled in a little—ever so little—and so it will go on filling by tiny recoveries, until you can face your own glorious life again.

a LARGE hug

from Tim

[May 29, 1961]
3 Connaught Square, Alderney

Dearest Mary,

I wonder how you are getting on? I myself have been having a sort of minor nervous breakdown or perhaps a change of life. I managed to get through New York on nembutals and tranquillisers, and put up quite a good shew, but when I got back at the end of January I decided I was becoming a drug fiend, so I switched over to brandy. For three months I managed to get *some* sleep and relief from misery by drinking a bottle a day—but then I decided I had changed from a drug fiend into a drunk! So I dropped that and am now back on one small nembutal a night and one tranquilliser a day—which I hope to discontinue soon. I have managed to bring my correspondence up to date, and pay my bills, and begin sunbathing and swimming (icy!).

Now, my dearest Mary, when I told you about my deaf-and-blind friends last autumn, you mentioned that you wouldn't mind coming here for a summer holiday to help with them. Do you still feel the same and could you come for a fortnight in late June or early July, if I can fix the tickets? It is an exhausting occupation, and for two of them you would have to learn the deaf-and-dumb language, if you don't know it already. The third can read ordinary handwriting written on the palm of her hand, as she is as clever as a monkey. You and I could get in quite a lot of our own conversation as well, because you can talk across or about them as if they were bits of furniture. There would also be bathing, if only this glorious weather keeps up, and after all, it would be a change. *Do* write and say you will come?

> Best love
> from
> Tim

Dearest Mary,

I have now grown absolutely *certain* that your sufferings about Pottës are based on a physical condition and exaggerated by the menopause. Don't take me up wrong. I am not suggesting that he was not worth all the mourning in the world—he was—but that your inability to accept the situation and put him out of your mind—as he, of all people, would most, most certainly have wished—is due to the change of life and nothing else. In a minute you will find out why. Before I get on to that, I want to get through rather a rigmarole. (1) Yes, I am publishing a book of poetry [*Verses*], also making a speaking gramophone disc for Argo, with some of it on it. [12] (2) In this book there is a poem I wrote during the last war, at a time when I had volunteered for the R.A.F. (they refused me) and thought I would have to go away to it. (3) The *only* thing I regretted leaving and was worrying about was my greatest love of the time, a red setter. (4) The poem ["Off to the Wars": see Appendix B] tells her, implores her, begs her on bended knees to forget about me utterly, not to repine and to go on being happy. It

252

says that the *only* way I can face death is if I know she is not mourning for me.

It might have been written by Pottës.

If there is any such thing as personal survival, you may be sure of one thing. Your unhappiness would be torturing Pottës—he would express his pain by a shew of arrogance, a restless, nervous shew of it—and the sooner you can stop making him helplessly miserable—helpless to help you—the happier he will be.

Decent people don't *want* to be remembered, if that means suffering to their loved ones.

Now about the menopause.

For the last twenty years I have had a bad leg, which has afflicted me in attacks which came about twice a year—sometimes from drinking too much, sometimes for thwarted love affairs, sometimes just for the change of season at spring and autumn, and sometimes for no apparent reason. Nobody could put a name to it. It produced a sort of cramp, numbness and spasm in the leg. Two months ago, I had my worst attack of it so far—it seems to be my Achilles Heel, which gets seized on when I am run down. I could not walk a step or put my foot to the ground. Julie's father-in-law, a physiotherapist from Wimpole Street, happened to be staying in Alderney. I have been going to him, off and on, ever since. My leg is still pretty lousy, though better, and the latest rumour, purely a rumour, is that it is what the late king died of.

Anyway, we got so exasperated with the anonymous nature of this complaint that we began treating me for practically everything there was! I said, "Do men have a menopause? Why am I so miserable? Is it worth having a shot at that?" He agreed that anything was worth trying once, so, on top of the massage, infra-red, ultra-violet and all that lark, he got me on to as much as eight Tofranils a day and also taught me to give myself intramuscular injections of a hormone called Gonan, with the needle. (I am secretly proud of being able to jab my own flesh once a week with this bloody great syringe—as you say I once told you, I can always do anything I have to do!) He also makes me touch my toes twenty times a day, a thing I never knew I would be able to do, and among other treatments prescribed by myself I am also slimming on some biscuits called Limmits.

Well, terribly slowly but surely—as you say, it is a question of months not weeks—I am getting a little better, a little less wretched, a little more active. I feel that without the Tofranils and perhaps the injections, it would have been a question of years, not months.

I think you *were* taking Tofranils? But had you pressed it up to as many as eight a day? Have you thrown yourself whole-heartedly into the full treatment for menopause?

My apparent trouble was mental, like yours. I had lost the heir on whom I had pinned all my love and trust [the boy called "Zed" in Warner's biography of White].

But I do think that when I have faithfully followed the menopause treatment for three months I shall be as much better as I would have been otherwise in twelve.

Incidentally, this doctor taught me one of the great discoveries of my life. I had been sleeping simply terribly, three hours or not at all. He said, "Sleep is a *habit*. Take two strong nembutals every night for at least ten days, then take one for ten days, then take them every other day, then knock off. You will find the habit has re-established itself."

So much for our common woes, mental and physical.

Julie [Andrews] and her husband are coming to stay tomorrow. On the 9th I am going to my cousins in Derby for the boy's half term. On the 15th I am going back to stay with the physiotherapist for more massage. I am spending Xmas with the cousins.

Yes, we got on famously and had a superb tour of France by car. We *all* adore each other—mother, father, 2 girls and 2 boys—and I found I liked the mother, my first cousin, almost most of all. My French accent and vocabulary became superb! Timmy, the boy, thinks I am the greatest living being and fortunately his mother does not object to my giving all of them all the presents I can think of. So far, Timmy has got away with (1) my own self-winding wrist watch, (2) my 14 ft dinghy Popsie, (3) a camera and millions of films, (4) skin diving apparatus, (5) a Chinese rat, (6) a red squirrel and (7) an alligator!

It is lovely to have a real family again and strange to have re-established a sort of contact with my dead father, from whom my awful mother estranged me for good at 14. They have given me his signet ring, which I wear proudly, and also his pedigree—quite a distinguished one. At any rate, I am descended in the direct male line, of which I am the senior representative, from one of Charles Lamb's best friends, about whom he wrote a good deal in the *Essays of Elia*. He was called James (Gem) White, and wrote a book called *The Letters of Falstaff*, and used to give an annual dinner to all the poor little chimney-sweeping boys. I am thinking of trying to revive something of the same sort. Can you think of anything equivalent to chimney sweeps?

My publisher and his wife [Michael and Patricia Howard] were here, helping with two of my deaf/blinds called Pat and Queenie. One afternoon poor Pat made a joke about having rum in his tea. This reminded me of "Rather Rum," which I had forgotten all over again and not read. So I rushed to find it, gave it to the publisher, and he had it re-typed. Unfortunately we find it too youthful, mannered and dated. We have decided to publish it posthumously, as a curio, to catch the market in the year of my death. I have written a little tribute to Potts in the introduction. PLEASE SEND ME THE DATE OF HIS DEATH. My diary and the memorial service are packed away in a parcel which I don't want to undo.

Now, Mary, I have shamed you by writing a longer letter than yours. Never again say I don't write to you.

One last thing. Please, PLEASE, PLEASE have the facial surgery done to your grand-daughter now, NOW, NOW—*before* she is conscious of the very *first* slight which she might suffer on account of it [a birthmark, which faded away in a few weeks].

    a hug from
    Tim

The circulatory problems that White had for years been experiencing were growing more serious. When White went on an extended American lecture tour, his traveling secretary was young Carol Walton, Julie Andrews's sister-in-law, who was obviously assigned to watch over him. Carol's father, a physician, had warned her that White might die at any time.

[March 3, 1962]
3 Connaught Square, Alderney

Dearest Mary,

I will write you a proper answer when things have cleared up a bit.

At present I have to have a fairly serious operation at St. Thomas's Hospital, but it seems I can't go there before April without becoming liable to English Income Tax as well as ours, while the surgeon himself is going on holiday during that month. It looks as if I may be there for the whole month of May. Things are a bit vague.

Puck is angry with you because you said you would write to her and have not. She thinks you heartless and won't listen to my explanations. Don't forget the poor darling is very isolated in her mind. I too have not written as I ought to have done. She has such troubles that she sometimes doesn't recognise those of other people, including me. If you want to be an angel and rectify this, her address is Miss Florence Collier . . .

I will try to fix about you and her as soon as I know whether I have survived or not! You might tell her so and give my apologies? I am as wretched as you!

    love from
    Tim

[postcard]

[September 20, 1963]
Cunard R. M. S. Queen Elizabeth
83,673 TONS

Dearest Mary—your invite to the wedding did not mention the *date*
but I doubt if I could have come any way, owing to the rush of
getting off to America on a lecture tour. I am taking 18 year-old
Carol Walton, the sister in law of Julie Andrews as a secretary or
protector and we have to cover practically the whole continent. It
will be exhausting and all the money will go on Carol's fares and
hotels, but at least it ought to be an experience. Please wish
William the best of luck and tell him to go on being the Potts
paterfamilias.

    love Tim

Soon after White's departure, Mary Potts left Cambridge for a trip
to Kenya and Kuala Lumpur; there were no further letters between
them.

At the end of December 1963, the SS *Exeter* sailed out of New
York on her way to Greece by way of Spain, Naples, Egypt, and
Lebanon. On January 17, 1964, in the port of Piraeus, an entry was
made in her Log Book reporting the death of a British subject,
apparently of acute heart disease. The passenger's name was
Terence Hanbury White. One might say T. H. White died as he
lived—on his way to new adventures, and alone.

The poem that he wrote after he had seen his merlin, Balin, die
of heart failure might well have been written of his own death:

Death was my first and only natural piece of Nature.
Death was as further as a birth and I went without fear.
I fell over sideways, I laid down the head which ever kept
    upright.
I went forward also, to learn under the dark wings and be there.

257

Appendix A: White's Comments on L. J. Potts's Poems

White made a full comment on Potts's poems. Each one is carefully analyzed, sometimes line by line, and the remarks are often humorous. Here are a few examples of L. J. Potts's poetry with White's comments.

Potts: "The Slaves of the Pyramid," 1923
           Our very souls are slaves . . .

White: This—by me much disliked—construction of "very" seems bred in your very bones, verily, for it crops out all through . . . Yes, forsooth, effstoons, and odd boddikins!

Potts: "Thoughts in Love-Fever," 1925
           I have dwelt within my bursting prison-house and knelt in anguish.

White: You kneel too much.

Potts: "Interlude," 1926
            . . . Do not yield
            To dregs of love or rake hope's embers through.
            Back to the battlefield!

White: All right, Browning, I'll do as you tell me.

Potts: "False Birth," 1926
            And yet there was no sickness on that morn.

White: Frankly, I think this is piffle. One day you will call
            the morning "the morn" once too often, and
            something will happen.

There were several poems that White liked, such as "G.S.K.,"
written in 1925:

G.S.K.

There is no bitterness in such a death,
  But reverent sorrow at his swift escape
  From all the rain, drought, and frost that shape
Our lives to sterner bents, and tame our breath.

The tree that slowly ripens to its fall
  Is tempest-warped, and feels the pruner's knife;
    The sapling is undrained as yet of life;
So he lost nothing till we lost him all.

                        (L. J. Potts, October 2, 1925)

T.H.W.'s comment: *Quite* beautiful. I would not alter a word.

Appendix B: A Sample of T. H. White's Poems

Invocation to Words

Now welled wide off-impulse, cleaned up, cleared up: my flighted
Fresh grey-dawn duck streaming the edgy birth of day:
My wingèd words, neck-stretched and sighted
Upon the certainty: glass-clear, first morning wind, first, first
    away:
Now spring, now up of the sun,
Brushing the cold cheek with an opening eye, kissing hair, gone:
O words, leap to me, opening, true, giving me, each one, one
Dart to the heart, the blue heart. Or I am done.
          (*The Listener*, March 25, 1931, p. 511.
              Enclosed in a letter to Potts,
                   September 1931.)

Indescribable Loneliness of Man

Indescribable loneliness of man in love and beauty!
Love crucified Christ and man is crucified daily,
I hourly: up-bolted, out-nailèd, to my dread destiny and duty.
My heart so swells, drags to the breast-bone from the nails,
Struggles like sparrow in hand, to burst, to bound toward thee,
To cover and clutch thee: but fails, and fails.
* * *

Some trick of the light eyes, some peach skin texture merely
Both dust decaying hourly and undurable,
So draw, so wrench and rend me really

That I am, feel, know, think only one thing:
Which God makes nothing.

(*The Listener*, October 21, 1931, p. 690.
See letter dated October 10, 1931.)

In the unpublished "You Can't Keep a Good Man Down," Dr.
Prisonface is the headmaster of St. George's, a prep school very
similar to St. David's, where White was teaching when he wrote
this poem.

Dr. Prisonface

This pretty boy, mischievous, chaste, and stupid,
With bouncing bum and eyes of teasing fire,
This budding atom, happy heart, young Cupid,
Will grow to know desire.

Affluent parent, think! He too must wander,
if he grows on, the labyrinth of lust.
He too is doomed to bear, perhaps to squander,
His fertile handful of extatic dust.

Anxious Mamma, discern the signs of rapture:
Observe his sensuous wriggles in the bath.
His plump brown legs design their future capture,
Their virgin quelled, their tenderness and wrath.

Happy immoral imp, if this continues
He will, no doubt, grow up a shameless sensualist.
He won't despise his genitals and sinews,
Won't know that it is "beastly" to be kissed.

Naturally stupid, he may think that living
Is sweet, with music, hunting, books and girls:

May think that seed's for sowing, gifts for giving,
And lips for laughing, kissing curves and curls.

*

Stuff him in Etons quick, and send him packing
To Dr. Prisonface his Surrey school.
That old rheumatic man with threats and whacking
Will justly bring this body to the rule.

Not quickly, but with tireless attrition,
He will be brought to heel and taught to know
Bodies are beastly, love a sneaking vision,
Beauty forbidden, foul, and fancy low.

*

Old Dr. Prisonface the triple blue
(Now grown rheumatic) knows his Maker well:
He knows that boys who keep their hands in pockets
Will go to hell.

He knows that Christian (not too Christian) gentlemen
Exist in packs in order to propel
Tight leather balls a distance of exactly
22 yards, or taste the fires of hell.

He knows that work is really not important
But must be done. He knows the chapel bell
Must summon infants twice a day to praying
Against their sterile bodies, lest they go to hell.

Music and books to Dr. Prisonface, if "classic,"
Compel a puzzled, grudging, right respect.
Dickens he's heard of, poetry makes him as sick
As any poet might expect.

Dr. Prisonface has never shot or hunted,
Walked roots or viewed a fox across a ride.

262

He has never been alone, or thought, or loved (he lusted);
He was always too busy playing for his side.

Dr. Prisonface, the grand discourager, discourages laughter:
Discourages all games unless, being organised, they cease to be
      games.
Dr. Prisonface's weak scowl obstinately discourages
The head, the heart, the reins.

Dr. Prisonface's wife (sensible woman) has run away from him,
But he consoles himself by thinking that her morals were not
      healthy.
It is all "not" with Dr. Prisonface, he has never said "Do,"
Never said "is," except "is filthy."

                              *

Send your bright dreaming angel then to Dr. Prisonface
So that he may be taught his "beastly" loins to rule,
So that he may be learned what is and isn't cricket,
So that he may be a product of the good old school.

His legs are beautiful but he must hate them,
Starve them till sterile and when past their prime
He may be allowed to marry somebody exactly like him,
And have a jolly good time.

Till then, for you can't quite kill his angel,
He'll fall at intervals and take a whore,
Shamefully take her in the night time and afterwards hate himself
All the more, and do it more.

He will convey the blight to his own marriage bed
Which will exactly resemble Dr. Prisonface's:
Surreptitiously wrestling with his wife in the darkness,
Putting her with averted eyes through hasty shameful paces.

Dark and remorseful and dirty will be his copulation,

In Dr. Prisonface's hell, among the wicked.
But never mind, he'll be a credit to the nation;
And we all hope, we all so hope, he will be good at cricket.*

Love Song for Lin

My long-rust Muse, in dark and bleaching weeds
Underdamped like an old coulter which once drove bright,
A land ship's forefoot housewifing for seeds
Which should grow upright, rampant and rife and right,
Now suddenly comes up and fits to plough,
Fitting, falling into place, finding home true,
Rust, scours, revolves, says once more here and now
I bring my tilth, my triumph, my teeming truth to you.

What to? To one, but in that one what teams,
What reams, what races, what real regiments and ranks
Of other-love, down dwelling in dark flames,
Lovely pervading unknown ocean streams:
Where this perturbed spirit may slip, dip, drown with sinking
    thanks;
May rest, now rest, mated, in love, not dreams.

(enclosed in a letter to Potts, January 18, 1936)

Poem, Looking into a Gas Fire, Alone in London

Just to sit and wait,
To accept this vast experience of the universe,
This enormous coincidence of contingencies narrowing down to
    minute points
Touching me.

*This is the complete poem. Nine stanzas (out of nineteen) appeared in Warner's
biography of White and in A Joy Proposed, p. 7. (Enclosed in a letter to Potts,
October 10, 1931.)

The huntsmen in America, the man in the remote moon,
    and God in the great starry bush of the firmament,
And Years, geological time, and geographical miles,
And everybody *else*, with their mysteries of mothers and
    mistresses,
Secret, multitudinous, outstanding and unnumbered,
With mountains, and oceans, and plains on plains,
    and all the waves one after the other,
Lapping into this one mind,
Coming, helpingly, into this one spark of consciousness,
This one little bright temporary star
That gleams out
A lighthouse
Over all those dark blue hateful miles of time and space
A pin prick
A light.

                (enclosed in a letter to Potts, February 2, 1936)

The following poem first appeared in a brochure appealing for funds for the restoration of the bells of St. Anne's Church in Alderney; White later included it in *Verses* (Alderney: privately printed, 1962, p. 23; *A Joy Proposed*, p. 60.) See letter of March 19, 1953.

Verses for Coronation Year

in aid of a Public Subscription
   to restore the church bells of
ALDERNEY, taken away by the GERMANS

Wind up the curling stairs
Set in the wall—
Ten, twenty, thirty, forty,
Hardly yet worn at all.

In this square, empty room,

Silently serene,
Lit from above, no view,
Is where the Bells have been.

Clean as a pin,
unstirred
By mouse or man,
Is the great box where they were heard.

They are to come back, they are,
From their long bundling and pilgrimage of war.

They are to swoop again, and must
Jollify marriages and mourn the ancestral dust.

Deep-tongued, re-hung,
Raucous and real,
They are to celebrate
Their liberation, jubilation, coronation peal.

Off to the Wars (2)
(1941)

Brownie, my Brownie, now that I am going—
This may be no good poem but it will be truth—
You have been to me mother and daughter,
Decency, kindness, love, beauty and youth.
Forget me then. Oh, forget me utterly.
Forget quick and be happy and live long.
If you remember for a minute, I shall die in badness,
Or live in ashes and beastly, remorseful, wrong.
Live you, tail flirting, eyes pleading,
In pleasure, in brownness, in trust of my race.
Only thus shall I live or die, my darling,
Not in disgrace.

(See letter of November 11, 1961.) This poem was published in *Verses*, p. 28; *A Joy Proposed*, p. 33.

Appendix C: L. J. Potts's Review of
The Elephant and the Kangaroo

This article originally appeared in *The Dial*, Michelmas Term, 1947. (See letter of December 28, 1947.)

T. H. White: *The Elephant and the Kangaroo*. G. P. Putnam's Sons, New York, 1947.

It is eighteen years since T. H. White published his first book, a small collection of poems, while he was still an undergraduate at Queens'. His latest and best book has not been published in this country yet; in these days, novelists who are lucky enough to be able to do so publish first in America in a large impression, and afterwards on our more modest scale at home.

Like all his books, this is a fantasy. The hero is a Mr. White, living on a farm in Ireland with its owners, Mr. and Mrs. O'Callaghan. (To avoid confusing him with his hero, I shall call the author T. H. W.) The Archangel Michael comes down the chimney, and tells them that there is going to be a flood, and that they are to build an ark. The O'Callaghans, according to their custom when they are faced with any crisis, leave it to Mr. White, who takes down the roof of the new hay-barn and turns it upside down to form the keel of the ark; and in due course it is completed, with accommodation for livestock, stores, and equipment to restart human life after the flood is over. When the flood comes, they embark and their craft floats; but almost at once Mr. White realises that the flood is not a mere waste of waters but an enlarged river, and that his ark will inevitably run into the first high bridge down stream and be wrecked. This duly happens: the party then takes to the water in barrels, pursued by a small body of admirers who hope for some reward in this world or the next if they can get admitted to the holy expedition; and by the hostility of the whole of the rest of Eire, roused against them by Father Byrne, the local priest, on account of their irregular behaviour. ("If there were to have been a flood, the announcement ought to have been made through the existing machinery, which was Father Byrne.") They float into the Liffey, through Dublin (in spite of the efforts of the Army and Navy to stop them), and out to sea, where they are picked up by the mail boat from Holyhead.

The main substance of the book consists of the interplay between the three chief characters. Mikey O'Callaghan, "a small, red-faced man of about sixty, who looked a little like the first Duke of Wellington and a little like a tortoise," was utterly lazy and incompetent, "but cheerful, affectionate, and kind. He adored Mr. White, and would have done anything not to be in his bad books— anything which did not involve work or danger. He was good-tempered, except when he lost his temper, and this he did only with inanimate objects, because live ones might have hit back." Mrs. O'Callaghan "was a tall thin woman, over fifty years of age, who never stopped working and never got anything done." The book becomes the story of her heroism. "Mrs. O'Callaghan had lived for twenty-three years in a fairly comfortable farmhouse, and she had paid £120 in installments on its Dutch barn. He had turned her barn upside down, filled it with the pick of the farm stock and all the implements, taken her away in it from the home in which she had lived all her married life, conveyed her a distance of five miles to Cashelmor, which she could have reached more easily by a détour in the pony trap, and had finally submerged the whole contrivance in the turbulent waters of the Slane. Perhaps she might have been forgiven if she had expressed some form of displeasure at this stage, or if she had only asked ironically, 'What next?'" She was not like that.

"Seeing his look of misery, she said, how generously: 'It was Mikey's fault, the way he wouldn't give you a hand with the beehive.'"

"Mikey exclaimed: 'I would give him a hand; but it was your

fault, because—because—because you left the keys on the dresser.'" (The favourite pastime of the O'Callaghans is putting the blame on each other in this way, quite irrelevantly.) As for Mr. White, he is a largely fictitious character, with some slight foundation in fact: closely related to Merlin in *The Sword in the Stone,* and the Professor in *Mistress Masham's Repose* (T. H. W.'s last book but one, which has just been published by Jonathan Cape). He is clever with his hands, and has a passion for solving complicated problems, and a stronger passion for converting his friends to his own beliefs and theories of the moment.

T. H. W. has become adept at anecdotes. The stories of the Archangel's appearance; of how Mr. White taught Mikey the art of water-divining and Mikey tried to teach it to Mr. Quin the postman, with disastrous results; of the attempt of Pat Geraghty to assassinate Mr. White; and of Mr. White's behaviour on the submerged bridge at Cashelmor when he is trying to tow his fellow-passengers from the wrecked ark ashore; and the final hysterical scene in Dublin, described in a kind of nightmare parody of James Joyce's *Ulysses*—are the high lights of the book. The attempted assassination is the best—indeed the very highest comedy; but it is too long to quote, and a summary would spoil it. The scene on the parapet of the bridge, as Mr. White walks downwards from the middle, where it is only just under water, towards the end, where the water is deep, is short enough to quote.

"The water hurled itself against his knees, feathering into a little curl upstream of each. It grew to his thighs, as each precarious pace diminished to a shuffle. It could be seen that he was unable to pass the right leg in front of the left one, because the current pressed them together. The mill race of water, hitherto silent there, made a harp of his legs and roared on it. He became isolated from all life but his own, wrapped up in the noise of his passage . . .

". . . He deliberately leaned forward into the water, saying, inaudibly, 'Aaaaah!' as the melted snow snatched at his breath like fire, and lay flat in it, like a swimmer, with his head upstream and his feet against the parapet. It was the only hope of getting along, to walk in a horizontal position, as if the current had deflected gravity from the vertical, which, indeed, it had.

"Mr. White began to look ridiculous and pathetic, if not

revolting, as all creatures with pelts do, when they have been soaked. His whiskers adhered to his chin. He appeared to be basking in the flood for sport, like a walrus, and making no progress at all. His movements were perverse, inefficient, broody. Nobody could see what he was about.

"Quite gracefully, and apparently on purpose, as if he had just invented a new plan, he put his head under water, erected his buttocks, waved to the spectators, turned on his back, spun round, vanished, and reappeared a moment later at the end of the rope. He had missed his footing.

"Mrs. O'Callaghan began to scream for Holy Mary as the rope spun out. She grabbed it and began to pull. Instead of pulling Mr. White back to the barrels, the rope pulled the latter after him. It was tied. It was impossible to let go. In the twinkling of a second the three barrels were spinning round like a roulette wheel, in the worst of the current below the bridge. A minute later the parapet was far behind. They were clear of Cashelmor itself, with half a mile of river on either side. Mr. White was swimming frantically for the barrels, while Mrs. O'Callaghan played him on the rope."

This is a book about Ireland; it will not be popular with any Irishman in whom patriotism has swallowed up a sense of humour. But T.H.W. has little use for nationalism (Irish or any other sort); and as the laugh is as often directed at Mr. White as at the natives, I hope some of them will enjoy it. It is in the best tradition of English comedy; and that tradition, after all, owes as much to Irishmen as to Englishmen.

L.J.P.

Appendix D: "Milk-a-Punch Sunday"

This article originally appeared in *The Dial*, Easter Term, 1948, the quincentenary number. (See letter of December 28, 1947.)

Alderney, the island on which I live, is the smallest, the most

270

barren, the most neglected, and by far the most charming of the three larger Channel Islands. During the last war it was evacuated and used as a concentration camp by the Germans. Even before the war its population was only about 1,400: it is now 900. At the best the island must always have been a cavernous, waste shore. Now, amid the gun-emplacements, ruined cottages, fortresses and general devastation, the returned nine hundred are doing their best to rebuild their own civilisation—in the teeth of the Privy Council, of beaurocracy, and of the present Government.

Theirs is a peculiar civilisation. The first Sunday that I ever spent in Alderney was the first Sunday in May. A Sunday is about the only day in Alderney when the pubs are theoretically supposed to close; so I asked my hosts at the small hotel whether they could recommend me to a pub with a convenient back door. They said, certainly they could; I was to come with them after dinner. We went together, to find in the bar a steaming jug of milk punch, made from rum, milk and nutmeg. After we and the other customers had drank gallons and gallons of this mixture free, I really began to feel that I ought to pay for something. I was not allowed to do so. "Don't you know," they said kindly, "that to-day is MILK-A-PUNCH SUNDAY?" I did not know, but I have found out since.

From the Middle Ages, from the time of William the Conqueror, or for that matter from the time of Duke Robert—from whom most of the customary laws of the Channel Islands still derive—Milk-a-Punch Sunday has persisted. In the old days, on the first Sunday in May, you were allowed to go out with a pail into any field, and to milk any cow. Then you were allowed to take the free milk to the nearest drink shop and to demand free rum. Nowadays the pubs even provide the milk—but this habit has been going on probably since *before* the first date in "1066 and All That."

Now that I am a property-owner in Alderney, I have a splendid means of defending my claims. Should anybody encroach upon my property, all I have to do is collect two witnesses, kneel on the church steps, recite the Lord's prayer, and cry with a loud voice, "Ha-ro! Ha-ro! à l'aide, mon prince! On me fait tort!" At this, Duke Robert (or his tradition) instantly comes to my aid. The man who is

271

building a house on my holding drops the brick from his hand. The Judge of Alderney pauses paralysed, with the fork half way to his mouth. Practically the whole life of the island stops. Until my plea has been investigated, and, if possible, satisfied, nothing can be done. Incidentally, one of the Kings of England—I think it was the Conqueror himself—was turned out of his own grave by this cry— which is called the *clameur de Haro*—and they were unable to bury him until the claimant to that grave-ground had been satisfied.

But to return to Milk-a-Punch Sunday. When we got back to the hotel from that orgy of rum-punch, we fell to talking in the midnight hours about witchcraft. I was foolish and rude enough to express some doubts about the existence of witches. My hosts were more shocked than insulted. "But, Mr. *White*," they said, in pained and earnest tones, "Margaret, in the corner there, was bewitched only ten years ago!" "How?" "Why, her mother fell out with Mrs. . . . . (and even I dare not tell you this wise woman's name, for fear of suffering the like disfavour), and on the morning afterwards Margaret was *covered with lice*. She was not lousy before," they explained—and this was only too obvious in so clean a house. "The lice came all at once," they said, "and in billions."

Since the midnight conversation I have discovered from books that Alderney witches have been famous from at least the end of the seventeenth century for just this particular feat. But here is the charming thing about it. The Alderney witches can't give you the evil eye, can't kill you or your cattle, can't afflict you with any diseases. The lice are the only trick they know—and, after all, there is D.D.T. for that.

T. H. White

Appendix E: The Works of T. H. White

Loved Helen and Other Poems (London: Chatto and Windus, 1929)
Dead Mr. Nixon (with R. McNair Scott. London: Cassell, 1931)

They Winter Abroad (by "James Aston." London: Chatto and Windus, 1932; New York: Viking Press, 1932)

First Lesson (by "James Aston." London: Chatto and Windus, 1932; New York: Alfred A. Knopf, 1933)

Darkness at Pemberley (London: Gollancz, 1932; New York: G. P. Putnam's Sons, 1933; reprinted New York: Dover, 1978)

Farewell Victoria (London: Collins, 1933; New York: G. P. Putnam's Sons, 1934)

Earth Stopped, or, Mr. Marx's Speaking Tour (London: Collins, 1934; New York: G. P. Putnam's Sons, 1935)

Gone to Ground (London: Collins, 1935; New York: G. P. Putnam's Sons, 1935)

England Have My Bones (London: Collins, 1936; New York: Macmillan, 1936; reprinted New York: G. P. Putnam's Sons, 1982; reprinted London: Macdonald Futura, 1981)

Burke's Steerage, or, The Amateur Gentleman's Introduction to Noble Sports and Pastimes (London: Collins, 1938; New York, G. P. Putnam's Sons, 1939)

The Sword in the Stone (London: Collins, 1940; New York: G. P. Putnam's Sons, 1939; reprinted London: Collins, Evergreen, 1977)

The Witch in the Wood (London: Collins, 1940; New York: G. P. Putnam's Sons, 1939)

The Ill-Made Knight (London: Collins, 1941; New York: G. P. Putnam's Sons, 1940)

Mistress Masham's Repose (London: Cape, 1947; New York: G. P. Putnam's Sons, 1946; reprinted London: Puggin Books, 1972; New York, Berkley Books, 1973)

The Elephant and the Kangaroo (London: Cape, 1948; New York: G. P. Putnam's Sons, 1947)

The Age of Scandal: An Excursion Through a Minor Period (London: Cape, 1950; New York: G. P. Putnam's Sons, 1950)

The Goshawk (London: Cape, 1951; New York: G. P. Putnam's Sons, 1952; reprinted London: Penguin Books, 1970)

The Scandalmonger (London: Cape, 1952; New York: G. P. Putnam's Sons, 1952)

273

The Book of Beasts (London: Cape, 1954; New York: G. P. Putnam's Sons, 1955; New York: Capricorn Books, 1960)

The Master: An Adventure Story (London: Cape, 1957; New York: G. P. Putnam's Sons, 1957; reprinted London: Puggin Books, 1971)

The Once and Future King (London: Collins, 1958; New York: G. P. Putnam's Sons, 1958; London: Fontana Books, 1962; New York: Berkley Books, 1981)

The Godstone and the Blackymor (London: Cape, 1959; published in America as *A Western Wind*, New York: G. P. Putnam's Sons, 1959)

Verses (London: Hertford and Harlow, The Shenval Press, 1962, privately printed, limited edition of 100 copies)

America at Last: The American Journal of T. H. White, with an introduction by David Garnett (New York: G. P. Putnam's Sons, 1965)

The Book of Merlyn: The Unpublished Conclusion to the Once and Future King, prologue by Sylvia Townsend Warner (Austin and London: University of Texas Press, 1977; London: Fontana/Collins, 1978; New York: Berkley Medallion Books, 1978)

A Joy Proposed: Poems by T. H. White, with an introduction, afterword, and notes by Kurth Sprague (London: Bertram Rota, 1980, limited edition of 500 copies)

The Maharajah and Other Stories by T. H. White, collected and with an introduction by Kurth Sprague (London: Macdonald Futura Publishers, 1981; New York: G. P. Putnam's Sons, 1981)

Notes

Chapter 1

1. Sylvia Townsend Warner, *T. H. White: A Biography* (London: Cape with Chatto and Windus, 1967; New York: Viking Press, 1968), p. 41.

2. *Loved Helen* (London: Chatto and Windus, 1929). White's inscription is: Mater Mea. Principium et Finis. Vita Corpus Caput. Felicitatis Meae. Accipe Hunc Librum qui Sine Te Nihil Esset.

3. See Appendix A for a sample of Potts's poetry and White's comments thereon.

4. From *The Complete Poems of D. H. Lawrence* (London: Heinemann, 1964), vol. 1, p. 392.

5. The poem was "Invocation to Words," *The Listener*, March 25, 1931, p. 511. It is reproduced in full in Appendix B.

6. With a few alterations, this poem appeared in White's *Verses*, p. 14 (Alderney: privately printed, 1962) under the title "Looking at the Skull of St. Andrew on the Altar at Amalfi" and in *A Joy Proposed*. The first and last stanzas are in *First Lesson*, p. 233 (London: Chatto and Windus, 1932).

7. *Hatter's Castle* was written by A. J. Cronin, *Afternoon Men* by Anthony Powell.

8. The solicited poem was "Indescribable Loneliness of Man," *The Listener*, October 21, 1931, p. 690. It is reproduced in full in Appendix B.

9. Warner, *T. H. White*, p. 55.

10. *Darkness at Pemberley* (T. H. White), *They Winter Abroad* (James Aston), and *First Lesson* (James Aston) were published in 1932.

11. Quoted in Warner, *T. H. White*, p. 58.

12. Warner, *T. H. White*, pp. 59–60.

Chapter 2

1. This diary was not found after L. J. Potts's death.

2. Sylvia Townsend Warner, *T. H. White: A Biography* (London: Cape with Chatto and Windus, 1967; New York: Viking Press, 1968), p. 76.

3. Warner, *T. H. White*, p. 81.

4. After this passage, which is quoted in her biography of White, Sylvia Townsend Warner comments: "The sexual autobiography for the benefit of other poor devils was not written. But between 1957 and 1961 he kept an intimate record of his own poor devil state. He considered this the most important of his books ('It has cost more') and made a special bequest of it with the hope that its publication (at a date when it could no longer distress those concerned) might contribute to a more enlightened and merciful outlook on sexual aberrants" (*T. H. White*, p. 83).

Unfortunately, this record is still under lock and key.

5. The books White mentions here are by R. S. Surtees: *Mr. Sponge's Sporting Tour* (1853), *Mr. Romford's Hounds* (1864), *Handley Cross* (1843), and *Jorrocks Jaunts and Jollities* (1869).

6. The poem White refers to is this:

Not, I'll not, carrion comfort, Despair, not feast on thee;
Not untwist—slack they may be—these last strands of man
In me ór, most weary, cry *I can no more*. I can;
Can something, hope, wish day come, not choose not to be.

Poems of Gerard Manley Hopkins (London: Oxford University Press, 1930), Poem 40, "Carrion Comfort," p. 61.

Chapter 3

1. *The Goshawk* (London: Cape, 1951). When Gos flew away, White decided that the book he had intended to write was useless; it was only in 1949 that Wren Howard of Jonathan Cape found the typescript under a settee cushion and advised White to publish it.

2. Much of the research mentioned in this letter and the following one was used in *The Goshawk*. White made use of this particular "small research" again later, in a long footnote to the "Assida" (ostrich) entry in *The Book of Beasts*.

3. David Garnett, *Beaney Eye* (London: Chatto and Windus, 1935). Mr. Butler is a living portrait of David Garnett's father.

4. Mary Potts remembers that her daughters were arguing; Weg said: "I never did!" and Betsy asked: "Never'd You?"

5. Mary Potts had a book in which she had written and illustrated stories for the very young. White was stimulated to add a story of his own, involving the adventures of Weg, Betsy, and William Potts when they dived into the sea and visited a welcoming character, called the white whale, in a warm and rosy cave. Mary had to set it to music and play while White read it aloud.

6. White wrote exactly the same story to David Garnett, using the same words. (See *The White-Garnett Letters*, London: Cape, 1968, p. 23.)

7. Francis Macdonald Cornford, *Microcosmographia Academica: Being a Guide for the Young Academic Politician* (Cambridge: Bowes and Bowes, 1908).

8. "The notice which you have been pleased to take of my Labours, had it been early, had it been kind; but it has been delayed till I am indifferent and cannot enjoy it, till I am solitary and cannot impart it, till I am known and do not want it." Letter of February 7, 1755, from *The Letters of Samuel Johnson* (Oxford: The Clarendon Press, 1952), p. 61.

9. In fact, Aldous Huxley had settled in the United States as early as February 1937. His pacifist views were well known and his bad eyesight would have prevented him from taking any active part in the war.

Chapter 4

1. The first chapter was finally reduced to seven pages. *The Queen of Air and Darkness* (as *The Witch in the Wood* was eventually re-titled) starts with a description of the queen's castle, where her sons, Gaheris, Gareth, Gawaine, and Agravaine, are telling the story of King Uther Pendragon. Morgause first appears on the fifth page, boiling a black cat alive so as to attempt to become invisible.

2. The fifth part of White's Arthurian tale has only recently been published: *The Book of Merlyn*, prologue by Sylvia Townsend Warner, illustrated by Trevor Stubley (Austin and London: University of Texas Press, 1977; London: Fontana/Collins, 1978; New York: Berkley Medallion Books, 1978).

3. George Townsend Warner was Sylvia Townsend Warner's father. He was a writer of history books, a teacher at Harrow, and a Fellow of Jesus College in Cambridge.

4. Unfortunately, this very humorous scene of the tilting at the quintain and tossing of the cabay on the ice, which ends with Morgause standing up to her knees in water, disappeared in the final version of *The Witch in the Wood*.

5. The poem White refers to is this:

> Her strong enchantments failing,
> Her towers of fear in wreck,
> Her limbecks dried of poisons
> And the knife at her neck,
> The Queen of air and darkness
> Begins to shrill and cry,
> "O young man, O my slayer,
> To-morrow you shall die."

The Collected Poems of A. E. Housman (London: Cape, 1939), p. 307.

6. "I should prescribe for Mr. Pontifex a course of the larger mammals. Don't let him think he is taking them medicinally, but let him go to their house twice a week for a fortnight and stay with the hippopotamus, the rhinoceros, and the elephants, till they begin to bore him." Samuel Butler, *Ernest Pontifex, or, the Way of All Flesh* (1903; rept. London: Methuen, 1964), p. 307.

7. White sometimes invested Mary Potts with everything he disapproved of; far from discouraging her daughter in her enthusiasm for creeping things, Mary helped Weg to build a snail zoo and never forbade her to take a snail to bed with her!

8. Professor Cook was vice-president of Queens', and the author of *Zeus: A Study in Ancient Religion* (Cambridge: University Press, 1914–1940). Both Dr. Cook (who, the Professor imagines, "had offered to mention him in a footnote to *Zeus*") and White's problems with "Trypharium" (mentioned later in this letter) were worked into *Mistress Masham's Repose*.

9. Two of the books Potts mentions working on were eventually published: *Comedy* (London: Hutchinson's University Library, 1949) and Aristotle's *Poetics*, with an introductory essay and explanatory notes (Cambridge: University Press, 1953).

Chapter 5

1. "Tears in the un-Romantic Age," *Life and Letters and The London Mercury*, July 1946, vol. 50, pp. 3–7. See also *The Age of Scandal*, chapter thirteen, entitled "Tears."

2. White put these cases and crates in a shed, where they were left during the very cold winter of 1946–47. When he opened them a year later, the shed had leaked and several of his Cambridge diaries and all L. J. Potts's letters, some of which he had kept for ten years, were completely ruined.

Chapter 6

1. *The White-Garnett Letters*, p. 231.
2. *The White-Garnett Letters*, p. 268.

3. Sylvia Townsend Warner, *T. H. White: A Biography*, p. 277.

4. White's diary on that period was published in the United States under the title *America at Last* (New York: G. P. Putnam's Sons, 1965).

5. This letter was not sent before June 20. To his letter to Mary, White added his answer to L. J. Potts's letter of June 13. The "freezing, flaming and operation-table ordeals" mentioned in the first sentence were, respectively, the bitter winter of 1947 (people skated on the river Cam), a fire in the Pottses' nursery, and an operation on one of L. J. Potts's ears.

6. This is what David Higham, White's literary agent, wrote: "The girl had cut off all communication. He could tell nothing about her except that she'd married. Several times during the next few years he asked me what I could discover, but there really wasn't any way I could enquire. After his death I did find out where she was living—in the house in which Tim had kept his goshawk." (David Higham, *Literary Gent*, London: Cape, 1978, p. 213.)

7. Jules Castier. But *Mistress Masham's Repose* was never translated into French.

8. Charles Crichton (Mary Potts's brother) wanted to film some of White's books, because, as he pointed out, White's humor was visual. The two men met at Michael Trubshawe's, but it soon became clear that White wanted to direct and produce the films himself!

9. "A link with Petulengro—Concerning Queen Victoria," *The Illustrated London News*, Christmas Number, 1953, pp. 32–34.

10. This "mortal enemy" was Dorothy Sayers, who had written to the *Times Literary Supplement* to protest about a point of translation in L. J. Potts's *Aristotle*.

11. In 1927 White had to be sent to Italy after a diagnosis of tuberculosis. Mr. Robin Laffan, senior tutor at Queens', had asked his colleagues to subscribe for a fund in order to help him, and L. J. Potts had given something very generous. More than thirty years later, White sent two hundred pounds back to Mary Potts.

12. *Poems: Read by the Author* (Argo EAF60, 1963).